Cooking *from the* Gourmet's Garden

Edible Ornamentals, Herbs, and Flowers

Coralie Castle & Robert Kourik

COLE
GROUP

Publisher	Brete C. Harrison
VP and Director of Operations	Linda Hauck
VP Marketing and Business Development	John A. Morris
Associate Publisher	James Connolly
Director of Production	Steve Lux
Senior Editor	Annette Gooch
Production Assistant	Dotti Hydue
Editorial Assistants	Linda Tronson and Susanne Fitzpatrick
Copyeditor	Sharon Silva
Cover Photography	Debbie Patterson
Illustrators	Darwen and Vally Hennings
Interior Design and Production	Nancy Simerly

This volume owes a great debt to Dr. Sinclair Philip and the staff of Sooke Harbour House, Sooke, BC, Canada, and to the many experts at Fetzer Food and Wine Center, Hopland, California, for having so generously shared their knowledge.

Distributed to the book trade by Publishers Group West.

Printed and bound in Singapore
Published by Cole Group, Inc.
1330 No. Dutton Ave., Suite 103, PO Box 4089
Santa Rosa, CA 95402-4089
(800) 959-2717 (707) 526-2682   FAX (707) 526-2687

A B C D E F G H
4 5 6 7 8 9 0 1

Library of Congress Catalog Card Number 93-3220

ISBN 1-56426-563-3

Contents

Foreword

Coralie Castle and Robert Kourik's book, *Cooking from the Gourmet's Garden*, is a celebration of the modern kitchen garden. These adventuresome authors lead us along an exciting landscape pathway into a kitchen where the treasures of the garden are transformed into the pleasures of the contemporary table. Hundreds of gardening books and cookbooks appear every year throughout the world, but, sadly, many of them are simply reworkings of old recipes and old themes. By way of contrast, *Cooking from the Gourmet's Garden* is a welcome addition to the libraries of creative gardeners and imaginative cooks alike.

At the Sooke Harbour House, our avant-gardeners and kitchen staff strive to investigate the most interesting plant varieties available and design our menus and gardens accordingly. As a result of the novel information brought forward in this book, everyone here is already plowing through new plans for several of our gardens and preparing to break new ground with our menus.

In the past, I have frequently referred to Robert Kourik's *Designing and Maintaining your Edible Landscape—Naturally*. Since the publication of that book, his gardening expertise has expanded to cover new plant materials. As a result, some of Kourik's landscape suggestions are so far-reaching that you may want to run right out and uproot your rhododendrons and replace them with a flowing drift of calendula or a splendiferous, mellifluous persimmon tree. Through his prose, it becomes clear that an apprenticeship in the new kitchen garden is an essential for any competent chef.

Coralie Castle's contribution is the ideal kitchen companion to the planting savoir faire of Robert Kourik. I have always been a big fan of this innovative cook. Her enthusiasm and vast experience in so many culinary endeavors are in evidence in every delicious, thought-provoking page of this book.

In the early stages of designing the kitchen gardens at the Sooke Harbour House, in addition to using Robert Kourik's book, we repeatedly referred to *The Edible Ornamental Garden*, coauthored by Coralie Castle. We found her first book to be an excellent resource and an indispensable guide to gardening, harvesting, and preparing nouvelle produce in the late 1970s and early 1980s.

Cooking from the Gourmet's Garden goes well beyond her original work to enter into an entirely new dimension in creative cooking. This compendium stresses that the building block essential to good cooking is the use of organic, ripe, seasonal, unadulterated raw materials at their peak.

The recipes in this book are easy to follow and are clearly laid out. Moreover, the book contains a wealth of information on compound butters; infused oils, vinegars, stocks, and honeys; bouquet garnis; and preserves.

If that weren't enough, *Cooking from the Gourmet's Garden* also features several exciting contributions from celebrity chefs. Ron Zimmerman of the Herbfarm, for instance, has contributed a wonderful sweet cicely sorbet that I very much enjoyed during my last trip to Fall City, Washington. Such legendary chefs as Alice Waters, Flo Braker, John Ash, Martin Yan, and even our team of chefs from the Sooke Harbour House have contributed some of their most tantalizing new recipes, adding a little more spice to an already comprehensive and well-thought-through selection of dishes.

Dr. Sinclair Philip
Innkeeper-Restaurateur-Gardener
Sooke Harbour House
Sooke, British Columbia
December 1992

The Gourmet's Garden, Food and Beauty Together Again

Why "harvest" only fallen leaves from your shade trees when you could gather aromatic, brown-skinned Hosui Asian pears? Why pick only ornamental zinnias when you could sprinkle your salads with a rainbow of such edible flowers as borage, violets, nasturtiums, roses, and geraniums? Any yard in any climate can be transformed into an edible landscape, a gourmet's garden yielding a bounty of both flavor and beauty.

In the past, farm families reserved an area of land adjacent to the house for flowers and a multitude of fruits and vegetables. Gradually these gardeners turned to the same place for their produce that everybody else did—the supermarket. Now the cycle has come full circle and more people on and off the farm are interested in home-grown food, but with the extra advantage of enhancing the look of their yards with ornamental plants. This approach, known as edible land-scaping, marries the utility of food gardening with the aesthetics of traditional landscape design.

To engage in edible landscaping is to combine the hedonism of great flavors and wonderful fragrances into a rich tapestry of seasonal color, thereby creating a landscape that is not only distinctive, but also productive. For the gourmet gardener, the culinary advantages of an edible landscape are no less compelling than the visual ones. Unequalled freshness, the sweet complex flavors of tree-ripened fruit, superior nutrition, and the chance to grow food without the use of questionable chemical pesticides—the edible landscape offers all these and more.

Here are a few important guidelines for a well-designed and productive gourmet's garden that includes edible ornamentals:

- Plan ahead: Spend some time getting the advice of other gardeners, landscape designers, or landscape architects. Draw designs on paper to prepare for the work ahead. Planning should always precede picking up the shovel.

- Structure is the core of good landscape design. Plan for brick walkways, arbors, stone walls, trellises, and/or wood-chip pathways to hold the overall plan together. The more vegetables you have in your design, the more dominant the permanent structural elements should be.

- Not every plant needs to be edible. Your design should have less than 50 percent edible plants. The intent is to integrate the food plants aesthetically into your overall plan.

- Start small. Select an area no more than several hundred square feet, and see how it fits into your lifestyle. Do not redo the entire backyard at once.

- Cluster the salad greens in one attractive place. If you scatter individual lettuce and other salad green plants randomly in a flower border, they'll be hard to find before they become bitter and bolt.

- Plant salad greens and culinary herbs close to the kitchen. They will be easy to see, so you will know when you need to harvest or replant them.

- Choose as many edible plants as possible that are relatively pest and disease free. You don't want to become a slave to your garden.

- Have fun. The main reason for an edible ornamental landscape is culinary hedonism. Take time to savor the pleasures of gardening and the banquet from your landscape.

Choosing from a Cornucopia of Edible Ornamentals

In 1919, Edward Lewis Sturtevant, in his *Sturtevant's Edible Plants of the World*, listed nearly three thousand condiments, staple foods, survival rations, beverage plants, and recreational herbals. He quotes one seventeenth-century source as guessing there were about five hundred varieties of apples. Most sources now agree there are at least six thousand named varieties of apples to tempt us. Some plant collectors have over two hundred varieties of pears in their orchards. Dried bean collectors have been known to grow at least two hundred fifty different selections in their own gardens. So given this cornucopia of choices, how did we choose which plants to feature in this finite volume?

Foremost, we selected those plants with the optimum blend of good flavor and attractive potential as a landscape plant. For example, English lavender offers the adaptability of being sheared to any shape, including a short hedge or small topiary, at the same time having attractive gray-green foliage, a fantastic and famous scent, and the culinary use of both flowers and foliage.

We have selected a range of ornamental plant types for every major design element in a landscape. There are trees that can be used to shade the house from the afternoon sun: persimmons, crabapples, and chestnuts. Some plants, such as grapes, kiwis, and chayotes, are fruiting vines well adapted to vertical trellises, overhead wire trellises, arbors, or an informal bower. Others are deciduous, or treated-as-deciduous, herbaceous perennials—artichokes, bronze fennel, cardoon, lovage—that can be the backbone of a renewable design.

We have included evergreen perennials—sweet bay, chives, feijoa, lavender, oregano, rosemary, sage—that make it easy to establish an overall perimeter or a visual "spine" for a garden that can be seen throughout the year. For ground covers we offer some of the previously mentioned plants along with parsley, thymes, and Buckler's sorrel. And because no garden is complete without the seasonal delights afforded by annual vegetables, we discuss, among others, scarlet runner beans, the soft lettuces, and that tasty bastion of any contemporary salad mix, arugula.

To add diversity and texture to both the landscape and the dinner plate, choose from among our plants those that have several edible parts. For example, cilantro is famous for its use as an essential chopped green in many Asian and Mexican dishes, but if the plant is allowed to form seed, the gardener has coriander, yet another useful seasoning. Lavender blossoms can be candied as a garnish for desserts, the flowers sprinkled directly on a fruit salad, and the foliage used to flavor ice cream, salads, and grilled meats.

Cooking the Bounty of the Gourmet's Garden

Whether you prefer refined gastronomical hyperbole, delicious preparations with unique seasonings, or traditional dishes for good ol' eatin', there are recipes in these pages that are guaranteed to intrigue you. All of them are designed to inspire you to develop your own repertoire of recipes that presents the edible ornamental landscape at its savory and visual best. And eye appeal is always of utmost importance, with every plate, bowl, and platter garnished artistically before it leaves the kitchen.

Information on Complementary Seasonings and Foods and a selection of Mini Recipes accompany nearly every plant description. A chapter of basic recipes provides directions for making everything from flower- or herb-infused honeys, vinegars, and oils to flavored sugars, pastry doughs, and a poaching liquid for fruits. The recipes rely on a variety of cooking methods, from classic oven roasting and quick sautéing to healthful steaming. An emphasis on good health is also reflected in the limited use of fats and salt.

Coupled with this contemporary approach to creating dishes that taste good and are good for you is an invitation to experiment with the pairing of wine and food in new and delightful ways. Some of the most exciting views on wine-and-food matching are being explored at the beautiful Fetzer Vineyards, located in northern California's wine country. The people at Fetzer believe that wines should mate with the predominate herb flavoring in a meal. For example, fresh snapper with lemon and dill provides the perfect partner to the citrus and herbal notes found in Sauvignon Blanc. In the spirit of such discoveries, the descriptions of many of the herbs in this book provide suggestions for appropriate pairing with wines.

Fetzer Vineyards has also developed experimental wine tastings that revolve around sampling fresh flowers and herbs with complementary wines that exemplify similar characteristics. A bite of the particular flower or herb followed by a sip of the wine expands the flavor of each. This might mean serving Fumé Blanc with anise hyssop blossoms or a Gewürztraminer with daylilies. Our section on edible flowers gives additional suggestions for tastings.

Using This Book

Read this book as a stepping-stone to experimenting with each plant's use in the landscape and in the kitchen. The plants are listed alphabetically by their most frequently used common name. The proper botanical name, in Latin, follows each main entry for the sake of accuracy and safety. When buying from your local nursery or ordering via a mail-order company, use only the botanical name, to avoid inadvertently acquiring a toxic plant (see page 217 for a partial list of common poisonous plants and page 218 for a list of mail-order sources). There are many common names for some plants. We have tried to select the most common of the common names and have listed some alternatives in the accompanying text.

Each plant entry begins with a description of the plant's ornamental virtues and uses, some cultivation tips, and, perhaps, a few special features. Pest and disease problems are occasionally mentioned; check with your local cooperative extension for the particulars about problems in your area. Suggested spray and control programs are based upon the least invasive techniques and on nonchemical compounds in order to protect the health of the gardener as well as the garden. To grow all these special plants and then spray them with toxic chemicals, or to apply systemic pesticides and herbicides to them, defeats the purpose of an edible landscape—fresh, safe, and poison-free produce.

You will notice most of the descriptive plant entries do not list a climate zone. The zone map found in most gardening books is a generic, macroscopic characterization of climate. With so many edible plants, the subtleties of microclimates make the difference between life or death, excellent flavor or an insipid taste, an abundant crop or a fruitless tree. Take the time to discuss the plants you're thinking of growing with local experts: the personnel at the nearest cooperative extension or farm advisor's office, the knowledgeable staff of a retail nursery, the members of gardening organizations, and longtime gardeners in your neighborhood.

Each plant also includes a review of when and how to harvest and proper preparation and storage in the kitchen, followed by a few tips on which foods complement the featured plant and some quick-and-easy recipes. And last, but most important, are recipes that display the virtues and unique flavors and textures of the edible ornamentals, herbs, and flowers featured in this book.

Basics

Many plants from the gourmet's garden landscape can be used for preparing basic ingredients. Instructions for preparing these culinary essentials, along with bouquets garnis, herb salt, candied flowers and leaves, and flavored sugars appear in the following pages. In addition, there are recipes for salad dressings, sauces, pastries, and other preparations called for throughout the book. Some of these recipes, such as a poaching liquid that calls for lavender, rosemary, or sweet cicely, use plants from the culinary landscape. Others, including a nonfat or low-fat yogurt cheese and a white sauce, enhance the harvest from the gourmet's garden.

Wash and thoroughly dry all fresh herbs, leaves, and flowers before preparing any of the following.

Infusions

Herbs, leaves, or flowers steeped in appropriate sweet or savory liquids impart a subtle flavor. The intensity of the infusion depends upon the amount of flavoring used and the length of the steeping time.

Stock: Simmer any kind of stock, uncovered, with fresh or dried herbs, leaves, flowers, or petals until flavored to taste, about 30 minutes. The stock will cook down slightly and become more concentrated. Use as you would any stock.

Oil: Choose the oils you use most frequently in salad dressings, marinades, and for stir-frying, sautéing, and grilling fish, poultry, and meat. Loosely pack herb sprigs, one kind or a combination, in a clean glass container, pour in oil to fill container, stretch a piece of cheese-cloth over the top, and place in a warm area or sunny windowsill 2 to 3 weeks. Strain the oil and taste. If the flavor is not strong enough, repack with fresh herbs and steep for an additional week. Strain, cap, and refrigerate up to 2 weeks. Bring to room temperature before using.

Garlic will complement almost all of the herbal oil infusions. To avoid the possibility of botulism developing, marinate the garlic in distilled white vinegar 24 hours, then drain and add it to the oil.

Vinegar: Use high-quality white wine, red wine, unseasoned rice wine, or cider vinegar and any herbs, flowers, or fresh or dried seeds, alone or in combination. For variety, add chopped shallots or lightly crushed garlic.

Lightly bruise the herbs, petals, or seeds. Loosely pack the herbs or petals in a clean glass bottle or jar with an acid-proof lid, or add 2 to 3 tablespoons seeds. Warm the vinegar slightly and pour into the bottle to fill almost to the top. Cap and place in a sunny window 2 to 3 weeks; check daily to make sure the herbs are immersed in the vinegar and add more warm vinegar as needed. Alternatively, to speed the infusing process, bring vinegar just to the boiling point and pour it over the herbs, petals, or seeds. Steep 1 week.

Strain the vinegar and taste. If the infusion is too strong, transfer the vinegar to a larger container and add more vinegar to dilute to taste. If it is not strong enough, strain and add fresh cuttings, petals, or seeds; let stand for another week. Strain (add a fresh sprig to the finished herb vinegar), cap, and store in a cool, dark area up to several months.

Honey: For color and fragrance, infuse honey with fresh or dried herbs, leaves, or blossoms. Allow approximately 1 tablespoon chopped fresh or 1 teaspoon crumbled dried flavoring for each pint of honey. If using leaves, lightly bruise before placing in a sterilized jar. Pour in honey and stand jar in a pan of barely simmering water for 10 to 15 minutes. Remove from water bath, cool, cap, and store in a cool, dark area at least 1 week before using. The infused honey will last many months.

Oil Concentrates

These concentrates are an excellent way to preserve herbs. They can be used as a base for marinades, or for sautéing or grilling fish, poultry, or meats. Allow 2 cups firmly packed chopped herbs, one kind or a combination, to 1/2 cup canola, safflower, or olive oil. The type of oil will depend upon its eventual use. Freeze in small containers and defrost as needed. The concentrate may be strained before using, if desired.

Compound Butters

Preparing compound butters is not only an easy way to preserve herbs, but also one of the best ways to add piquancy when cooking or saucing eggs, vegetables, fish, poultry, and meats. Full-flavored herbs or seeds make the best compound butters.

Allow approximately 1 tablespoon chopped fresh herb(s) or 1/2 teaspoon seeds for each 1/4 pound butter, preferably unsalted. Pound the herb(s) or seeds in a mortar with a little salt and blend into softened butter. If desired, gradually incorporate other ingredients such as minced shallots or garlic, onion juice, fresh lemon or lime juice, vinegar or Worcestershire sauce, mustard, freshly grated nutmeg, and/or salt and pepper. Alternatively, blend in a food processor fitted with a metal blade. Pack into crocks, or form into a log, and refrigerate at least 3 hours to mellow the flavors. Use within 3 days, or wrap well and freeze up to 3 months.

Herb Salt

Herb salt, which can be used as you would plain salt, should be made with kosher salt, sea salt, or noniodized table salt. Use only one herb, or try different combinations.

To make herb salt with fresh herbs, use equal parts firmly packed chopped herb(s) and salt. Crush the herb(s) in a mortar, blender, or mini processor with a little of the salt, and then mix thoroughly with the remaining salt. Spread the mixture on a baking sheet and place in a preheated 200° F oven until dry, about 45 minutes. Stir often to break up lumps, and make sure the herbs are evenly distributed. Remove from oven, let cool, and stir in 1/2 to 1 teaspoon paprika, if desired. Store in tightly capped glass container in a cool, dry area up to 3 months.

To make herb salt with dried herbs, mix ground or crumbled herbs with salt (5 to 8 tablespoons to 1 cup salt) and a little paprika. Store in a sealed glass container in a cool, dry area.

Bouquets Garnis

Bouquets garnis, sometimes called faggots, are herb or spice combinations used for flavoring long-simmered dishes. The classic French bouquet garni consists of parsley, thyme, bay leaf, and sometimes marjoram, but any mixture can be used as long as the elements are compatible and they complement the dish they are seasoning.

When your garden is in full production, make bouquets garnis with fresh herbs. If using the bouquet garni within a day or two, make a bundle of herbs, enclose in a wrapper of leek leaves or nest between two celery ribs, and tie securely. Otherwise, wrap the herbs in a square of double-thick cheesecloth and tie the top closed. Seal the cheesecloth bags in a plastic bag and freeze up to 6 months. When ready to use, defrost and pound lightly with a flat mallet to release oils before adding to dishes. If using dried herbs to make bouquets garnis, tie them in cheesecloth and store in an airtight container in a cool, dark place up to 3 months.

Chiffonade

The word *chiffonade* refers to both a style of cutting and a preparation. To chiffonade herb leaves—basil, sage, sorrel—and leafy vegetables— lettuce, Swiss chard—wash and remove stems and any damaged leaves. For a very thin cut, roll a single leaf into a tight cylinder and cut crosswise into fine shreds. For a coarser cut, loosely roll several leaves together and cut crosswise.

Once the herbs or vegetables have been cut, they may be added raw to soups and salads, or cooked and served as a garnish, or a chiffonade.

Flavored Sugars

Pound granulated or superfine sugar and minced fresh flower petals or herb leaves in a mortar, or whirl in a food processor. Transfer to a jar, cover, and let stand 1 week. Use as you would any sugar.

Candying

If possible, choose a nonhumid day for candying flowers, fruits, or leaves. Select white or brightly colored flowers with simple petal arrangements, small fruits such as grapes and hardy kiwifruits, and any small, attractive leaves. Beat egg white until frothy and, using a feather brush, paint egg white on flowers or petals to cover completely. Then, using tweezers, dip into extrafine sugar.

Place coated items, not touching, on a fine-mesh wire rack. Let dry in a warm place such as an unlighted gas oven or an electric oven set at lowest heat and with the door slightly ajar. Timing will vary depending upon weather conditions and the items being candied. When thoroughly dry, store in airtight containers up to 3 or 4 months. Use for garnishing desserts.

Sealing and Storing Jams, Jellies, and Preserves

Remove jam or other preserves from heat and immediately ladle into hot, sterilized jars, filling to within 1/4 inch from top of jar. Wipe edges of jars with a clean, damp cloth and seal with sterilized canning lid and screw top. Tighten completely and place on a kitchen towel on a tray or work surface. Let stand undisturbed 24 hours. If properly sealed, lids will be slightly depressed (you will hear a light pop when they seal). Touch lightly with fingertips to check for seal. Store jars in a dark, cool place. Those jars that have not sealed properly should be refrigerated immediately and stored as indicated in individual recipes.

Basics Recipes

Herb Vinaigrette

6 tablespoons olive oil

1/4 cup red wine vinegar

1 teaspoon Dijon-style mustard

1/2 to 1 teaspoon pressed garlic

2 teaspoons minced oregano or 1 teaspoon minced basil or tarragon

Pinch sugar

Salt and freshly ground black or white pepper, to taste

A good all-purpose dressing for green salads.

In a bowl whisk together all ingredients thoroughly. Jar, cover, and refrigerate at least 4 hours or up to 1 week. Bring to room temperature and shake well before using.

Makes about 1/2 cup

Herbed Tomato Vinaigrette

1/2 cup firmly packed parsley leaves and tender stems

1 1/2 tablespoons chopped thyme leaves

l or 2 large cloves garlic, chopped

1 1/2 cups peeled, seeded, and diced very ripe tomatoes

1 tablespoon fresh lemon juice

1 to 3 tablespoons olive oil

Salt and freshly ground pepper, to taste

A delicious dressing for freshly cooked pasta, navy beans, or sautéed polenta squares. If using this tangy vinaigrette on salad greens, add an additional 1 or 2 tablespoons olive oil. Thinly chiffonade-cut basil can also be added.

✦

*I*n a blender combine parsley, thyme, and garlic and whirl until minced. Add tomatoes, lemon juice, 1 tablespoon oil, and salt and pepper and purée until vinaigrette is well mixed and slightly thickened. Add additional oil as needed for desired consistency. If not using immediately, jar, cover, and refrigerate up to 1 week. Shake well before using.

MAKES ABOUT *1 1/2 CUPS*

Balsamic Vinaigrette

6 tablespoons balsamic vinegar

1 teaspoon Dijon-style mustard, or to taste

1/4 cup olive oil

2 tablespoons finely minced shallot or green onion (optional)

2 teaspoons finely minced dill or basil (optional)

Fresh lemon juice, salt, and freshly ground white pepper, to taste

The proportion of vinegar to oil can be adjusted to your taste. Serve on greens or lightly steamed vegetables.

✦

*I*n a small bowl whisk together vinegar, mustard, and oil. Add shallot and/or dill (if used). Season with lemon juice, salt, and pepper and mix well. Jar, cover, and refrigerate up to 1 week. Bring to room temperature and shake well before using.

MAKES ABOUT *2/3 CUP*

Hoisin Salad Dressing

2 tablespoons each hoisin sauce
and unseasoned rice
wine vinegar

1 teaspoon each fresh lemon
juice and Asian sesame oil

Dash chili pepper oil or
hot-pepper sauce

This simple Asian dressing is especially good on salads made with bean sprouts, Chinese cabbage, ornamental kale, or bitter greens. The ingredients can be adjusted to individual tastes. Hoisin sauce, which is based on fermented soybeans, is slightly sweet and quite thick. It can be purchased at Asian food stores.

✦

*I*n a small bowl whisk together all ingredients thoroughly. Transfer to a jar, cover, and refrigerate up to 1 week. Shake well before using.

MAKES ABOUT *1/3* CUP

Yogurt Salad Dressing

1/4 cup Yogurt Cheese (see
page 22)

1 1/2 tablespoons olive oil

1 tablespoon fresh lemon juice,
or more to taste

1/4 teaspoon grated lemon zest

Celery salt and freshly ground
white pepper, to taste

1 to 2 tablespoons chopped
fennel feathers, chives, or
other herbs

A simple, low-calorie mayonnaiselike dressing that can be used whenever a creamy dressing is appropriate.

✦

*I*n a small bowl whisk together all ingredients until thoroughly blended. Taste and adjust seasonings with additional lemon juice and/or herbs. Jar, cover, and refrigerate up to 1 week. Whisk briefly before using.

MAKES ABOUT *1/3* CUP

Yogurt Fruit Salad Dressing

3 tablespoons olive oil

1/4 cup Vanilla Yogurt Cheese
(see page 23)

4 teaspoons basil, anise hyssop,
salad burnet, or other herb
vinegar (see page 14)

1/2 to 1 teaspoon fresh
lemon juice

1/2 teaspoon sugar

Salt and freshly ground white
pepper, to taste

Fresh orange juice (optional)

*Spoon over Asian pears and top with feta cheese or over a dish of
fresh blueberries.*

◆

*I*n a small bowl whisk together all ingredients except orange juice until
thoroughly blended. Taste and adjust seasonings. Jar, cover, and
refrigerate up to 3 days. Just before serving, thin, if desired, with a little
orange juice.

MAKES ABOUT 1/2 CUP

Mixed Herb Pesto

1/2 cup walnuts or pine nuts

2 to 3 large cloves
garlic, chopped

1/2 teaspoon salt

1/4 cup chopped green onion

1 cup firmly packed chopped
lemon basil or basil

1/3 cup firmly packed
chopped parsley

1/4 cup firmly packed
chopped oregano

2 tablespoons firmly packed
chopped summer savory

1 tablespoon firmly packed
chopped lemon thyme

5 tablespoons freshly grated
Parmesan cheese

2 tablespoons shredded
Gruyère cheese

1/2 cup olive oil

Freshly ground white pepper,
to taste

Most commonly prepared with basil or basil and parsley, pesto has assumed many new guises in the culinary world with recipes based on sun-dried tomatoes, olives, mint, and a host of other ingredients. This basic recipe uses a mix of aromatic fresh herbs. Experiment with other herbs such as thyme, as well as other herb combinations, using parsley as the flavor stabilizer. Depending upon the dish with which the pesto is to be served, use olive, canola, or safflower oil. If lemon basil and lemon thyme are unavailable, add a little fresh lemon juice to the finished pesto.

Use pesto as a sauce for steamed clams, pasta, or rice. Substitute pesto for butter in sandwiches, or use a dollop of it atop scrambled eggs, poached fish, or veal chops. Thin pesto with Yogurt Salad Dressing (see page 19) for a green salad or with rice wine vinegar for shredded cabbage salad. Stuff pesto under the skin of chicken before roasting, or mix with ricotta cheese as a filling for crêpes. Stir pesto into vegetable soups just before serving, or mix it with hard-cooked egg yolks for deviled eggs.

*I*n a blender or a food processor fitted with metal blade, combine walnuts, garlic, and salt and process 1 minute. Add green onion and all the herbs and process 1 minute longer. Add cheeses and process just until well blended. With motor running slowly pour in oil in a thin stream. Process to form a smooth paste. Add pepper, taste, and adjust seasonings. Jar, cover, and refrigerate up to 4 days or freeze up to 3 months. Defrost in refrigerator and stir well before using.

MAKES ABOUT 1 CUP

White Sauce

1 tablespoon each butter and olive or canola oil

1/4 cup finely minced onion

1/2 teaspoon dry mustard

2 tablespoons flour

1 cup evaporated low-fat or skimmed milk or 1/2 cup each milk and rich stock, plus milk or stock for reheating, if needed

1 tablespoon snipped dill, chives, or other herb of choice

Salt, freshly ground white pepper, paprika, and freshly grated nutmeg, to taste

Here is a low-fat adaptation of béchamel sauce. Use it for preparing dishes such as creamed Swiss chard, orach, onions, or peas, or similar dishes.

◆

*I*n a skillet or saucepan over medium heat, melt butter with oil. Add onion and sauté, stirring occasionally, until onion is soft, about 5 minutes. Sprinkle with mustard and flour and cook, stirring occasionally, 3 minutes. Remove from heat and slowly stir in milk.

Return to low heat and cook, stirring often, 10 minutes; sauce will have thickened to a creamy consistency. Stir in all remaining ingredients and heat gently. Taste and adjust seasonings.

If not using immediately transfer to container, cool, cover, and refrigerate up to 3 days. Reheat gently, thinning with additional milk or stock, if needed.

MAKES ABOUT 1 1/2 CUPS

Mornay Sauce

*A*dd 1 cup shredded Monterey jack or Cheddar cheese (about 1/4 lb) to sauce once it has thickened. Remove from heat and stir until cheese melts. Then add dill and seasonings and proceed as directed.

Yogurt Cheese

Draining the whey from yogurt results in a solid dairy product that can be used as a substitute for sour cream in dishes such as beef Stroganoff, for whipping cream in soups, and for whipped-cream toppings. Special yogurt strainers are now on the market, but a sieve or colander lined with a coffee filter or cheesecloth will work as well. For this recipe use yogurt that contains no gelatin.

◆

*S*poon plain nonfat or low-fat yogurt into a special yogurt strainer or lined sieve or colander (see recipe introduction) and refrigerate the empty carton and lid. Cover and refrigerate to drain overnight or up to

24 hours. Spoon yogurt back into reserved carton, close lid tightly, and refrigerate, upside down, up to 10 days or more. Storing the yogurt upside down will lengthen its life considerably. Use only clean utensils when measuring and do not return any yogurt to a carton that has been unrefrigerated for any length of time.

Jar the whey and refrigerate up to 3 days or freeze up to 3 months. Use in sauces, yeast breads, and soups.

One pint of yogurt will yield approximately 1 cup cheese and 3/4 cup whey. Yields vary depending upon how long the yogurt is drained.

Vanilla Yogurt Cheese

Follow directions for Yogurt Cheese, substituting plain nonfat or low-fat vanilla yogurt for plain yogurt. Use to make frozen yogurt desserts or in toppings for fruit compotes and salads.

Fritter Batter

1/2 cup flat beer, white wine, milk, or milk in which flowers or herbs have been infused

2 eggs

1 cup unbleached flour

1 teaspoon baking powder

1/2 to 1 teaspoon sugar (optional)

1/4 teaspoon salt

Almost any edible blossom or leaf can be dipped in batter and deep-fried. For savory items such as clary sage leaves, make the batter with beer, omit the sugar, and serve with meat or poultry dishes. For sweet items such as rose petals or geranium or sweet cicely leaves, use white wine or milk, add the optional sugar, and use to garnish desserts. The batter, which must be refrigerated for two hours, may be made a day in advance.

◆

In a blender combine all ingredients. Process, stopping often to scrape down sides of container, until smooth. Cover and refrigerate 2 hours before using.

MAKES ABOUT 1 CUP

Poaching Liquid

1 cup Chardonnay

2/3 cup water

1/2 cup sugar

4 slices lemon

4 whole cloves

4 coriander seeds,
lightly crushed

1 cinnamon stick (3 in. long),
broken into 3 or 4 pieces

12 lavender leaves

Depending upon the recipe being prepared, scented geranium leaves or herbs such as sweet cicely, lemon or lime thyme, pineapple sage, or rosemary can be substituted for the lavender leaves. Adjust the number of these other leaves according to the intensity of their flavor. This recipe makes enough poaching liquid for two pounds of Asian pears, Fuyu persimmons, or quinces. It can also be reduced to a light syrup over high heat, cooled slightly, and used for steeping feijoa slices or orange sections.

◆

*I*n a large, nonreactive saucepan over medium-high heat, combine all ingredients and bring to a boil, stirring to dissolve sugar. Reduce heat and simmer, stirring occasionally, 10 minutes. Let cool, cover, and refrigerate up to 1 week.

MAKES ABOUT *1 2/3* CUPS

To Poach Fruit:

Halve or slice peeled and cored fruit and add to liquid in saucepan. Cover with a lid slightly smaller than the circumference of saucepan to immerse the fruit in the liquid, and place over medium heat. Bring to a gentle boil and simmer until fruit is tender (10 to 25 minutes). Timing will depend upon the type of fruit.

Let cool in liquid, cover, and refrigerate up to 3 days. To serve, transfer fruit to serving dish and strain liquid over the top.

Custard Sauce

2 cups low-fat or evaporated low-fat milk

2 to 4 herb sprigs or flower leaves or blossoms

6 egg yolks

1/3 cup superfine sugar

Lighten this sauce with Vanilla Yogurt Cheese (see page 23), if desired, and serve as a topping for fresh or poached fruits or berries, or mix into fruit purées and serve, warm or cool, over meringues or angel food cake. Keep in mind that some herbs are stronger than others, so adjust the amount accordingly. Choose such herbs as lavender, mint, basil, anise hyssop, or sweet cicely. If you use a flavored sugar, the bouquet of the custard will be intensified.

◆

In a heavy saucepan over medium heat, combine milk and herb sprigs and bring just to a boil. Remove from heat and set aside for at least 10 minutes or up to 1 hour.

In a mixing bowl whisk together egg yolks and sugar until thickened, creamy, and dark yellow. Remove herb sprigs from milk and discard; reheat milk just to boiling point and, whisking constantly, slowly pour into yolks. Return yolk mixture to saucepan and place over medium-low heat. Using a wooden spoon, stir constantly until sauce thickly coats back of spoon (8 to 10 minutes or 170° F on a candy thermometer). Do not allow custard to boil and do not overcook.

If using soon after preparing, transfer to top pan of double boiler over hot water to keep hot; stir occasionally. If not using at once, cover with plastic wrap, pressing it directly onto surface to prevent skin from forming. Let cool and refrigerate up to 2 days. Reheat in top pan of double boiler over simmering water.

MAKES ABOUT *2 1/4 CUPS*

Pizza Dough

1 tablespoon active dry yeast

1/4 cup lukewarm water (105°
to 115° F)

1/2 teaspoon sugar

1/2 cup milk, scalded and
cooled to lukewarm

2 tablespoons olive oil

1 1/4 cups unbleached flour, or
as needed

1/2 teaspoon salt

A thin, crispy, easy-to-make basic dough for any kind of pizza.

✦

*I*n a large mixing bowl, sprinkle yeast over lukewarm water and stir in sugar. Let stand until yeast is creamy (about 5 minutes). Stir in milk and oil. Add 1 cup of the flour and the salt and beat vigorously with a wooden spoon 3 minutes. Gradually beat in remaining 1/4 cup flour.

Turn dough out onto lightly floured board. Knead until smooth and elastic (about 10 minutes), using as little additional flour (no more than 1/4 cup) as necessary to keep dough from sticking.

Form dough into a ball and place in large oiled bowl. Turn to coat on all sides with oil, cover with tea towel, and let dough rise in warm place until doubled in bulk (about 1 1/4 hours).

Punch down dough, knead briefly, and form into a ball, or halve and form into 2 balls. Cover with a tea towel and let rest 10 minutes. Roll and pat dough as directed in individual recipes.

MAKES ONE MEDIUM PIZZA CRUST

Basic Pastry

1 cup unbleached flour

1/2 to 1 teaspoon
sugar (optional)

1/4 teaspoon salt

1/4 cup unsalted butter, cut into
24 uniform cubes and chilled

3 tablespoons plain nonfat
yogurt, chilled

A food processor makes this recipe foolproof if you follow the directions carefully. When preparing this dough for a savory dish, omit the optional sugar and add, if desired, 1/4 to 1/2 teaspoon crumbled dried herb of choice.

◆

In a food processor fitted with metal blade, combine flour, sugar, and salt. Pulse several times to mix. Strew butter cubes evenly over flour and pulse until mixture is consistency of tiny peas. Rub mixture between your fingertips to check for proper consistency. Distribute yogurt evenly over flour-butter mixture and process only until dough starts to gather on one side of work bowl (5 to 8 seconds). Do not overprocess or dough will toughen; it is better to undermix than overmix.

Carefully remove dough from bowl. Press gently into a loose ball, gathering up any stray bits of dough from sides of bowl. Flatten ball into a disk, wrap well in waxed paper, and place in a plastic bag. Refrigerate at least 1 hour, or overnight.

Remove disk from refrigerator and let rest 3 to 4 minutes, or 10 minutes if dough has been refrigerated more than 2 hours. Place on lightly floured board and, using lightly floured rolling pin, roll from center of disk outward, pressing gently (do not slide rolling pin across surface of dough) and gradually radiating strokes around entire disk to make a round.

When round is about 8 inches in diameter, slip a long, thin-bladed spatula under it, lift up, flip round over onto your hand and forearm, lightly flour board, and then slip dough back onto board so side on which you were rolling is now facing the board. Continue rolling out dough with light strokes. The final round should be 1/8 inch to 1/4 inch thick, depending upon recipe.

When round is the approximate size needed, fold it in half and gently lift it from board. Set it down on half of the pie pan and unfold. Lifting edges of round as you work, press dough lightly to sides of pan. Trim edges evenly to leave an overhang of 1/4 to 1/2 inch. Firmly fold overhang onto edge of pan to make a rim, then flute with fingertips.

MAKES ONE 10-INCH PIE SHELL OR 9-INCH DEEP-DISH PIE SHELL

To Partially Bake or Fully Bake Pie Shell:

If time allows, wrap the pastry-lined pan in plastic wrap and freeze several hours; defrost in refrigerator 15 minutes before baking. Otherwise, refrigerate 30 minutes.

Preheat oven to 400° F. Carefully line chilled shell with a circle of lightweight aluminum foil large enough so it can be easily lifted out. Fill foil-lined shell with metal pie weights or raw rice or legumes to reach halfway up sides of shell. To prevent overbrowning, crimp the foil so that it covers exposed crust rim.

Bake shell 10 minutes. Lift out weights and foil, prick entire bottom surface of shell with tines of fork, and return shell to oven. For a partially baked shell, bake an additional 5 minutes, remove from oven, place on wire rack, and let cool completely before filling. For a fully baked shell, after removing weights and pricking shell, lower oven heat to 350° F and bake shell until golden (15 to 20 minutes). Cool on wire rack.

The partially baked or fully baked shell will keep at room temperature for 6 hours. Unbaked, partially baked, and fully baked shells may be frozen, well wrapped in aluminum foil or plastic wrap, 3 to 4 weeks.

Walnut Pastry

1 cup whole-wheat pastry flour

1/3 cup unbleached flour

1/2 cup finely chopped walnuts

1/2 teaspoon salt

1/3 cup canola oil

1/4 cup nonfat milk, or
as needed

This nut crust can be filled with a variety of fruits and topped with Custard Sauce (see page 25) or with Vanilla Yogurt Cheese (see page 23) lightened with a little cream or fruit juice. Chop the walnuts with a knife or chopper, not in a food processor.

✦

Preheat oven to 425° F.

In a food processor fitted with metal blade, combine flours, walnuts, and salt. Pulse several times to mix. Add oil and milk and process just until blended. Pinch a bit of dough between your fingers; if dough does not readily stick together, add a little more milk and process 1 or 2 seconds.

Remove dough from processor and form into a ball. Place ball on large piece of waxed paper and cover with a second piece of waxed paper. Press down to flatten into a disk and, using a rolling pin, roll into a round about 14 inches in diameter. Discard waxed paper and center pastry round in a 10-inch pie pan. Gently pat pastry evenly onto bottom and sides of pie pan and flute edges. Should cracks form, pinch together to seal.

Prick bottom and sides of dough with tines of fork and bake until just starting to turn golden (about 14 minutes). Let cool on wire rack before filling.

MAKES ONE 10-INCH PIE SHELL

Plants and Recipes for the Gourmet's Garden

Globe Artichoke

Cynara scolymus

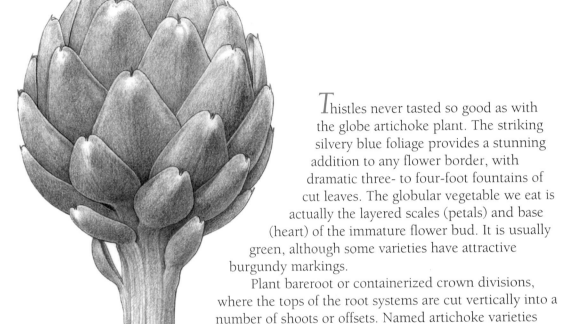

Perennial herbaceous plant; foliage naturally dies back each summer. Best in coastal zones with mild, nearly frost-free winters.

Plant crown divisions, either bareroot in winter or in a container in the spring and summer.

Prefers rich, well-drained soil.

Apply regular fertilizer each fall.

Protect from ravenous gophers.

*T*histles never tasted so good as with the globe artichoke plant. The striking silvery blue foliage provides a stunning addition to any flower border, with dramatic three- to four-foot fountains of cut leaves. The globular vegetable we eat is actually the layered scales (petals) and base (heart) of the immature flower bud. It is usually green, although some varieties have attractive burgundy markings.

Plant bareroot or containerized crown divisions, where the tops of the root systems are cut vertically into a number of shoots or offsets. Named artichoke varieties such as 'Green Globe', 'Purple', and 'Early Green Provence' can be true to form only if grown from crown divisions, not from seed.

In their native Mediterranean habitat, artichokes are not irrigated even though there is little or no summer rain. The foliage bounds forth in the early spring, the crop is harvested before summer, the tops die back to the soil during the heat of summer, and the winter rains rejuvenate the foliage from the massive root system. Plant an attractive evergreen ornamental plant in the foreground to mask the summer absence of the foliage.

The first artichoke heads, or globes, that form in the spring or early summer are generally the largest of the season. Harvest the first

*Complementary
Seasonings and Foods*

Basil, bay leaf, cilantro, mint,
oregano, thyme; lemon juice;
cheese and egg dishes; garlic,
chayotes or summer squashes,
mushrooms, onions, tomatoes;
seafood, poultry, lamb, veal.

globe when full sized, but before the scales begin to pull away from the head, by cutting the stem several inches below the base. The plant will respond with either more globes from the stem beneath the harvested head or with new flower shoots. The secondary crop is borne on flower stems that resemble a candelabra. Each subsequent flush of artichokes is proportionally smaller than the previous crop.

Soak the cut artichokes in salted ice water for at least 30 minutes to rid them of any insects that may be nesting in the scales. Rinse well and, using a sharp stainless-steel knife, cut the stems flush with the bases. Pull or cut off the small lower scales and cut off the top one fourth of the artichoke. Using scissors, snip off remaining scale tips halfway down. To avoid discoloration, immediately place in acidulated water to cover (one tablespoon lemon juice or vinegar per quart of water). If desired, pull the center scales apart to loosen, scoop out (use a sturdy melon baller) and discard the choke, and tie the artichoke back together with kitchen string. For recipes calling for only artichoke bottoms, remove the leaves and discard the choke. Trim, if needed, for appearance. To trim an artichoke so the entire globe is edible, select tiny artichokes (1 to 1 1/2 ounces each). Discard all tough scales down to the pale, tender heart and cut off about 1/2 inch from tops.

Always use nonreactive utensils when cooking artichokes. Large artichokes are sometimes boiled in water to cover to which lemon juice has been added, but most frequently they are arranged on a steamer rack, topped with fresh or dried herbs, minced garlic, and a drizzle of fresh lemon juice and olive oil and steamed over boiling water. Steamed tiny artichokes may be marinated, pickled, or added to stews or roasts. They may also be braised, sautéed, or dipped in batter and deep-fried.

To test large artichokes for doneness, pull a scale from the middle of the globe; it should pull out readily and the edible portion should be tender. Pierce the artichoke bottom with the tip of a sharp knife or a cake tester; it should slip in easily.

Mini Recipes

Fill cooked artichoke bottoms with Savory Chestnut Purée (see page 68) and bake in preheated 350° F oven until heated through (10 to 15 minutes). Garnish with chopped hard-cooked egg white.

Remove and discard chokes from whole cooked artichokes and fill with chicken, turkey, or shrimp salad prepared with small cubes of Monterey jack cheese; potato salad prepared with sliced radishes and capers; or orzo pasta salad prepared with chopped sun-dried tomatoes.

Stir together light cream cheese, Yogurt Cheese (see page 22), and fresh lemon juice. Pull leaves of uniform size from cooked large artichokes. Spoon 1/2 teaspoon of cheese mixture on fleshy part of each leaf and top with a dab of lumpfish caviar, a tiny strip of lemon zest, and a dill feather. Arrange leaves in spoke pattern on round serving plate and serve as hors d'oeuvres.

Fill cooked artichoke bottoms with creamed Swiss chard and sprinkle with freshly grated Romano cheese and paprika. Bake in preheated 350° F oven until heated through (10 to 15 minutes).

Layer sliced cooked artichoke bottoms in casserole dish, cover with Mornay Sauce (see page 22), and sprinkle with freshly grated Parmesan cheese. Bake in preheated 400° F oven until heated through and lightly browned (about 15 minutes).

Artichokes Stuffed with Herbed Lamb

Lamb Stuffing:

1/2 cup minced shallot

4 large cloves garlic,
finely minced

1 tablespoon olive oil

1 egg white

1 tablespoon cornstarch

1/2 cup fine fresh bread crumbs

1/2 cup plain nonfat yogurt

1/4 cup each finely chopped
basil and parsley

1 ounce feta or Gorgonzola
cheese, crumbled

1 pound lean ground lamb

1/4 teaspoon salt

1/8 teaspoon freshly
ground pepper

4 medium-large artichokes,
trimmed and chokes removed

Acidulated ice water, to cover

1/2 tablespoon olive oil

1 onion, minced

4 cloves garlic, minced

2 cups lamb or chicken stock

4 slices lemon

4 sprigs oregano

If there is any meat mixture left after stuffing the artichokes, form into small balls and sheet-freeze for a future appetizer. Tiny new potatoes, cooked along with the artichokes, or crusty French bread and a green salad dressed with Balsamic Vinaigrette (see page 18) make perfect accompaniments. The stuffing precludes the need for a dipping sauce for the artichoke leaves.

◆

*I*n a bowl combine all stuffing ingredients and mix well. Place a small amount in a small dish, place dish on steamer rack over boiling water, cover pot, and steam 5 minutes. Taste and adjust stuffing seasonings with basil, salt, and pepper. Cover and refrigerate stuffing mixture to blend flavors.

Soak artichokes in acidulated ice water to cover 30 minutes. Following directions on page 32, scoop out and discard choke of each artichoke. In a nonreactive saucepan just large enough to hold artichokes snugly, heat olive oil over medium heat. Add onion and garlic, cover, and cook until onion is soft (about 5 minutes). Add stock and bring to a simmer.

Meanwhile, drain artichokes and gently loosen leaves without detaching. Spoon some of the stuffing between the rows of leaves and then fill centers of artichokes with more stuffing, mounding it slightly. Stand artichokes upright in the simmering stock, top each with a lemon slice and an oregano sprig, and baste with a little of the stock. Bring to a boil over medium-high heat, lower heat, cover, and cook at a gentle boil, adding additional stock if needed to maintain original level, until artichokes are tender (about 25 minutes).

Discard lemon slices and oregano sprigs. Using tongs, transfer artichokes to individual serving plates. Spoon a little stock over the top of each.

Serves 4

34

Braised Artichokes with Mustard and Tomatoes

1 tablespoon olive oil

12 tiny artichokes (about 1 1/2 oz each), trimmed and halved

2/3 cup finely minced onion

4 large cloves garlic, finely minced

1/4 teaspoon salt

1/8 teaspoon freshly ground white pepper

1 cup stock of choice

1 tablespoon Dijon-style mustard

12 cherry tomatoes, peeled (if desired) and halved if large

3 tablespoons minced parsley

2 tablespoons snipped chives

1/3 cup freshly grated Parmesan cheese

The braising liquid forms a sauce that can be tossed with freshly cooked pasta or spooned over a bed of polenta or steamed rice, barley, or bulgur.

◆

Heat oil in a large skillet over medium heat. Add artichokes and sauté, turning often, 3 minutes. Add onion and sauté 2 minutes. Add garlic and sauté 1 minute. Sprinkle with salt and pepper, raise heat slightly, and add stock and mustard. Stir well, cover, lower heat, and cook until artichokes are tender (about 10 minutes). Timing will depend upon size and freshness of artichokes.

Add tomatoes, cover, and cook until tomatoes just start to soften (1 to 2 minutes). Sprinkle with parsley, chives, and cheese and serve immediately.

SERVES 4

Asian Pear

Pyrus ussuriensis and P. serotina

Standard tree reaches 35 to 40 feet tall and 25 feet wide; dwarf trees are as small as 12 feet by 8 feet.

Plant bareroot tree in winter.

Prefers well-drained soil; will tolerate clayey soil better than most fruit trees.

Shape and prune limbs for a wide angle of attachment. Fruit forms on the same fruiting spur clusters each year for five or more years.

Use nontoxic spray for codling moth and leaf caterpillars as needed.

Watch for blackened leaves and oozing twigs, which indicate fireblight.

Variously known as a salad pear, pear-apple, Oriental pear, apple-pear, and Korean pear, the proper name for this extraordinary fruit is Asian pear. While a "new" fruit to most Americans, this pear has been grown for over a thousand years throughout the Orient. These wonderfully scented, deliciously flavored fruits are usually round like an apple, yet are members of the pear family.

One's first impression upon sampling a tree-ripened fruit is how superbly juicy it is—succulent enough to dribble down your chin. The flesh is also amazingly crunchy without being mealy or grainy, as with the traditional European pear. Even more amazingly, the Asian pear, unlike the European pear, fully ripens *on* the tree without developing a rotten core.

There are two major categories of Asian pears: those with russeted, brown skin and those with smooth yellow skin. The flesh of some of the brown-skinned Asian pears is flushed with a unique aromatic perfume and complex mixture of exotic flavors. One such variety, 'Hosui', has an intense aroma and a taste that is similar to an earthy

*Complementary
Seasonings and Foods*

Mint, anise hyssop, pineapple
sage, sweet cicely; ginger,
orange and lemon zest;
almonds, pecans; berries,
kiwifruits, oranges; Jarlsberg,
Port-Salut, Gouda, Stilton, Brie,
provolone, Gruyère cheese; dry
or sweet red wine, amaretto,
brandy, pear brandy.

brandy flavor blended with the subtle essence of other ripened fruits. The tasty '20th Century' Asian pear, called 'Nijisseiki' in Japan, is one of the green-yellow varieties. In all, you can order nearly 30 varieties of Asian pear trees from mail-order catalogs.

Any garden where the typical European pear grows, except for the extremes of cold and warm winters, can expect Asian pear trees to fruit well at least three out of five years, or better. The trees offer an intense blaze of hot yellow fall color and are awash in pure white during spring bloom. Unlike their European cousin, many Asian pear-tree varieties sport an attractive burgundy tinge on new spring growth.

Perhaps the most difficult thing to learn about Asian pears is when to harvest for the best flavor, texture, and juiciness. The season is August through October, depending upon the variety. Fortunately, the longer the fruit is on the tree, especially with the russeted types, the better and more complex the flavor. For the russeted fruits, wait at least until the greenish undertone is almost fully covered by the darker, rich brown overtone. Yellow-green varieties should be left until the yellow covers the entire fruit and a hot yellow, almost orange-yellow, blushes the sunny side of the fruit. To harvest, pluck the fruit from the tree when it can be lifted 45 degrees to the side and the stem easily separates from the twig's spur cluster.

After cutting into a pear, rub with lemon juice to prevent surface discoloration, and, unless the skin is unsightly or especially tough, or a recipe so specifies, do not peel. Core, slice or dice, and drizzle with a little fresh lemon juice and/or honey, or combine with other fruits in a fruit cup or salad.

Asian pears may be spiced, canned, or dried, and they make delicious chutney or butter. If using in baked goods, note they have a higher water content than European pears. Serve pear wedges with Brie or Camembert cheese, or for dipping into cheese fondue. Chop and add to quick bread or muffin batter.

Mini Recipes

Toss diced Asian pears with other diced fresh fruits, lightly toasted chopped blanched almonds, and minced anise hyssop leaves and/or flowers, pineapple sage leaves, and/or sweet cicely feathers.

Toss diced Asian pears with Yogurt Fruit Salad Dressing (see page 20) and serve on bed of lettuce with garnish of mint sprigs.

Combine sliced Asian pears with cranberries or rhubarb in a cobbler, pie, or tart.

Toss Asian pear and jicama slices with fresh lemon or lime juice and arrange on lettuce leaves. Garnish with cilantro sprigs.

Poached Asian Pears with Rose Geranium Leaves

Poaching Liquid (see page 24 and recipe introduction)

Boiling water, as needed

4 Asian pears, peeled, halved, cored, and rubbed with fresh lemon juice

Rose geranium leaves, for garnish

Because Asian pears are very firm and thus difficult to core, you may want to core them after they are poached. When preparing the liquid for poaching, substitute 6 sweet cicely sprigs, mint sprigs, or pineapple sage for the lavender leaves. Serve poached pears plain or with Custard Sauce (see page 25), chocolate ice cream, or frozen yogurt.

◆

*I*n a saucepan prepare Poaching Liquid and bring to a boil. Gently lower pear halves into liquid. Add boiling water as needed for pears to float in liquid. Cover with lid slightly smaller than circumference of saucepan to keep pears immersed in liquid, reduce heat, and simmer, turning pears once, until tender when pierced with cake tester (15 to 25 minutes). Timing will depend upon variety of Asian pear.

Cool pear halves in poaching syrup and refrigerate, basting and turning occasionally, 3 hours or overnight.

To serve, using a slotted utensil transfer pears to 4 serving plates. Strain poaching syrup evenly over top. Garnish with leaves.

SERVES 4

Asian Pear Sorbet with Rosemary

Poaching Liquid (see page 24 and recipe introduction)

4 or 5 Asian pears (about 2 lb), peeled, cored, and coarsely chopped (4 cups)

1 teaspoon fresh lemon juice

1 egg white

Mint sprigs or sweet cicely feathers, for garnish

A perfect sorbet to serve between courses, in which case spoon into six chilled parfait glasses. For dessert, serve in four chilled crystal bowls. When preparing the liquid for poaching, add 2 slices lemon or 3 slices fresh ginger and substitute 3 sprigs rosemary for the lavender leaves.

✦

In a saucepan combine Poaching Liquid and pears. Cover and cook over medium heat until pears are soft (15 to 25 minutes). Using a slotted spoon transfer pears to a shallow metal dish. Strain liquid, cover, and refrigerate. Place pears in freezer until frozen almost solid (3 to 4 hours).

In a food processor fitted with metal blade or a blender, combine frozen pears and lemon juice and purée. Add reserved liquid, blend well, and return to dish. Place in freezer and freeze, stirring with fork several times, until solid (3 to 4 hours).

Beat egg white just until soft peaks form. Return pear purée to food processor and blend until smooth. Transfer to mixing bowl. Fold in egg white, spoon mixture into freezer container, and refreeze until solid (3 to 4 hours) or up to 3 days.

Just before serving, return to processor and blend until smooth (3 or 4 seconds). Spoon into glasses or bowls and garnish each serving with a mint sprig.

Makes about 4 cups

Pear and Grape Waldorf Salad

1/4 cup Yogurt Cheese
(see page 22)

2 teaspoons fresh lemon juice

Pinch each salt and sugar

Freshly ground white pepper,
to taste

1 to 1 1/2 cups diced Asian pear

2/3 cup halved seedless grapes

1/2 cup diced celery

1/4 cup each raisins and
chopped walnuts

1/2 cup crumbled chèvre

1 teaspoon each snipped
rosemary and minced
pineapple sage

Looseleaf lettuce leaves

Cilantro sprigs, for garnish

Vary this refreshing version of Waldorf salad by adding cubed Poached Chicken (see page 72). If a lighter dressing is desired, thin with buttermilk.

✦

In a large bowl combine Yogurt Cheese, lemon juice, salt, sugar, and pepper. Using a fork stir in all remaining ingredients except lettuce and cilantro. Taste and adjust seasonings. If not serving immediately, cover and refrigerate up to 3 hours. Bring to room temperature before serving.

Arrange a bed of lettuce on serving platter. Mound salad on lettuce and garnish with cilantro sprigs.

SERVES 4

Basil

Ocimum basilicum

An annual grown from seed or transplants each season.

Plant once all danger of frost is past. Prefers warm soil to germinate and for good growth.

Prune or harvest regularly to extend the season of leafy greens and delay flowering.

Protect young seedlings from slugs, snails, and earwigs.

Flowers as well as leaves are edible.

What was once known as just an ingredient in Italian pesto is now prized for its broad range of flavors and its uses in a host of cuisines, from Thai and Mexican to Indonesian and Vietnamese. Traditional sweet basil has been joined by varieties with the extra scent and taste of lemon, cinnamon, and licorice.

Of even more interest to the gourmet gardener is the fact that basil comes in many ornamental forms and colors. Perhaps the cutest and most novel basils are the emerald 'Greek Mini', 'Basil Fino Verde Compatto', and the 'Piccolo' varieties with their mature half-globe shape of from 6 to 12 inches. These compact plants maintain their tight, well-behaved form with no pruning and with leaves as small as 1/2 inch long. They make exquisite, tidy, attractive path borders or miniature "hedges." The irony is that although these small forms demand little maintenance in the landscape, they require tedious preparation in the kitchen and *many* more plants than their larger kin to make the same amount of pesto. Reserve the petite basils for their unique ornamental value, and use the larger basils for cut-and-come again harvesting.

When you cut the outer foliage of a basil plant it will look unattractive until the new leaves grow. If you love pesto, consider

*Complementary
Seasonings and Foods*

Oregano, thyme, parsley, garlic; egg and cheese dishes; salads and salad dressings; melons, strawberries, oranges ('Cinnamon Basil', 'Anise Basil'), sweet peppers, broccoli, cabbage, carrots, cauliflower, eggplants, parsnips, peas, potatoes, rice, squash, tomatoes; seafood ('Lemon Basil'), poultry and game birds, lamb, beef, veal; Gamay Beaujolais, Zinfandel, Sauvignon Blanc, Cabernet Sauvignon, White Zinfandel, Gewürztraminer ('Cinnamon Basil'), Fumé Blanc ('Anise Basil'), Chardonnay ('Lemon Basil').

secreting a large basil plot in the landscape for an easy, bountiful harvest. You can still have various basil plants sprinkled throughout the garden for a colorful and textural addition.

For rich burgundy-purple foliage, plant the regularly leafed 'Opal' or the frilly 'Purple Ruffles'. The unique color of the purple basils provides an interesting counterpoint to plants with lime green or yellowish foliage.

Some basil plants have distinctively shaped foliage for yet another ornamental pattern in your garden. 'Lettuce Leaf' basil was once considered an old-fashioned variety, but is now part of a revival that values its large, four-inch crinkled leaves with smooth edges. 'Basil Napoletano' has large, pale green, almost pendulous crinkled leaves. One form, 'Mammoth', produces spectacular leaves large enough to wrap fish for grilling or to stuff like a cabbage leaf.

There is no need to stop harvesting once the plants begin to bloom. The young, tight buds along the flower stems offer concentrated, intense flavor similar to the flavor of the foliage and make an excellent addition or garnish to a salad of mixed baby greens.

Harvest only what you need and when you need it, for basil wilts quickly. To keep it fresh, stand the sprigs in a glass of water, cover with a plastic bag, and refrigerate for perhaps two days. Tearing the leaves instead of chopping them will lessen their tendency to discolor, as will cutting in chiffonade.

To insure a supply until next year's crop, prepare compound butter, oil concentrate, and/or infused oil or vinegar (see pages 13 to 15). 'Purple Ruffles' makes a particularly colorful vinegar. Thinly chiffonade-cut leaves may also be stuffed into ice cube trays, the trays filled with water, and then frozen; add cubes directly to stews or soups.

Mini Recipes

Thread cubes of firm white fish alternately with basil leaves on skewers. Grill over charcoal, basting with a mixture of fresh lemon juice and basil oil.

Make a salsa of diced ripe tomatoes, finely minced garlic, thinly sliced green onion, snipped chives, chiffonade-cut basil, balsamic vinegar, salt, and pepper. Serve with roast lamb.

Toast bread rounds and top each round with a basil leaf, a thin slice of chèvre, and a thin slice of cherry tomato.

Bread, Tomato, and Basil Salad

3 thick slices Italian bread (about 9 oz)

1/3 cup finely diced sweet red or white onion

1 large clove garlic, finely minced

1 cup peeled, seeded, and diced cucumber

3 or 4 large ripe tomatoes, peeled, seeded, and diced

1/4 cup firmly packed chiffonade-cut basil leaves

2 tablespoons each red wine vinegar and olive oil

1 tablespoon balsamic vinegar

Salt and freshly ground pepper, to taste

A loaf of dense, country-style bread will make this Tuscan salad, called panzanella, *truly authentic.*

◆

*I*n a bowl place bread and add water to cover. Let soak 15 minutes.

Squeeze bread to remove excess moisture. Tear into 1 1/2-inch pieces and place in salad bowl. Add all remaining ingredients, cover, and refrigerate 2 hours or up to 6 hours.

Toss just before serving.

SERVES *4*

43

Pesto Spiral Bread

1 tablespoon active dry yeast

1/3 cup lukewarm water (105° to 115° F)

3 tablespoons honey

3 tablespoons unsalted butter, at room temperature, cut into bits

1/2 cup nonfat milk, scalded

1/2 cup potato water or water

1/3 cup noninstant nonfat dry milk

2 tablespoons soy flour

2 teaspoons salt

3 cups unbleached flour, or as needed

Mixed Herb Pesto (see page 21)

Using water left over from boiling potatoes imparts a lightness to the bread and the soy flour helps keep the loaf fresh. The pesto may be prepared one day in advance, covered, and refrigerated.

◆

*I*n a large bowl sprinkle yeast over lukewarm water, stir to dissolve, and let stand until creamy (about 5 minutes).

Meanwhile, in a separate bowl, stir honey and butter into milk until melted. Stir in potato water, let cool to lukewarm, and add to yeast.

Sift together dry milk, soy flour, salt, and 1 1/2 cups of the unbleached flour; stir into yeast mixture. Beat vigorously with a wooden spoon until air bubbles form (about 3 minutes). Gradually beat in remaining 1 1/2 cups flour to form stiff dough.

Turn out onto floured board and knead, adding additional flour as needed to reduce stickiness, until smooth and pliable (about 5 minutes). Try not to use more than 1/4 cup additional flour.

Form dough into a ball and place in large oiled mixing bowl; turn ball to coat with oil. Cover with tea towel and let dough rise in warm place until doubled in bulk (about 1 1/4 hours). Punch down, turn out onto floured board, and knead briefly.

Oil a 4 1/2-by-8 1/2-inch loaf pan. Pat and roll dough into a rectangle approximately 12 by 8 inches. Spread 3/4 cup of the pesto on rectangle, leaving a 1-inch border around edges. The pesto should cover dough evenly; use more if necessary.

Starting at one short end, carefully roll rectangle like a jelly roll; tuck in ends, pat into loaf shape, and place seam side down in prepared pan. Cover with tea towel and let rise in warm place until almost doubled in bulk (about 1 hour).

Preheat oven to 350° F. Bake until top is golden brown and loaf sounds hollow when tapped with fingers (35 to 40 minutes). Remove bread from pan and return loaf to oven rack until bottom is golden brown (5 to 10 minutes). Cool on wire rack before slicing.

MAKES 1 LOAF

Bay
Laurus nobilis

In the garden, an evergreen tree from 12 to 30 feet tall.

Start from container-grown plant.

Use as an individual specimen tree or a formal or informal hedge. Can be shaped to any topiary form.

Requires rich, well-drained soil and plenty of sun. Plant on a slightly raised mound or in as large a container as possible. Place where there is good air circulation, and no chance of frost.

Foliage is damaged below 30° F and tree can be killed at 10° to 20° F.

*T*he pallid dried leaves that most cooks pull from a tiny jar pale in comparison to the savory, robust flavor of freshly harvested bay leaves. Look for the true sweet bay. A tree native to the West called California bay laurel or pepperwood is a distant cousin to sweet bay and has a harsh, inferior flavor.

In the landscape, the mature "true" culinary bay tree ranges from 12 to 30 feet tall, depending upon the soil and climate. The dark green glossy foliage adds a richness to the landscape and provides a good backdrop for more colorful flowers and plants in the foreground. Thus, sweet bay trees are often planted close together and clipped to smallish or medium-sized hedges to define areas of a garden, like small rooms, or to form the perimeter of a planting.

The Mediterranean origins of this handsome tree have infused it with a sensitivity to hard freezes. Fortunately, the plant can be easily grown in a container and moved indoors during winter. (It can even be cultivated year-round indoors in a sunny bay or south-facing window.) Plant a seedling in a pot at least as big as a one-gallon plastic milk jug. The larger the container, the easier it will be to care for the plant and the greater your harvest of leaves. Clip the foliage frequently, water every day or two, and lightly fertilize at least monthly. The clippings, of course, become fodder for a sauce or soup.

45

The bay leaf's combined flavor of pepper, vanilla, and cloves allows the herb to adapt to sweet as well as savory dishes. The leaves need long cooking or marinating to release their subtle flavor, so make them an essential ingredient of bouquets garnis. Use the leaves in marinades, when curing or pickling meats or vegetables, or to infuse stock, milk, or cream. Add bay leaves to the cooking water for tongue or corned beef, potatoes, rice, pasta, and soup stock. Make a bed of bay leaves under meat loaf before baking or steaming, or line a tureen or pâté mold with the leaves. Neither fresh nor dried leaves soften in cooking, however, so leaves must be discarded before a dish is served.

Complementary Seasonings and Foods

Bouquet garni herbs; blueberries, oranges; tomatoes; fish, venison, poultry and game birds, liver.

Mini Recipes

Marinate turkey cutlets in fresh lemon juice, chopped green onions, and crumbled bay leaves for several hours. Remove from marinade, dip in beaten egg and then in flour or fine dried bread crumbs, and brown on both sides in butter and garlic olive oil.

Alternate fresh-picked bay leaves and chunks of firm white fish on skewers; grill over hot coals, basting with fresh lemon juice and olive oil.

Marinate pork kabobs in dry white wine, onion chunks stuck with whole cloves, lightly crushed peppercorns, minced garlic, and bay leaves. Grill over hot coals, basting with marinade.

Marinate slices of calves' liver in dry sherry, minced onion, and crumbled bay leaves 3 to 4 hours. Remove liver from marinade; arrange slices in a shallow heatproof dish and cover with thinly sliced onions. Place dish on rack set over boiling water, cover pot, and steam 10 to 15 minutes.

Veal and Bay Leaf Kabobs

4 veal escalopes (about
2 1/2 oz each)

1 tablespoon fresh lemon juice

2 ounces *caciocavallo, pecorino,*
or *locatelli* cheese

1 tablespoon olive oil

1/2 cup finely minced onion,
plus 1 whole onion

3/4 cup fine dried bread crumbs

3 tablespoons chopped, lightly
toasted pine nuts

2 teaspoons minced parsley

1 teaspoon minced sage

1/4 teaspoon salt

1/8 teaspoon freshly
ground pepper

16 bay leaves

Metal or bamboo skewers can be used for assembling these Italian-inspired kabobs. When using the latter, soak in cold water to cover for about 30 minutes before loading. You can substitute pork, beef, turkey, or chicken for the veal.

✦

Cut each escalope in half lengthwise. You should have 8 pieces each about 4 inches long and 2 1/2 inches wide. Place each piece between layers of plastic wrap. Using a flat meat mallet, pound gently until 1/8 inch thick. Transfer to shallow dish, pour lemon juice over escalopes, and let stand 30 minutes.

Grate enough of the cheese to measure 1/4 cup; cut the remainder into 24 uniform cubes. Set grated and cubed cheese aside.

In a skillet over medium heat, warm oil. Add minced onion and sauté until soft (about 5 minutes). Remove from heat and stir in bread crumbs, grated cheese, pine nuts, parsley, sage, salt, and pepper; mix well. Taste and adjust seasonings.

Cut whole onion lengthwise into eighths. Pull each eighth apart to form individual layers about 1 inch wide and 1/4 inch thick. You will need 16 pieces; any leftover onion can be refrigerated for another use. Set onion pieces aside.

Pat veal slices dry with paper toweling and place flat on work surface. Divide crumb mixture evenly among slices, spreading it to cover, then top each slice with 3 cheese cubes. Starting at narrow end closest to you, roll tightly like a jelly roll. As you work, place rolls seam side down on work surface. (Rolls may be made several hours ahead, covered, and refrigerated.)

Prepare a charcoal fire, or preheat broiler.

To assemble the kabobs, have ready eight 6- to 7-inch skewers. Thread ingredients onto each skewer in the following order: an onion section, a bay leaf, a veal roll, a bay leaf, and an onion section. Grill kabobs over hot coals or under broiler, turning often, until rolls are lightly browned (about 10 minutes). Serve hot.

Serves 3 or 4

Snap Bean

Phaseolus vulgaris

*Annual planted
from seed in late spring after all danger of
frost is past and the soil has warmed.*

Plant in full sun only.

*Build sturdy arbors or trellises to handle
heavy mature vines.*

*Watch for beetles and caterpillars that
eat the leaves; control with appropriate
organic spray.*

*Beans and flowers of 'Hyacinth' and the
various runner beans are edible.*

There seem to be more types of garden beans than political promises during an election year. In fact, one collector of heirloom beans, John Withee, maintains over two hundred fifty named varieties. One way of dividing up this superfamily is to break them loosely into two categories, dried and snap. Snap beans are those in which the entire fresh pod and the immature seeds it holds are prepared in the kitchen. When the pods are broken into pieces, one hears a distinctive "snap," hence the name. Dried beans are separated (shelled) from the desiccated, fibrous pod and usually stored for use in soups, baked bean dishes, and casseroles. Another category is the shell or shelly bean, where the seed is larger than in an ideal snap bean pod but not mature or dry enough to be called a dried bean. Some beans, such as the 'Scarlet Runner' varieties, can span all three categories.

For drama in your edible landscape, plant pole-type runner beans. The most famous of these prolific vines is the 'Scarlet Runner' or 'Red Knight Runner' (*Phaseolus coccineus*), which grows to 10 feet and is covered with highly ornamental, edible orange-red blossoms. Unlike other bean plants, these blossoms can be appreciated from a distance *and* lure hummingbirds to the garden. 'Scarlet Runner' beans are rapid growers and will cloak an arbor or bean tepee with luxurious green foliage and a long season of dramatic bloom. 'Thomas Famous White

Dutch' and 'White Knight' pole beans have the same characteristics, but with pure white blossoms. A relatively rare variety, 'Painted Lady', offers the option of salmon or white flowers.

Another attractive pole bean is the 'Hyacinth' or 'Lab Lab' bean (*Dolichos lablab*). A prolific vine that can reach 20 feet, it is draped in cascades of fragrant lavender-purple or white blossoms. This tropical bean was grown by Thomas Jefferson in his Monticello home garden. Gardeners without trellises or arbors can grow a shorter, bushlike form of the red runner called 'Hammond Scarlet Runner Bush'.

In mild winter climates where the ground doesn't freeze, 'Scarlet Runner' and 'Thomas Famous White Dutch' runner beans can become perennials. These legumes make small, oblong beige tubers just beneath the soil that, if grown in very well-drained soil, resprout each spring. Like their distant legume relative jicama, some of these tubers can be harvested as food and the vines will continue to resprout. To experiment in the kitchen, prepare the tubers as you would a potato or tuberous nasturtium "spud." Even in mild winters, the foliage dies back to the ground each fall and new shoots bound forth from the tubers in the spring.

Once you have sampled a 'Scarlet Runner' or 'Hyacinth' bean blossom, your supply of beans will diminish as you begin harvesting the tasty flowers. Surprisingly crunchy, sweet, tangy, and similar in taste to the bean itself, the blossoms impart flavor, texture, and color to salads, vegetables, sauces, and stews.

Pick snap beans when they are four to six inches long, before they mature to the point where the pods begin to fill out. Watch 'Scarlet Runner' beans closely, for they quickly get woody. Wash, snip off the top and tail, and pull out the string, if any, along one side. Leave whole, slice across or on a diagonal, or halve lengthwise.

If you want to allow some of your snap beans to mature to shell beans, leave on the vine until the pods are about 10 inches long and the shapes of the shell beans are visible. Pick and store, unshelled, in a plastic bag in the refrigerator for up to three days. Shell the beans and steam, boil, or braise as you would lima or fava beans, or use them in your favorite succotash recipe. Shell beans take considerably less time to cook than dried beans and do not increase in volume. For recipes

Complementary Seasonings and Foods

Savory, basil, oregano, rosemary, thyme, tarragon, sage, chives; Dijon-style mustard, balsamic vinegar, lemon juice, vinaigrette; Parmesan cheese, toasted sliced almonds, chopped walnuts, sesame seeds, garlic, fresh ginger, water chestnuts, chayotes, onions, tomatoes, mushrooms; ham, bacon, lamb.

calling for cooked beans, simply boil gently in water until softened to taste (8 to 12 minutes). The addition of onion, garlic, and/or herb sprigs will heighten the flavor.

Snap beans can be blanched, parboiled, steamed over boiling water, butter-steamed, or cooked in rapidly boiling water until just tender. Save cooking water for adding to soup stocks. For a special flavor, slip a sprig of summer or winter savory in with the beans as they cook. After cooking, season beans to taste with salt or herb salt and freshly ground white or black pepper, or with butter and finely minced herbs. (Do not salt until after cooking or beans will toughen.)

Mini Recipes

Stir-fry cut snap beans with garlic and fresh ginger; toss in sliced water chestnuts or jicama and a few drops of Asian sesame oil.

Toss steamed or boiled snap beans with sliced onions sautéed in olive oil, minced thyme, and balsamic vinegar.

Dress steamed or boiled snap beans with Mixed Herb Pesto (see page 21) or anchovy paste thinned with a little olive oil, or toss with minced garlic and crumbled chèvre.

Niçoise Salad

1 1/2 pounds uniform-sized potatoes, peeled or scrubbed

5 large cloves garlic, bruised

4 sprigs thyme or lemon thyme

1 1/2 recipes Balsamic Vinaigrette (see page 18)

2 tuna fillets (about 3/4 lb each and 1 in. thick)

No main-dish salad is better known than the Niçoise and none is more challenging to the creativity of the cook. The presentation described here can be altered to suit individual taste.

Firm fresh tuna is a must. It should be broiled just before assembling the salad so it is still slightly warm when served. Marinate tuna no longer than 30 minutes. The other ingredients should be at room temperature. Peel thick-skinned potatoes before boiling; serve thin-skinned new potatoes unpeeled or peel after boiling.

Serve the salad with baguettes and unsalted butter or olive oil infused with garlic. Follow with fresh fruits such as Asian pear and cheese.

3 tablespoons each olive oil and fresh lemon juice

1/4 teaspoon each salt and freshly ground white pepper

2 sprigs rosemary

1 pound snap beans, halved crosswise if very long

'Lolla Rossa' or other soft lettuce, for lining platter

3 to 4 tablespoons well-drained capers

3 ripe tomatoes, peeled and each cut into 8 wedges

3 hard-cooked eggs, each cut crosswise into 8 slices (optional)

1 can (2 oz) anchovy fillets packed in olive oil (optional)

1/2 cup Niçoise-style black olives

Roasted red sweet pepper strips (see page 160)

Minced parsley

♦

Place potatoes in saucepan with 3 of the garlic cloves and the thyme sprigs and add water to cover. Bring to a boil over high heat, cover, lower heat to medium, and boil gently until potatoes are just tender (15 to 20 minutes). Drain (reserve water for soup stocks or yeast breads) and return potatoes to heat for 1 or 2 minutes to boil away any water left in pan.

When cool enough to handle, peel potatoes, if desired, and cut into 1/4-inch-thick slices. Place in bowl and pour about 1/4 cup of the dressing over top. Toss with fork, taste, and adjust seasonings, adding more dressing if desired. Set aside.

Rinse tuna fillets, pat dry with paper toweling, and place in nonreactive shallow dish. In a small bowl stir together olive oil, lemon juice, remaining 2 garlic cloves, salt, pepper, and rosemary sprigs. Pour over tuna. Marinate at room temperature, turning once, 20 minutes.

Preheat broiler. Meanwhile, arrange beans on steamer rack set over boiling water, cover pot, and steam until barely tender (3 to 4 minutes). Drain, immerse in ice water, drain again, and pat dry with paper toweling. Place in bowl and set aside.

Remove tuna from marinade and place on broiler pan. Broil, turning once, until done (about 5 minutes per side). Meanwhile, arrange lettuce on a large platter and drizzle with a little of the vinaigrette. Mound potatoes in center of lettuce bed and sprinkle capers over potatoes. Toss beans with dressing to taste. Gather them into 6 small bunches and arrange in spoke pattern radiating out from potatoes.

Remove tuna from broiler to cutting board. Using a fork gently break each fillet into 3 equal portions. Place a piece of tuna equidistant between "bean spokes." Along one side of each tuna piece, arrange 4 tomato wedges in a line parallel to bean spoke. Along other side, arrange 4 egg slices in same fashion (if used). Drain anchovy fillets (if used) and arrange as a garnish on tuna. Tuck olives and red pepper strips in and around other ingredients and generously sprinkle salad with parsley.

Serve immediately. Pass remaining vinaigrette in small bowl.

SERVES 6

Blueberry

Highbush (*Vaccinium corymbosum*); Lowbush (*V. angustifolium*);
Rabbit Eye (*V. ashei*)

Perennial shrub that prefers full sun.

Plant bareroot plants in winter and container plants in spring and summer.

Add plenty of acidic leaf mold or peat moss to the planting spot.

Water frequently and use an acid-stimulating mulch such as pine needles.

Fertilize with cottonseed meal, an excellent acidic nitrogen fertilizer.

Leave unpruned for first three years after planting, then prune out three or more of the older shoots that have already fruited.

Blueberry shrubs are a colorful addition to any hedgelike element in a landscape. The shrubs' fall leaves flush hot with oranges, yellows, and reds. As the autumn color falls to the ground, many types of blueberry shrubs, especially the highbush varieties, reveal warm red stems that continue to provide an accent of color in winter. Spring growth begins with a bronzy, metallic tint to the foliage. Pale pink, heart-shaped flowers soon follow. Well-fertilized and properly watered plants offer a rich, glossy green foliage throughout the summer.

All blueberry shrubs share a trio of main desires: plenty of moisture, plenty of humidity, and a highly acidic soil. The planting of blueberry shrubs typically involves incorporating large volumes of peat moss into the soil because peat is acidic and it retains moisture. Regular irrigation at least two or three times per week will help these bog-loving plants to prosper. Soil pH should be between 4.0 and 5.0 for most blueberry varieties. Blueberries also like *full* sun, except for certain lowbush types. Because of the acid soil requirements and special water needs, these plants must be clustered in a spot reserved just for them.

*Complementary
Seasonings and Foods*

Cinnamon, coriander, ground
ginger; cream cheese, cottage
cheese, custard; oranges,
kiwifruits, rhubarb, peaches,
pears, apples.

Blueberry shrubs fall into three main types, but their biggest distinction is size. Highbush, or swamp, blueberry plants love plenty of moisture and can reach 12 feet (usually 5 to 6 feet), with a September crop of full-flavored, large, blue-black berries. Not all varieties of highbush blueberries are hardy in colder climates; have your local nursery select the best one for your area. Lowbush blueberry plants, which are native to many parts of the country, grow from half a foot to several feet tall, can tolerate some shade, thrive in shallow soils, yield a sweet reddish or dark blue berry in August, and require plenty of water. Rabbit eye varieties, which may reach 20 feet (15 feet is common) and are widely cultivated in the southeastern United States, are not as hardy as highbush types, withstand heat better than other cultivars, require less irrigation to be happy, and yield a complex-flavored black berry.

Blueberries are best eaten fresh, either plain or with cream and a little sugar. Use as soon as possible after picking. Wash under running water, drain well, and pat dry with paper toweling. If it is necessary to store the berries, place them in a basket lined with paper toweling, cover loosely with plastic wrap, and refrigerate for up to one or two days. When using blueberries in batters, toss the berries with a little flour just before adding so they will not sink to the bottom.

Store sheet-frozen blueberries in airtight bags in the freezer for up to three months. Use in pies or in waffle or muffin batters; fold into softened sorbets or sherbets; or make blueberry vinegar (see page 14).

Mini Recipes

Fold blueberries into Custard Sauce (see page 25), pour into a fully baked Walnut Pastry shell (see page 29), and top with sliced kiwifruits or feijoas.

Season sieved ricotta cheese with freshly grated orange zest and honey or sugar. Combine blueberries with a little orange juice or red wine and spoon over cheese mixture. Serve for dessert.

Fold blueberries into low-fat lemon yogurt that has been thinned with fresh lemon juice and sweetened with honey or sugar. Serve over angel food cake or pound cake.

Blueberry Tortoni

1 egg white, at
room temperature

Pinch cream of tartar

4 tablespoons sugar

1 cup whipping cream, chilled

1 teaspoon rose water, violet
water, or vanilla extract

1 pint (3 cups) blueberries

Violets, for garnish

A simple do-ahead dessert that is as attractive as it is delicious. Chill the serving bowls or glasses. If you have no violets, garnish with any colorful edible flower blossom or with mint sprigs or sweet cicely feathers.

In a bowl combine egg white and cream of tartar and beat until stiff peaks form. One teaspoon at a time, beat in 2 tablespoons of the sugar and continue beating until egg white mixture is smooth and satiny (about 2 minutes). Set aside.

With clean beaters and a clean bowl, whip cream until stiff peaks form. Gradually beat in remaining 2 tablespoons sugar and the rose water. Gently fold cream into egg white, transfer to shallow container, cover, and freeze until edges are solid (1 to 2 hours).

Stir with fork and fold in blueberries. Return to freezer until mixture is frozen almost solid (2 to 3 hours).

Using a wire whisk, beat blueberry mixture to soften slightly. Spoon into chilled crystal bowls or stem glasses. Garnish with violets.

SERVES 8

Blueberry Corn Muffins

1 cup fine-grind nondegerminated cornmeal

1 cup whole-wheat pastry flour

1 to 2 tablespoons sugar

2 teaspoons baking powder

3/4 teaspoon salt

1/2 teaspoon each baking soda, ground cinnamon, and ground coriander

2 eggs

1/4 cup canola oil

1 1/4 cups buttermilk

1/2 pint (1 1/2 cups) blueberries

All-purpose flour for dusting

Serve these sunny yellow muffins warm for breakfast or with a luncheon salad. Any that are left over may be stored in a sealed plastic bag for a day or so and reheated in a warm oven. Or they may be well wrapped and frozen for several weeks; defrost and reheat in a warm oven.

◆

Preheat oven to 400° F. Oil 16 muffin-tin wells or line with paper cupcake liners. Set aside.

In a large bowl stir together cornmeal, pastry flour, sugar, baking powder, salt, baking soda, and spices. In a smaller bowl lightly beat eggs with a fork. Beat in oil and buttermilk. Make a well in dry ingredients and pour in wet ingredients. Stir just to moisten; do not overmix. Batter should be slightly lumpy.

Toss blueberries in all-purpose flour to coat lightly and quickly fold into batter. Fill prepared muffin tins two-thirds full.

Bake until cake tester inserted in center of a muffin comes out clean and muffins are golden brown (18 to 20 minutes). Turn out onto wire rack, turn right side up, and let cool briefly before serving.

MAKES 16 MUFFINS

Cardoon

Cynara cardunculus

Perennial herbaceous plant. Prospers in coastal zones with mild, nearly frost-free winters; can be grown as an annual in cold winter areas.

Grow from seed or containerized seedlings.

Plant with a wire basket to protect from ravenous gophers.

Provide rich, well-drained soil.

Fertilize and water regularly.

Cut dead foliage back to soil each fall and mulch heavily in cold winter areas.

Cardoon, or *cardi* in Italian, is a little-known vegetable in America, but one no self-respecting Italian gardener could do without. Its prolific silver-blue foliage, which spews forth like a seven-foot-tall fountain flash-frozen in all its majesty, makes a sensational addition to any yard. A relative of the artichoke plant, cardoon grows with more vigor, more height, and more drama than its kin. While the foliage dies back to the ground each fall, each spring a rapid renewal of growth bursts forth from the massive, fibrous root system.

The typical cardoon flower stalk can reach well over seven feet and is covered with a dozen or more flower heads that resemble small, woody globe artichokes. The flowers, which are inedible, share the same vibrant purple of an uneaten artichoke blossom. Do not let the flowers set mature seed, as cardoon can become an invasive plant from wind-blown seed. Cardoon is best placed in the mid to deep background of a planting so its tall, imposing foliage doesn't overwhelm smaller plants. Display the silver leaves next to a dark green plant such as sweet bay or rosemary.

Oregano, chives, parsley; olive oil, lemon juice, mustard; Fontina and Parmesan cheeses; garlic, onions, leeks, spinach, tomatoes, Swiss chard; anchovies.

The edible portion of the plant is the ribbed stalk at the base of each leaf, which is blanched as the plant grows. Some gardeners blanch the entire plant; others just whiten the lower 12 to 18 inches. One approach, which is done in the late summer three weeks prior to harvest, calls for bundling the lower portion with string, wrapping the bundle with five or more sheets of newspaper, and then tying them in place to exclude light. Another approach is to cover the plant with a tall, narrow upside-down bucket with its bottom cut out.

Cardoon should be harvested when it reaches two to four feet in height. Cut the plant as close to ground level as possible. Using a sharp knife, cut away and discard all the leaves, spurs, tough outer stalks, and any wilted stalks. Rinse the tender stalks in water, shake off the excess, wrap in paper toweling, and store in a plastic bag in the refrigerator crisper for up to one week.

Just before cooking, trim the top and bottom off each stalk and then scrape the entire length of the stalk to remove all strings. As each stalk is trimmed, rub it with a cut lemon or immerse it in acidulated water (one tablespoon lemon juice or vinegar to one quart water) to prevent discoloration. Be careful to cut out all leaves, even those growing in the heart, for they are bitter.

Cardoon can be steamed, boiled in water or stock, braised, or deep-fried. For most recipes, the stalks and heart should first be cut into two- to three-inch lengths and parboiled in salted water with a little lemon juice. Cooking time will depend upon the maturity and freshness of the cardoon, as will the yield. To cook fully, simmer cut-up cardoon in stock to cover until tender. Again, cooking time will depend upon the age and freshness of the vegetable; about 20 minutes is average. Cardoon is salty in itself, so be careful when seasoning.

Mini Recipes

Add diced, cooked cardoon to potato salad.

Sauté parboiled cardoon pieces in butter and olive oil, season with salt and pepper, add a little stock, cover, and braise until tender. Sprinkle with minced parsley.

Cook parboiled cardoon pieces, julienne-cut Canadian bacon, minced garlic, and diced onion in olive oil in covered skillet; add chopped ripe tomatoes and simmer to blend flavors.

Add diced, cooked cardoon to White Sauce or Mornay Sauce (see page 22), transfer to casserole dish, sprinkle with freshly grated Monterey jack cheese, and bake in 375° F oven until heated through and cheese melts (10 to 15 minutes).

Cardoon Gratin

1 pound trimmed cardoon, cut into 2-inch lengths and cooked in stock until tender

2 teaspoons olive oil

2/3 cup minced onion

2 large garlic cloves, minced

4 large ripe tomatoes, peeled, seeded, and diced

6 ounces Italian Fontina cheese, coarsely shredded

Cardoon is popular with both Italian and French cooks. Here it is prepared in a gratin with creamy Italian Fontina, but Montery jack or Gruyère would also be a good choice. Serve with mashed potatoes laced with onion and garlic, potherbs, and veal chops.

✦

Preheat oven to 375° F. Lightly oil a baking dish and arrange cardoon pieces in it. Set aside.

In a small skillet over medium heat, warm olive oil. Add onion and garlic and sauté until onion is soft (about 5 minutes). Scatter onion-garlic mixture over cardoon and top evenly with tomatoes.

Bake until bubbly (15 to 20 minutes). Strew cheese evenly over top and return to oven until cheese melts (about 5 minutes). Serve at once.

SERVES 6

Chayote

Sechium edule

A rampant deciduous perennial vine; grows to 40 feet in all directions. Grown mostly in mild winter areas.

Plant the fruit on its side so the dimpled end is just barely covered with rich, sandy or loamy, well-drained soil.

Supply plenty of water and fertilizer to sustain the prodigious vining growth.

Provide a sturdy trellis, arbor, or fence to support the vines.

Watch for beetles eating on the leaves and spray to control.

Fruits, tubers, and tendrils are edible.

Variously called chayote, chocho, and chuchu, vegetable pear, christophine, and mirliton (the Cajun word), these strange-looking pear-shaped fruits are found in the Asian or Hispanic produce section of the supermarket. The chayote isn't a fruit like an apple, but more like a vining summer squash. A member of the gourd family (*Cucurbitaceae*), it most closely resembles a zucchini in its flavor and use.

Chayotes have a dimpled bottom, weigh from half a pound to nearly three pounds, can be smooth, wrinkled, or covered with soft, short spines, and are pastel green, Granny Smith apple green, or rich dark green. They are produced on an enormous maze of vines, and a single vining plant, growing from its perennial tubers, has been known to cover an entire garage or 60 feet of a fence in a single summer and to yield over one hundred fruits.

This is one of the most multipurpose plants in cultivation. The flesh is used raw, much like a jicama, or prepared any way you cook zucchini. The single large, soft, flat seed inside each fruit can be steamed, sautéed, or marinated and has a slightly nutty taste and a richer flavor than the flesh. Perennial edible tubers resembling long yams form underground and can be cooked in virtually any way you

59

*Complementary
Seasonings and Foods*

Chives, tarragon, thyme, marjoram, oregano, parsley, basil, mint, chile powder, fresh ginger; lemon or lime juice; cheese, eggs; rice, pasta; chile or sweet peppers, corn, eggplants, potatoes, peas, garlic, onions, shallots, tomatoes, dried beans; pork, chicken, shellfish.

would prepare potatoes. The tender tips (called tendrils) of each leading vine can be steamed or boiled like an asparagus spear or snap bean and are the tastiest part of the plant.

The young tendrils can be harvested at any time. Fruiting begins in late summer and continues until frosts kill the vines. Pick fruits when only one or two inches in diameter for pickling and when four inches long for most other uses. Clip the stem near each fruit; don't bruise the fruit while harvesting. Mature fruits are good for stuffing. Fruits that exude a sticky sap when cut are too old and should be discarded. An occasional tuber can be dug up in the summer while the vines are growing.

Fruits for eating can be stored in the coolest part of the refrigerator for weeks; fruits for seed for the next year can be refrigerated for most of the winter. Experiment with freezing the young tendrils.

Chayote absorbs little oil in cooking and holds its shape and crispness even when reheated. Cut in half lengthwise for stuffing or slice or dice and boil, steam, bake, sauté, or braise. Substitute lightly steamed sliced chayote for potato in potato salad, or for eggplant in eggplant parmigiana. Dress steamed cubed chayote with chopped walnuts that have been lightly browned in butter. Stuff halves with any stuffing suitable for zucchini, sweet peppers, eggplants, or onions.

Mini Recipes

Toss lightly steamed sliced chayote in vinaigrette with halved cherry tomatoes, blanched peas or snow peas, and sliced ripe olives. Serve on bed of 'Red Oakleaf' lettuce.

Heat steamed diced chayote and cooked corn kernels in butter. Season with fresh lime juice and minced thyme, then mix in peeled, seeded, and diced ripe tomato.

Steam sliced chayote and slices of sweet red onion until tender. Layer in shallow dish and top with shredded Monterey jack cheese; bake in 350° F oven until bubbly and cheese melts (10 to 15 minutes). Serve at once.

Lamb Shanks and Chayote in Mustard-Horseradish Sauce

Flour seasoned with salt, freshly ground pepper, and paprika

4 large lamb shanks, cracked and trimmed of excess fat

2 tablespoons canola oil, or as needed

2 large onions, thinly sliced

3 large cloves garlic, minced

3 cups lamb or beef stock, or to cover

2/3 cup American-style mustard

1/2 cup prepared horseradish

Bouquet garni of 2 sprigs oregano, 2 sprigs parsley, 1 sprig savory, 3 lovage leaves, and 1 sprig lavender (see page 15)

2 chayote squashes (about 6 oz each), cut into 1 1/2-inch pieces

Salt and freshly ground pepper, to taste

Minced chives and parsley, for garnish

The combination of horseradish and mustard imparts a pleasant tang to this hearty main course. Repeated testing revealed that French's Classic Mustard is a must for this recipe. Begin preparing the dish a day in advance of serving. The flavor of the lamb shanks improves upon reheating, plus the chilling allows easy removal of any fat released during cooking. Polenta with Sweet Pepper and Savory (see page 202) is an ideal accompaniment.

✦

Spread seasoned flour on waxed paper. Roll shanks in flour to coat evenly and shake off excess flour. Heat oil in a large nonstick saucepan or dutch oven over medium-high heat. Add shanks and, without allowing them to touch, brown on all sides. Work in batches if necessary. Remove shanks and set aside. Add onions to same pan, along with additional oil if needed to prevent sticking, and cook until nicely browned (6 or 7 minutes). Stir in garlic and cook 1 minute.

In a mixing bowl stir together stock, mustard, and horseradish. Return lamb shanks to saucepan and pour in stock mixture, adding additional stock if needed to cover shanks. Place bouquet garni on top, bring to a boil, lower heat, cover, and cook slowly until meat starts to fall off bones (about 1 1/4 hours). Remove from heat, cool to room temperature, cover, and refrigerate overnight.

The next day, lift off and discard any fat that has congealed on the surface. Reheat lamb shanks over medium heat and discard bouquet garni. Increase heat slightly and add chayote. Cover and cook until chayote is just tender (about 10 minutes). Season with salt and pepper and transfer to large heated platter. Sprinkle with chives and parsley.

SERVES 4

Chervil

Anthriscus cerefolium

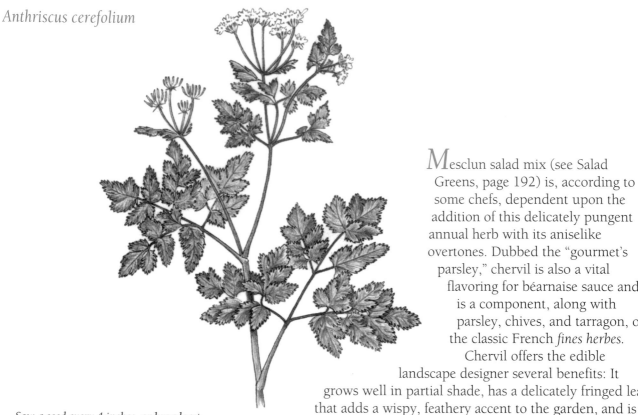

Sow a seed every 4 inches, or broadcast seed, for this annual (sometimes biennial); plant in late summer in mild climates or early spring in harsh winter regions.

Grows well in most soils.

Keep well watered.

Tolerates partial shade, and requires it in hot summer climates.

Allow some plants to make seed to ensure a self-seeding crop for years to come.

Mesclun salad mix (see Salad Greens, page 192) is, according to some chefs, dependent upon the addition of this delicately pungent annual herb with its aniselike overtones. Dubbed the "gourmet's parsley," chervil is also a vital flavoring for béarnaise sauce and is a component, along with parsley, chives, and tarragon, of the classic French *fines herbes*. Chervil offers the edible landscape designer several benefits: It grows well in partial shade, has a delicately fringed leaf that adds a wispy, feathery accent to the garden, and is quick to fill in around other annual and perennial plants. The pale green to somewhat dark green foliage looks like dainty, finely cut parsley leaves.

The leaves, tender stems, and flowers of chervil are edible; they can be used interchangeably in a wide range of dishes. Harvest shortly before use, or, if need be, stand sprigs in a glass of water, cover with a plastic bag, and refrigerate for up to one or two days. The best way to preserve chervil is to make compound butter (see page 15), which can be frozen up to four months and used on freshly cooked vegetables, fish, and chicken.

Sprinkle snipped chervil on finished dishes, mix into sautéed or braised dishes, stews, consommés, or cream soups and chowders at the last moment, or add to deviled eggs, cottage or cream cheese, twice-baked potatoes, or seafood salads. Use whole sprigs as garnishes and in marinades, or to make chervil vinegar (see page 14).

Complementary Seasonings and Foods

Tarragon, parsley, chives, anise hyssop, thyme, sage, lemon verbena; nutmeg, aniseed; lemon juice; yogurt, cream cheese; egg and cheese dishes; salad greens, beans, beets, carrots, corn, mushrooms, peas, potatoes, sorrel, spinach, tomatoes; seafood (especially oysters), chicken, rabbit, veal, lamb.

Mini Recipes

Whisk Dijon-style mustard, fresh lemon juice, and snipped chervil and chives into Yogurt Cheese (see page 22). Toss with cold sliced beets.

Toss chervil leaves into a mixed green salad with Buckler's sorrel, sliced cucumber, raw tiny cauliflower florets, and Yogurt Salad Dressing (see page 22).

Add a bouquet garni (see page 15) of chervil and parsley sprigs, chives, and bay leaf to the pot when making court bouillon.

Three-Cheese Chervil Omelet

4 whole eggs plus 2 egg whites

1 tablespoon water

4 tablespoons coarsely snipped chervil, plus chervil sprigs, for garnish

1 tablespoon minced anise hyssop flowers (optional)

2 tablespoons freshly grated Parmesan or Romano cheese

1/3 cup nonfat cottage cheese

Dash each salt and freshly ground white pepper

1/2 teaspoon unsalted butter

1 teaspoon olive oil

1/2 cup finely shredded Monterey jack, Gruyère, Italian Fontina, or Cheddar cheese

Fresh eggs at room temperature (at least two hours out of the refrigerator) and a well-seasoned skillet are prerequisites for a perfect omelet. Beat the eggs lightly and use immediately after beating. Chopped herbs may be added to the egg mixture, or the herbs may be incorporated into the filling.

✦

*I*n a mixing bowl combine whole eggs, egg whites, water, 2 tablespoons of the snipped chervil, hyssop flowers (if used), Parmesan cheese, cottage cheese, salt, and pepper. Using a whisk, beat lightly until blended.

Heat a 9-inch nonstick skillet over medium-high heat until hot. Add oil and butter, swirling pan to cover pan bottom. When pan is hot pour in eggs and cook, shaking skillet to prevent sticking, until edges begin to set (30 to 40 seconds). As eggs cook on bottom, using a spatula, lift up their edges and tilt skillet to allow uncooked eggs to run under cooked eggs. Continue in this manner until all egg mixture is set but top is still moist.

Sprinkle jack cheese evenly over eggs and top with remaining 2 tablespoons snipped chervil. Fold one third of omelet over and then slide it out onto heated plate, tilting skillet so omelet folds over itself and rests seam side down. Garnish with chervil sprigs.

SERVES 2 OR 3

Chestnut

American (*Castanea dentata*); Chinese (*C. mollissima*);
Japanese (*C. crenata*); European (*C. sativa*)

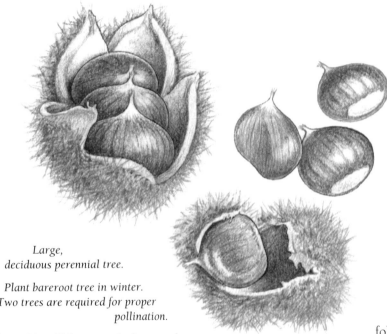

*Large,
deciduous perennial tree.*

*Plant bareroot tree in winter.
Two trees are required for proper
pollination.*

*Space 20 to 40 feet apart in deep, good-
draining fertile soil. Plant on a raised
mound 12 to 18 inches high by 3 to 5
feet wide.*

*Water well when tree is young. Can
become naturalized in the arid West or
elsewhere if well mulched.*

*Starts bearing nuts within the first
four years.*

*Few diseases other than a blight fungus.
Watch for the chestnut weevil, which
bores into the nuts.*

With a height of 40 to 100 feet and a majestic spread of large limbs paralleling the ground for up to 60 feet, the chestnut tree is not for the small yard. Yet few trees offer what the chestnut can: a symmetrical, uniformly shaped canopy, a distinctive and attractive branching pattern, and an overall imperial posture. The large, dark green oval leaves have a toothed edge and turn a wonderful ruddy yellow in the fall. The blaze of autumnal yellow from a single tree against the evergreen foliage of an adjacent conifer can be seen for miles.

These trees demand a royal setting and can be used to shelter the home from summer's afternoon heat. They provide shade for outdoor barbecues and can act as a sheltering arbor, a place to hitch a hammock, or a canopy for an ornamental planting.

The American chestnut, which once flourished in over 200 million acres of forest, has been almost entirely destroyed by a canker-forming blight introduced to New York City from Asia. Every year there is a rumor of the discovery of an isolated healthy grove of American chestnuts. Seedlings grown from blight-free trees in the Pacific Northwest are sold by some mail-order nurseries.

*Complementary
Seasonings and Foods*

Chives, parsley, thyme; sugar;
eggs; cream cheese; garlic,
cabbage, mushrooms, potatoes;
veal, bacon, game.

Basically, the Chinese chestnut, the smallest of all chestnut varieties, reaching only 40 feet tall, has replaced the American chestnut in the garden. These trees are resistant to the dreaded chestnut fungal blight and can tolerate winter temperatures down to -15° to -20° F. The crop of nuts is seldom affected by late frosts because the catkins full of pollen and the inconspicuous flowers don't open until early summer.

There are a number of trees that have been developed by crossing the Chinese, European, and/or American varieties and these have some resistance to the blight. One particularly successful cross, the 'Colossal', grows quickly, and the mature mother tree produces over four hundred pounds of nuts each fall.

Japanese chestnuts produce the largest-sized nuts, but have the least appealing flavor. The European chestnut, also called the Spanish or French chestnut, has much the same susceptibility to chestnut blight and is seldom sold by nurseries. This variety can be grown in the West where the chestnut blight has never been recorded, but should not be planted east of the Rocky Mountains.

Chestnuts are ready to eat when they start falling from the tree. While it may seem troublesome to separate the nuts from their spiny seed coverings, their delicious flavor makes the work worthwhile. The nuts can be prepared, raw or cooked, in a variety of ways. To peel, make a deep X on the flat side of each chestnut. Working with a dozen or so at a time, place them in a saucepan, add water to cover, and boil until the hard outer skins can be peeled off with a sharp knife, about 7 minutes. Be sure to keep them hot while you work, or the inner brown, furlike, bitter skin, which must also be removed, will not come off easily.

To cook, arrange peeled chestnuts in a single layer in a large skillet. Add water to cover, cover skillet, and bring to a simmer. Cook, shaking pan occasionally, until tender (about 45 minutes). Drain, cool, transfer to a storage container, cover, and refrigerate for up to two days. Slice and serve with cream sweetened with sugar and brandy. Use chopped or puréed chestnuts in stuffings, especially for game birds.

Mini Recipes

Cut an X on flat side of each chestnut. Roast in 350° F oven for 20 to 30 minutes. Let your guests peel their own.

Wrap boiled, peeled whole chestnuts in bacon, thread on skewers, and grill until bacon is crisp. Serve as an appetizer, or for breakfast or brunch with scrambled eggs.

Soften Savory Chestnut Purée with sour cream or Yogurt Cheese (see page 22). Using a fork stir in chopped hard-cooked eggs and minced parsley. Serve as a spread for crackers.

Sweet Chestnut Purée

1/2 pound chestnuts, peeled and finely chopped

1/3 cup sugar

1 teaspoon rose water

2 thin slices orange peel

2 rose geranium leaves

2 sprigs sweet cicely

3 tablespoons water, or as needed

2 to 3 tablespoons Vanilla Yogurt Cheese (see page 23)

2 to 3 tablespoons whipping cream or half-and-half

This rich purée makes a wonderful topping for ice cream, frozen yogurt, Custard Sauce (see page 25), cake. Just before serving, sprinkle generously with freshly grated orange zest and garnish with tiny mint sprigs.

*I*n a nonstick saucepan combine chestnuts, sugar, rose water, orange peel, geranium leaves, sweet cicely sprigs, and water. Bring to a gentle boil over medium heat, stirring to dissolve sugar. Cover, lower heat, and simmer until chestnuts are tender (about 20 minutes). Add water if pan becomes dry.

Let cool slightly, then transfer to a blender or a food processor fitted with metal blade and purée. Pour into mixing bowl and stir in Yogurt Cheese and cream. If not using within several hours, cover and refrigerate up to 3 days.

MAKES ABOUT 1 CUP

Savory Chestnut Purée

1 pound chestnuts, peeled and finely chopped

Bouquet garni of 3 stalks celery and leaves, cut into large pieces; 1 onion, quartered; 6 to 8 whole nutmeg geranium leaves; 4 lovage leaves; 2 sprigs lemon thyme; 2 whole cloves; and 1 bay leaf, crumbled (see page 15)

1/2 cup water, or as needed

1 tablespoon cider vinegar

1/4 teaspoon salt

1/8 teaspoon freshly ground white pepper

2 to 3 tablespoons unsalted butter

1/3 cup whipping cream, or as needed

Pipe a mound of this elegant purée alongside roast venison or other game, or fill heated artichoke bottoms with the purée and serve as a garnish for any meat, game, or poultry dish. A sprinkling of minced parsley will add the needed touch of color.

◆

In a saucepan combine chestnuts, bouquet garni, water, vinegar, salt and pepper. Cover, bring to a gentle boil over medium-high heat, lower heat, and simmer until chestnuts are tender (about 20 minutes). Add water if pan becomes dry.

Discard bouquet garni and stir in butter and cream. Transfer to a blender or a food processor fitted with metal blade and purée. Let cool slightly, then place in a saucepan and reheat gently. Taste and adjust seasonings. If too thick (it should be the consistency of whipped cream), thin with additional cream.

MAKES ABOUT *1 1/2* CUPS

Chive

Allium schoenoprasum
Garlic Chive (A. tuberosum)

The green grasslike foliage of the perennial chive plant is subtle in both its looks and taste. Prior to bloom, the tufty foliage resembles a more open and slightly coarse version of the ornamental mondo grass, famous for its use as a soft billowy ground cover in Japanese gardens. Once chives bloom, mid-spring to early summer, they are far from subtle. The lollipop-shaped flower heads present a bold, flashy rosy pink floral display, and the edible blossom's intense flavor is not for the weak of heart (or, more accurately, palate).

Use the chive plant as a decorative "skirt" growing out from beneath other herb plants or perennial ornamentals. While chives can withstand some neglect, they prefer rich, well-drained soil and steady irrigation. Place with other plants with the same cultural needs, such as cilantro, fennel, French tarragon, or French sorrel. Arrange a chive planting in rambling drifts, with far more plants than you would need solely for culinary purposes. Chives are also suited to individual plantings scattered throughout the flower or herb border as a color accent. They don't need deep soil if well fertilized and regularly

A hardy perennial with mounded foliage to 12 to 16 inches; evergreen in mild winter climates, deciduous elsewhere.

Plant from divisions, potted plants, or seed.

Keep well watered and provide regular fertilizer or compost; mulching helps the plant thrive.

Prefers full sun, but tolerates some morning shade.

Cut foliage to the ground once a year in the early spring.

69

watered. With some care, chives thrive in pockets of soil on top of stone walls, between patio flagstones, or in terra-cotta pottery.

Garlic chives, also known as Chinese chives, have a coarser, flatter leaf, foliage 18 to 24 inches tall, and looser heads of pure white blossoms. The blooms lend a regal accent to an ornamental planting. The foliage is more upright and not nearly as mounding or dense as that of the regular chive. Bloom period is mid- to late summer.

Regular cutting of chive blades will delay, reduce, or prevent blossoming. Once a year, cut the entire plant to the ground to remove woody and dead foliage.

Harvest chive blades and flowers as you need them, wash, and snip into tiny pieces. Use as last-minute additions to soups, or add to vinaigrettes or mayonnaise, batter bread dough, or to pasta, potato, or grain salads. Chives lose much of their flavor when dried or frozen; preparing chive butter (see page 15) is the best way to preserve them. Use the butter on steamed vegetables, fish, or poultry.

If your chive plants have multiplied and you have an abundance, pull out some of the bulbs and use them as you would green onions.

Mini Recipes

Sprinkle snipped chives on salad of cucumber and red onions dressed with Yogurt Salad Dressing (see page 19).

Pass bowls of snipped chives and cottage cheese to use as topping for baked potatoes, or mix into twice-baked or mashed potatoes.

Prepare chive or garlic chive compound butter (see page 15) with finely minced, well-drained oil-packed sun-dried tomatoes and fresh lemon juice.

For an appetizer, offer slices of smoked salmon, rye bread, crumbled goat cheese, and snipped chives. Let guests help themselves.

*Complementary
Seasonings and Foods*

Basil, chervil, mint, parsley, tarragon; egg and cheese dishes; asparagus, beets, carrots, cauliflower, corn, cucumbers, garlic, onions, peas, potatoes, spinach, tomatoes; seafood, poultry, meats; Fumé Blanc, Zinfandel, most other wines.

Shrimp with Chives and Chèvre

2 pounds large shrimp (about 25), peeled and deveined

2 tablespoons unsalted butter

1 tablespoon olive oil

1/4 cup minced parsley

1/2 teaspoon salt

1/4 teaspoon freshly ground white pepper

1/4 teaspoon paprika

1/3 cup dry sherry

2 to 3 ounces chèvre, crumbled

1/3 cup minced chives or garlic chives

To avoid overcooking the shrimp, ready all the ingredients and accompaniments before you begin cooking. Spoon over freshly steamed rice and serve with a salad of bitter greens dressed with Hoisin Dressing (see page 19). Feta cheese can be substituted for the chèvre.

◆

Pat shrimp dry with paper toweling and set aside. In a large skillet over high heat, melt butter with oil. When butter is bubbly, add shrimp and sauté quickly, stirring constantly, until they start to turn pink and opaque (about 3 minutes). Add parsley, salt, pepper, and paprika; cook, stirring, 1 minute. Do not overcook.

Add sherry, stir in well, then toss in cheese and chives. Serve immediately.

SERVES 4 TO 6

Poached Chicken

1 chicken (2 1/2 to 3 lb)

3 slices lemon

8 garlic chive bulbs and tops or green onions and tops

6 slices fresh ginger

6 large cloves garlic, bruised

1 teaspoon salt

6 white peppercorns, lightly crushed

This method of poaching chicken produces a flavorful, moist chicken for salads, pasta dishes, or casseroles, or for a simple entrée. The amount of water needed depends upon the size of the pot. Truss the chicken, then select a pot that will just hold the bird. Have a kettle of boiling water handy in case you need to add more to cover. Plan ahead so there is time for the chicken to cool enough to handle.

◆

Trim visible fat and loose skin from chicken. Rinse under cool running water and stuff cavity with lemon slices, chive bulbs and tops, ginger, garlic, salt, and peppercorns. Secure cavity closed and truss chicken by tying legs and wings against body. Place chicken in pot, add water to cover, and remove chicken.

Over medium-high heat bring water to a rolling boil. Lower chicken into water breast side down, adding more boiling water if necessary to cover chicken completely. Bring water back to a boil and boil 5 minutes, skimming off any scum that rises to surface. Lower heat, cover, and simmer 15 minutes. Remove from heat and let stand in poaching liquid 1 hour; do not remove lid.

Lift chicken out of pot and place on wire rack. When cool enough to handle, remove skin and strip meat from bones. Slice or cut up as desired. Cover and refrigerate up to 2 days.

MAKES ABOUT 3 CUPS CUBED CHICKEN

Cilantro

Coriandrum sativum

Tender annual herb; all zones if planted after late-spring frosts.

Plant from seed; will self-sow if some flowers are left to seed.

Prefers full sun and heat, but tolerates some shade.

Prospers in rich, fertile, well-drained garden loam.

Grows 12 to 36 inches tall and up to a foot wide.

Plants with dense, attractive foliage should be used in the foreground to mask the bare stems of older cilantro plants.

Common names for plants often confuse the home gardener and cook alike. The confusion is doubled with cilantro because the same plant yields two very distinctive and useful herbs. The fresh leaves are commonly called cilantro or Chinese parsley and are used in soups, salads, with seafoods, and in various dips and salsas. Coriander is the well-known spice made from the small brown seeds of the mature plant and is used in curries, chilies, pickling, breads, and salad dressings.

Cilantro, a delicately foliaged plant with fernlike leaves, grows with abandon in summer. A fountain of dark green foliage frosted with pink, lacy flowers, it makes a lovely filler among other plants, like ferns in a flower bouquet. The pale blossoms provide a nice backdrop to more intensely colored specimens such as clear red poppies, mauve cosmoses, or royal blue bachelor buttons.

Foliage can be harvested from young plants once they are more than six inches tall. Older plants will yield leaves with a slightly more pungent, untamed flavor. In either case, clip the outer two to three inches of ferny foliage. Cilantro will quickly bolt (begin to flower)

73

*Complementary
Seasonings and Foods*

Parsley, basil, mint, curry
powder, cumin; oyster sauce,
hoisin sauce, Asian sesame oil;
lemon juice; mild cheeses;
garlic, tomatoes, tomatillos,
chiles, onions, avocados; pork,
chicken, lamb, beef, sausage;
Gewürztraminer, White
Zinfandel, Sauvignon Blanc,
Fumé Blanc, Zinfandel,
Cabernet Sauvignon,
Gamay Beaujolais.

during the heat of summer. Repeated plantings every week or two will insure a ready supply of the young leaf.

Some find cilantro's tangy bite an acquired taste, but appreciate it mixed with other herbs and foods in small amounts. Use cautiously until you are sure you like the flavor. To store cilantro sprigs briefly, stand them in a glass of water, cover with a plastic bag, and refrigerate for up to two days. Cilantro leaves do not retain their flavor when dried, but may be frozen with some success. Make oil concentrate (see page 14) or compound butter (see page 15) with chopped leaves and freeze for up to three months.

The ripe coriander seeds drop out of the seed head, which falls apart easily (called shattering); harvesting early in the morning will help prevent this problem. To dry the seeds, tie the seed heads in bundles and hang them upside down in a paper bag in a dry, airy spot. Let them dry until they are hard, six to eight days. Toast some of the seeds and grind; leave others whole, toasting lightly before using. Store in airtight containers in a dark place for up to three months.

Although cilantro leaves and coriander seeds cannot be used interchangeably, they do combine well in a number of dishes. Use them together in marinades and curries.

Mini Recipes

Sauté cilantro leaves and minced garlic and fresh ginger in peanut oil; add fresh lemon juice and serve over fish or prawns.

Tuck cilantro leaves between leaves of whole artichokes before steaming; serve with cilantro butter (see page 15) for dipping.

Stuff a handful of cilantro and crushed garlic cloves in cavity of chicken before roasting.

Add chopped cilantro leaves to a frittata made with cooked corn kernels, shredded zucchini, and julienned sweet peppers; garnish with halved cherry tomatoes and cilantro sprigs.

Steamed Turkey with Cilantro

1 egg

2/3 cup well-drained soft tofu

2 cloves garlic, very
finely minced

1 teaspoon very finely minced
fresh ginger

1/2 cup minced cilantro, plus
cilantro sprigs, for garnish

1/4 cup minced parsley

1/4 cup fine fresh bread crumbs

2 teaspoons soy sauce

1/2 teaspoon Asian sesame oil

2 teaspoons cornstarch

1/2 teaspoon salt

1/4 teaspoon freshly ground
white pepper

1 pound ground turkey

2 or 3 dried shiitake
mushrooms, soaked in warm
water to cover 20 minutes,
drained, stemmed, and cut
into slivers

1 ounce Canadian bacon, cut
into slivers

Most often prepared with ground lean pork, this Chinese-inspired dish can also be made with ground dark chicken meat. Spoon the turkey and juices directly from the dish onto steamed white rice and serve with stir-fried snow peas.

✦

In a large bowl beat egg lightly. Add tofu, garlic, ginger, minced cilantro, parsley, bread crumbs, soy sauce, sesame oil, cornstarch, salt, pepper, and turkey. Stir with fork, or mix with fingers, to combine well. Mixture will be moist and rather soft.

Place a small amount of the turkey mixture in a small shallow dish. Set dish on steamer rack over boiling water, cover pot, and steam 5 minutes. Taste and adjust seasonings.

Pat turkey mixture into an attractive shallow dish approximately 9 inches in diameter and 2 inches deep. Form a slight indentation in center. Arrange mushroom and bacon slivers in spoke pattern on top of meat mixture. Place dish on steamer rack set over boiling water, cover pot, and steam 20 to 25 minutes.

Remove from steamer, garnish with cilantro sprigs, and serve directly from dish.

SERVES 4

Coriander Cookie Wreaths

1 pound margarine, at
room temperature

1 cup granulated sugar

1 teaspoon rose water

3 1/2 cups unbleached flour, or
as needed

1 1/2 to 2 teaspoons
ground coriander

3/4 teaspoon salt

1/2 cup finely ground almonds
or walnuts

Confectioners' sugar

These delectable cookies, which literally melt in your mouth, can be stored at room temperature for several days or frozen in an airtight tin for several months; they taste even better when eaten directly from the freezer. If your coriander is freshly ground, use the smaller measurement.

✦

In a large bowl and using a wooden spoon, or in the bowl of an electric mixer, cream margarine until smooth. Gradually beat in granulated sugar until mixture is creamy and smooth. Beat in rose water.

Sift together 1 cup of the flour, coriander and salt. Stir into margarine mixture along with almonds. Gradually beat in remaining 2 1/2 cups flour, blending well after each addition. A little at a time, add additional flour as needed to form a soft dough. The dough should not be quite as firm as pie dough.

Shape dough into a thick disk, wrap well in waxed paper, place in plastic bag, and refrigerate at least 1 hour. If refrigerating more than 2 hours or as long as overnight, let stand at room temperature 10 to 15 minutes before proceeding.

Preheat oven to 350° F. Working in batches, force dough through a cookie press fitted with the star disk to form long, continuous ropes on work surface. Break off pieces approximately 3 1/2 inches long. Form each into a ring and place on ungreased baking sheet, spacing rings about 3/4 inch apart.

Bake until cookies just start to brown (10 to 12 minutes). If using 2 baking sheets, halfway through baking switch sheets on racks, then rotate each sheet 180 degrees.

Using a spatula remove cookies to wire racks and sprinkle with confectioners' sugar. Let cookies cool completely before transferring to cookie tins.

Makes 15 to 16 dozen cookies

Crabapple

Malus sp.

Medium to large deciduous tree, up to 30 feet tall and wide.

Grows in most zones.

Plant bareroot tree in winter on raised mound. Tolerates moist or clayey soils.

Position in full sun, where flowers are easily viewed in spring.

Mulching is helpful, but supplemental fertilizers are not often needed.

Can become fairly drought resistant; water prudently.

Overwatering or overfertilizing may induce pest and disease problems. Watch for apple scab, mildew, and fire blight, and for the following pests: codling moths, caterpillars, apple maggot, San Jose scale, aphids, and soil mealy bug.

Fruits and flowers are edible.

*H*ow crabapples got stuck with such an uncomely name remains veiled in history, but the name is surely unjust given these trees' billowing fountain of extravagant spring color. From hot crimson, to wine red, to clear pink, to the palest of pinks, crabapples are blessed with a wide range of colors. Crabapple bloom comes in single crepe paperlike petals and opulent double-petaled flowers. The wonderfully sweet fragrance from a full-sized tree can waft to several houses down the street on a warm spring afternoon. As the bloom wanes, petals cascade to the ground to coat the lawn, sidewalk, or flower border like a late spring snowstorm of pink snow.

If the name *crabapple* was selected solely because of the fruit, whoever picked such a denigrating moniker certainly didn't sample the tasty flesh of cultivars such as 'Dolgo', 'Transcendent', 'Red Flash', and 'Centennial'. Such trees not only offer the same range of attractive foliage and bloom as an ornamental crabapple tree, but also offer the additional benefits of good eating, with flavors ranging from sharp to sweet to almost nutlike.

Crabapple trees come in a wide variety of shapes, from somewhat columnar, to mushroomlike, to cascading. With a wide selection of rootstocks, you can choose a tree that reaches 30 feet tall by 30 feet wide or as small as 8 by 8 feet. A common ornamental variety known solely for its prodigious pure white bloom is the Japanese flowering

77

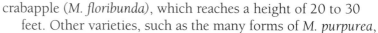

crabapple (*M. floribunda*), which reaches a height of 20 to 30 feet. Other varieties, such as the many forms of *M. purpurea*, are known for their distinctive range of purplish leaves or dark green leaves with reddish veins. Many ornamental crabapple trees make excellent pollenizers for all types of regular apple trees and crabapples. Check with your local nursery for the best pollenizer for your climate.

Crabapple trees demand generous space and should be treated as accent plants for the spring season. Place where the floral display can be easily observed by both the household and the neighbors. They do better planted in a lawn than most trees, but they should have a four- to eight-foot radius of permanent mulch or a planting of shade-tolerant ornamentals around the trunk. Don't place a crabapple tree where its canopy overhangs walkways, driveways, decks, or patios, as the fruit can discolor the surface and make a slippery, dangerous mess. The smaller forms can be planted close together as a deciduous hedge or summer windbreak.

Crabapples share with apple trees an ability to tolerate fairly heavy soils. There are many clones of rootstocks, each with a slightly different soil tolerance. Your local nursery can help with the selection.

All types of caterpillars love to graze upon the spring and summer foliage of apple and crabapple trees. Whole trees have been practically defoliated by these hungry pests. Use *Bacillus thuringiensis*, a commonly available spray harmless to humans sold under various trade names, to control all moth and butterfly caterpillars.

Gather the flowers shortly after the buds open; wash and dry with paper toweling. Harvest the apples just as they start to fall from the tree and refrigerate no longer than two or three days. Because the crabapple is too sour and tart to eat raw, it is often used with other fruits, adding tang to cobblers and puddings. The edible flowers can be dipped in Fritter Batter (see page 23), deep-fried, and sprinkled with sugar.

When cooking crabapples whole, leave stem on and cut out blossom end; prick skins in a few places to prevent apples from bursting. For jellies, remove the stem and cut in halves or quarters; for cobblers, slice the crabapples in half lengthwise and remove cores.

Mini Recipes

For breakfast, brown pork or turkey link sausages, remove from pan, and add crabapple slices to pan. Cook a few minutes, adding brown sugar to taste. Return links to pan, cook until heated through, and serve with scrambled eggs.

Mix grated crabapples and flaked crab meat into cream cheese softened with Yogurt Cheese (see page 22); serve as a dip for crudités or as a spread for plain crackers.

Combine cored and sliced crabapples with large apples when making apple pie seasoned with pumpkin pie spice.

Spiced Crabapples

2 cups sugar

1 to 1 1/4 cups white vinegar or white wine vinegar

1/4 cup water

2 lemon slices

1 tablespoon whole cloves

One cinnamon stick (4 in. long), broken

3 slices fresh ginger

1/2 teaspoon whole allspice

6 cups crabapples

Serve these spicy little apples as a garnish for meat or poultry dishes. Strained leftover syrup is excellent on ice cream or frozen yogurt.

✦

In a heavy, nonreactive pot over medium heat, combine all ingredients except crabapples. Bring to a boil, stirring to dissolve sugar. Lower heat and boil gently 10 minutes. Remove from heat and let cool slightly.

Using tines of small fork, prick crabapples in several places. Return pot to medium heat, add crabapples and heat syrup to 180° F. Turning apples often and maintaining 180° F temperature, cook until easily pierced with a cake tester (about 10 minutes).

Immediately ladle apples and syrup into hot, sterilized jars and seal and store as directed on page 17. Do not use for at least 2 weeks. Refrigerate unsealed jars no longer than 2 weeks.

MAKES ABOUT 3 HALF-PINTS

Crabapple Jelly with Sweet Cicely

3 pounds crabapples, halved or quartered

4 cups water

2 tablespoons pickling spice

1/2 to 3/4 cup sugar

Sweet cicely feathers or rose geranium leaves

The lovely color and spicy flavor will surprise and delight your family. For a firm jelly, use 3/4 cup sugar for each cup of juice. For a thinner jelly, use 1/2 cup sugar.

✦

In a large, nonreactive pot over medium-high heat, combine apples, water, and pickling spice. Bring to a boil, lower heat to medium-low, cover, and cook, stirring occasionally, until apples are soft when pierced with a fork (about 20 minutes). Mash apple mixture with potato masher.

Wet a jelly bag and wring out well. Transfer mashed apples to bag and hang over medium-large nonreactive saucepan. Let drip overnight to extract as much juice as possible. Do not squeeze.

Place the saucepan over medium-high heat and bring juice to a boil. Skim off and discard any scum that rises to surface and boil 5 minutes. Add sugar, stir to dissolve, and boil rapidly 8 minutes. Start testing at this point by placing a small amount of syrup in a wooden spoon and cooling it 4 or 5 seconds. Tip spoon and let syrup drop from side of spoon back into saucepan. As syrup thickens, 2 drops will form along edge of spoon on either side. When drops run together and fall as one, the firm jelly stage has been reached (220° to 222° F on candy thermometer).

Place 1 or 2 sweet cicely feathers in the bottoms of hot, sterilized jars and immediately ladle in jelly. Seal and store as directed on page 17. Refrigerate unsealed jars no longer than 2 weeks.

MAKES ABOUT 5 HALF-PINTS

Dill

Anethum graveolens

Annual herb.

Grow from seed.

Has a long taproot and prefers deep, fertile soil; doesn't need much extra fertilizer.

Plant in full sun every three weeks for a continuous harvest.

Must be consistently moist to extend the harvest of the leaf and delay flowering.

Do not let mature seed form as the plant can become a weed.

Plant in a sheltered spot or stake if windy.

Foliage may be attacked by swallowtail butterfly caterpillars; handpick or use Bacillus thuringiensis spray (see Crabapple).

Dill, with its feathery green or bluish green foliage, originated in Europe, but grows throughout the Americas. The fernlike leaves, which closely resemble anise and fennel, grow to four feet and are prized for their culinary value. Once flowering starts in mid-summer, the quality of the foliage as a fresh herb declines. The flower heads, shaped like parasols, are an attractive hot, clear yellow.

The wispy foliage makes a good backdrop for more colorful plants. Position dill in the medium background to fill in the area around plants that look unattractive or die to the ground in late summer such as artichokes, or use as a filler throughout the garden, much like cilantro. If planted near fennel, the two will cross and make seed that represents neither of the original plants.

Some varieties such as 'Bouquet Dill' are grown not for their foliage but for the seed, which also has many culinary uses. Other types, including 'Dukat Dill', are grown specifically for the leaves, sometimes called dillweed.

Letting some dill plants go to flower will enhance the populations of beneficial insects. Do not let dill form mature seed, as it can become a pesty weed.

*Complementary
Seasonings and Foods*

Mint, chives, fennel, parsley,
sage; egg and cheese dishes;
green and root vegetables,
onions, squashes; apples;
seafood, lamb, pork, beef;
Johannisberg Riesling, Fumé
Blanc, Chardonnay,
Chenin Blanc.

Treated by most gardeners as an annual herb, in warm winter climates, dill will grow as a biennial or perennial, although the foliage dies to the ground with the coming of frost. The trick to a continued harvest of the fresh leaf is to keep plants always moist.

To harvest snip off as many sprigs as needed and, if not using immediately, stand them upright in a glass of water, cover with a plastic bag, and store in the refrigerator for up to one day. Dill sprigs may be frozen whole; snip off only what you need. Crumbled dried dill, stored in airtight containers, will retain a degree of flavor for up to four or five months.

Use kitchen shears to snip the fragile foliage of fresh dill into tiny lengths. Add to dishes toward the end of cooking, or sprinkle over finished dishes. Dill makes a good salt substitute, and is used in pickling and in Greek salads, Indian *raitas*, borscht, and many other ethnic dishes. It also adds spice to tomato soup, chicken fricassee, mashed potatoes, and numerous other preparations.

Dried seeds (follow directions for drying coriander seeds on page 74), which are slightly bitter and stronger in taste than the leaves, can be stored in airtight containers in a cool, dark place for up to five or six months. Ground dried seeds will retain their flavor for up to three or four months. Add seeds to vegetables such as green beans, beets, or sauerkraut; to stews, long-cooking soups, fricassees, and meat pies; to boiled beef, tongue, or corned beef; and to court bouillon. Add ground seeds to breads or coffeecakes; to cream or cottage cheese; to appetizer sauce for prawns; to dressing for coleslaw or avocado salad; or to the poaching liquid for fish.

Beef Piroshki

Basic Pastry made with 1 tablespoon dried dill (see page 27)

1 teaspoon canola oil

1/3 cup minced onion

1 large clove garlic, finely minced

1/2 pound lean ground beef

1 tablespoon beef stock or water

1/2 tablespoon flour

2 tablespoons snipped fresh dill

1/4 teaspoon salt

1/8 teaspoon freshly ground pepper

1 extra-large egg, hard-cooked and finely chopped

2/3 cup Yogurt Cheese (see page 22)

1 small egg, beaten with 1 tablespoon cold water

These luncheon pastries are so pleasantly rich that one will suffice for a serving. Note that both dried and fresh dill are called for in the recipe and that the pastries may be made several hours in advance. Place on a baking sheet, cover with plastic wrap, and refrigerate until it is time to slip them into the oven.

✦

Prepare the pastry dough, adding dried dill with the flour. Wrap in waxed paper and refrigerate at least 1 hour.

In a skillet over medium heat, warm oil. Add onion and sauté until soft (about 5 minutes). Add garlic and cook 1 minute. Crumble beef into skillet and stir in stock, breaking up meat with fork as you do. Cover and cook, without allowing meat to brown and stirring occasionally with fork, until meat loses color (about 5 minutes).

Sprinkle with flour and cook, stirring, over medium-low heat 3 minutes. Season with fresh dill, salt, and pepper. Remove from heat and, using a fork, stir in hard-cooked egg and Yogurt Cheese. Taste and adjust seasonings. Set aside, or cover and refrigerate up to 24 hours.

Following directions in pastry recipe, roll out pastry dough into a rectangle 1/8 inch thick. Cut into 6 rounds each 5 1/2 inches in diameter, gathering and rerolling scraps to make last round. Place 1/3 cup filling on each round and fold over to make half-moon. Seal edges and crimp with tines of fork. Transfer to baking sheet, cover with plastic wrap, and refrigerate at least 20 minutes or up to 4 hours.

Position oven rack in the top one third of oven. Preheat oven to 375° F.

Brush pastries with egg-water mixture and bake 10 minutes. Lower heat to 350° F and bake until pastries are golden brown (about 20 minutes). Serve immediately.

MAKES 6 PASTRIES

Gravlax

Salmon fillets

Coarse salt

Sugar

Fresh dill

Gravlax can be made with either a pair of fresh salmon fillets with skin intact or with a whole salmon that has been scaled and gutted, then carefully filleted. Be sure to check fillets for any hidden bones. Fresh dill is a must.

✦

Rinse fillets in cold running water and pat dry with paper toweling. In a shallow glass or ceramic dish, place 1 fillet, skin side down. For each pound of salmon, combine 1 tablespoon coarse salt (not iodized) and 1/2 to 1 tablespoon sugar. Sprinkle salt mixture evenly over surface of fillet and cover completely with a generous layer of snipped dill. Sprinkle with lightly crushed white peppercorns and cover with second fillet, skin side up.

Cover salmon with plastic wrap and then aluminum foil. Place a weight, such as a brick wrapped in aluminum foil, unopened canned goods, or other heavy objects, on top. Refrigerate 48 hours, turning sandwiched fillets over and basting cut sides with juices several times a day.

If desired, the last 24 hours strew minced thyme, chervil, and/or tarragon, or finely minced drained green peppercorns, between fillets.

To serve the gravlax, scrape off seasonings and pat dry with paper toweling. Place fillets, skin side down, on large serving platter or board. Surround fish with lemon wedges and parsley and/or dill sprigs. Arrange bowls of unsalted butter, drained capers, and/or green peppercorns, finely minced sweet onion, and cream cheese softened with Yogurt Cheese (see page 22) around platter. Place a tray of assorted bread rounds such as rye, black, or pumpernickel and/or sliced bagels on the table. Guests slice the salmon on the diagonal and add their own garnishes.

To store any uneaten salmon, fold skin over untouched portion, wrap in plastic wrap and then aluminum foil, and refrigerate up to 4 days. The salmon can also be frozen, but the texture will not be the same; use only as an ingredient for dips or spreads.

Elaeagnus

Elaeagnus multiflora and *E. philippinensis*

Perennial shrub, small tree; tolerate mild to moderately cold winters.

Grow from seedlings, cuttings, or layered cuttings; purchase as a container plant.

Plant in a sunny location in well-drained soil.

Needs little extra fertilizer or water, except in the arid West.

Prune to shape.

Use bird netting to protect the crop each summer.

*T*he *Elaeagnus* genus contains a handful of multipurpose trees and shrubs that can serve many functions in the edible landscape. The tastiest elaeagnus fruits, however, come from a small tree most frequently called goumi (*E. multiflora*, the deciduous form, or *E. philippinensis*, the evergreen form). The name *goumi* has been associated with every species of edible-fruited elaeagnus, but is more frequently associated with these two attractive large shrubs or small trees. The pale green, narrow, oval leaves of the evergreen form are dotted with silver highlights on the underside so that, much like a white poplar tree, when the wind ruffles the leaves the pale white flickering enlivens the landscape.

The berries are up to 3/8 inch in diameter and are a pale burgundy glazed with a patina of silver spots. The berry's flesh is a cranberry color, moist, and has a tropical sweet-tart flavor. Some people eat the fruits fresh off the tree, but most reserve them for sweet sauces, pies, tarts, jams, or jellies. The branches can become laden with prolific clusters of the fruit, which makes for another colorful highlight in the mid- to late summer.

The goumi, like all elaeagnus species, prefers full sun or a sunny south- or west-facing wall. The evergreen variety reaches only about 6 feet, while *E. multiflora* grows to 10 feet. Left unpruned, the limbs of the evergreen form can grow into a rangy form that promises enough strength to support the ample crop. Plant near a dark wall to show off the attractive foliage; a lighter wall will make a better backdrop for the fruit.

Harvest the fruit berries when they are clear red and readily separate from the bush. Wash in a colander, stem, and dry with paper toweling. If not using at once, wrap unwashed berries in paper toweling, place in a plastic bag, and refrigerate for no more than two days.

Elaeagnus Sauce

4 cups elaeagnus berries

1/4 cup water

1/3 cup sugar, or as needed

The spectacular color lends eye appeal to this natural sauce. Its flavor complements game and poultry dishes, and it makes an excellent topping for ice cream, frozen yogurt, or Custard Sauce (see page 25).

✦

*I*n a heavy, deep, nonreactive pot over high heat, combine berries and water. Bring to a boil, lower heat to medium, cover, and cook, stirring occasionally, until berries are very soft (about 20 minutes).

Using a spoon or potato masher, mash berry mixture and then force through a fine-mesh sieve into clean, nonreactive pan. Alternatively, pass through food mill into pan.

Add sugar and stir to dissolve. Bring to a gentle boil over medium-high heat. Cover, lower heat to medium, and cook, stirring often, until thickened (about 10 minutes). Taste and adjust with more sugar if needed.

Ladle into sterilized jars. When cool, cover and refrigerate up to 1 week or freeze up to 6 months.

MAKES ABOUT 1 CUP

Herbed Cornish Hens with Elaeagnus Sauce

Marinade:

1/3 cup dry vermouth

2 tablespoons fresh lemon or lime juice

1 cup chopped green onion and some tops

1 large clove garlic, chopped

1/3 cup chopped parsley

2 teaspoons minced thyme

2 large Cornish hens

Salt, freshly ground white pepper, and paprika, to taste

1/2 cup Elaeagnus Sauce (see page 86)

2 tablespoons each dry vermouth and fresh lemon or lime juice

Spearmint sprigs, for garnish

Although Cornish hens have a relatively low fat content, you may want to skin them before cooking. The marinade will keep them moist. Plan ahead so the hens can marinate the designated time. The marinade can be made several hours ahead, covered, and refrigerated. Crabapple Jelly with Sweet Cicely (see page 80) may replace the Elaeagnus Sauce, in which case the jelly should be heated with the vermouth and lemon juice just until dissolved.

Wild rice cooked in chicken stock and steamed snow peas complement this colorful entrée.

✦

To prepare marinade, in a blender combine vermouth, lemon juice, green onion, garlic, parsley, and thyme. Purée until smooth.

Halve hens and trim off visible fat and loose skin. Rinse hens under cool running water and pat dry with paper toweling. Place hens in shallow nonreactive dish and pour vermouth mixture over them. Cover and marinate, turning several times, 4 to 6 hours at room temperature, or in refrigerator overnight.

Preheat oven to 400° F. Remove hens from marinade and place, cut side up, in shallow baking pan; do not crowd. Pour half the marinade over; reserve remainder. Sprinkle hens with salt, pepper, and paprika.

Roast hens for 20 minutes. Turn halves over, pour remaining marinade over, and roast 15 minutes longer.

In a small bowl stir together Elaeagnus Sauce, vermouth, and lemon juice and spoon over hens. Return to oven and roast until juices run clear when thigh is pierced (about 15 minutes). Let stand 5 minutes before serving. Garnish with spearmint sprigs.

SERVES 4

Elaeagnus Jelly

5 quarts elaeagnus berries

2 2/3 cups water

1 1/3 cups sugar

The fact that the berries do not retain their bright red color when cooked in no way detracts from the wonderful flavor of this jelly. Delicious on toast, biscuits, and English muffins and in grilled cheese sandwiches.

✦

In a large, deep, nonreactive pot over medium-high heat, combine berries and water. Bring to a gentle boil, lower heat to medium-low, cover, and cook, stirring occasionally, until berries are very soft (about 20 minutes).

Mash berry mixture with a potato masher and proceed as directed in Crabapple Jelly with Sweet Cicely (see page 80). Refrigerate unsealed jars no longer than 1 week.

MAKES ABOUT 4 HALF-PINTS

Feijoa

Feijoa sellowianna

Small evergreen tree to 30 feet, or shrub to 10 feet. Hardy down to 12° F.

Purchase named varieties in containers. Plant two varieties to ensure good fruiting.

Prospers in fertile soil, but also tolerates clayey loams.

Water and fertilize often until fruiting.

Bears fruit on the ends of new growth; no need to prune for a crop.

Responds well to pruning into any shape.

What used to be known as pineapple guava, feijoa is no relation to either the pineapple or the guava. The name derives from the fruit's tropical flavor, which is reminiscent of both pineapples and guavas. The flavor is fantastic as both a seedless, soft fresh fruit and, *if you have enough fruits left over after "grazing" the landscape*, a wonderfully mellow, smooth juice.

The leaves' dark green tops and silver-gray undersides lend a unique ornamental touch among fruit trees. The stunning reddish brown bark has a rough but not wild texture. Pruning the foliage to display some of the trunkline greatly enhances the plant's ornamental value. The pinkish white flowers, which also make delicious eating, are borne in late spring or early summer and are not too visible from a distance. Up close, the fleshy white petals and dominant shocking red stamens make an attractive display. The thick petals have all the tropical flavor of the fruit and are a "crop" unto themselves. The fruits, which range from pale lime green to olive and are two to four inches long, hang unobtrusively from beneath the foliage.

The small evergreen feijoa is one of the most versatile ornamental edibles in a gardener's plant repertoire. If trained as a standard, with a single limbless trunk up to a rounded canopy, the feijoa can reach 20 to 30 feet and act as a small shade tree or accent plant. The fully ripe fruits don't easily break open when they fall, and so are not messy when planted over private sidewalks, patios, decks, and porches—where people don't step on the fallen fruit.

The plant prefers to grow as a multitrunk tree or shrub, which offers many options to the garden designer: an individual well-pruned specimen where the shapely, curvy trunklines are revealed; a tightly trimmed evergreen hedge; a half sphere-shaped background planting up to 10 feet tall and wide; a bonsailike planting in a large terra-cotta pot; or a classically trained espalier against an earth-toned wall. Plus, fejoias have no serious pest or disease problems.

Feijoas are perhaps the most tropical-tasting fruit a gardener can grow outside of Florida, southern California, or Texas. The mature plants tolerate down to 12° to 18° F. Younger plants need protection. Drape old sheets or blankets over, but not touching, the plant to fend off unseasonable frosts. The addition of a light bulb beneath the covering is an added measure of defense.

The two premier commercial varieties have the self-boosting names 'Mammoth' and 'Triumph'. Water and fertilize thoroughly and on a regular basis. A well-tended plant will take several years to begin to form mature fruit. The plant can tolerate a fair amount of water around its roots and a relatively heavy soil.

The proper degree of ripeness of the fruits is especially important so that their rich, tangy sweetness is brought out. Fortunately for the home gardener, feijoas ripen one at a time over many weeks. Check for ripeness by gently squeezing the largest, plumpest fruits. Ripe fruits give gently to pressure, but are not flaccid. Or wait until a few fruits fall and then check the hanging feijoas for ripeness. Many times, fallen fruits have already discolored from the early stages of overripeness.

Ripe fruits can be stored in the refrigerator only a few days. Purée an abundance and freeze up to three months, or poach lightly (see Poaching Liquid on page 24) and then purée, sieve, and freeze up to six months. Use sweetened purées as a sauce for vanilla ice cream or sponge cake or as a base for sorbets, ice cream, or frozen yogurt. Halve feijoas and eat as you would a melon, or peel, slice, and serve over breakfast cereals. The fruit also combines well with other fruits, including avocados, and with herbs such as sweet cicely and mint.

Feijoa Meringue with Fresh Berries

Meringue:

4 egg whites, at
room temperature

1/4 teaspoon cream of tartar

1/2 teaspoon cider vinegar

1/8 teaspoon salt

3/4 cup superfine sugar

Filling:

4 egg yolks

1/2 cup superfine sugar

1 teaspoon freshly grated lemon
or lime zest

1/3 cup fresh lemon or
lime juice

3/4 cup whipping cream

1 cup finely chopped feijoa

Topping:

1/4 cup whipping cream

1/2 cup Vanilla Yogurt Cheese
(see page 23)

2 tablespoons superfine sugar

Whole strawberries, raspberries,
or blueberries, for garnish

Freshly grated lemon or lime
zest, for garnish

Mint sprigs or sweet cicely
feathers, for garnish

This delicately perfumed dessert, especially eye-catching when the meringue is baked in a glass dish, makes a suitable ending to an elegant dinner party. It must be made ahead, so it allows ample time to prepare dinner without having to worry about a last-minute dessert.

✦

To prepare meringue, preheat oven to 225° F. In a large bowl, combine egg whites, cream of tartar, vinegar, and salt and beat until stiff peaks form. One tablespoon at a time, beat in sugar; continue beating until egg whites are smooth and glossy.

Spoon meringue into a round dish with sloping sides about 11 inches in diameter and 3 inches deep. Spread meringue to cover center of dish about 1 inch deep and build meringue along sides of dish to a thickness of 1 1/2 to 2 inches. Bake until edges of meringue just start to turn golden (about 1 1/4 hours). Let cool on wire rack.

To prepare filling, in top pan of double boiler, beat together egg yolks, sugar, and lemon zest and juice until smooth, slightly thickened, and deep yellow. Place over gently boiling water and cook, stirring almost constantly with a wooden spoon, until custard thickens (15 to 20 minutes). The custard is ready when it pulls away from pan sides and lightly coats spoon; do not overcook. Set custard aside to cool, stirring occasionally.

Whip cream until stiff peaks form. Fold feijoa into custard, then fold in whipped cream. Pour into meringue shell, cover tightly with plastic wrap, and refrigerate 20 to 24 hours.

Shortly before serving, prepare topping. Whip cream until stiff peaks form. Whip Yogurt Cheese with a fork until light and mix in sugar. Then gently stir in whipped cream. Spread over filled meringue and arrange strawberries decoratively on top. Sprinkle with lemon zest and tuck mint sprigs around edges.

SERVES 10 TO 12

Bronze Fennel

Foeniculum vulgare dulce
var. rubrum

Few herb plants can compete with bronze fennel's striking fountain of foliage. The feathery fronds reflect a multitude of colors: bronzy red, musky purple, and the parts of the rainbow one sees in the sheen of a spot of oily water. This incomparable herb is often placed as a single, well-displayed plant to show off its unique colors.

Because the foliage dies to the ground in the fall, or is pruned back to tidy up the garden, the fresh flush of foliage in the spring is rapid and theatrical. This is another good filler to mask those plants—artichokes, squash, tomatoes, eggplants—that can look ratty by mid-summer. Bright yellow umbels arrive at the same time and hover a foot or more above the three to four feet of ferny leaves. In addition to delighting the eye, flowers offer tiny beneficial insects a place to feed before they hunt down and eat or parasitize pests.

Fennel foliage tastes best before the plant begins to bloom. Heat and drought stimulate flowering, so sustain the harvest of the herbal leaves by maintaining consistent moisture. You can also make several successive plantings to stretch the harvest.

Annual herb in all zones; perennial in mild winter climates.

Plant seeds or seedlings in fertile, well-drained soil.

Water well to sustain the harvest of the herbal foliage.

Can become weedy; cut off seed heads before they scatter seed.

Watch for swallowtail butterfly caterpillars; handpick or use a Bacillus thuringiensis spray (see Crabapple).

92

The feathery fronds, tender stalks, and seeds are all edible and impart a mild anise flavor. Harvest the feathers at any time after the plant is established. Use as soon as possible, or stand in a glass of water, cover loosely with a plastic bag, and refrigerate for up to one or two days.

The delicate flavor of fennel feathers is destroyed by high heat, so use as a garnish or in marinades, or chop and add to stuffings, soups (especially fish), salads (especially white bean), salad dressings, vegetable dishes (especially cabbage and potatoes), and egg dishes.

The feathers do not dry or freeze well, so depend upon the seeds for culinary endeavors after the plant has died back. Harvest the seeds when they have turned from a yellow-green to brown. To dry them, follow the directions for drying coriander seeds on page 74. Separate the seeds from the heads and store in airtight containers in a cool area for up to three or four months.

Both the feathers and the seeds can be used in fish, sausage, or duck dishes. Season barley, rice, and lentils with fennel feathers, or make fennel butter (see page 15) or cheese spread. Use the seeds in soups, sauces, and stews, or grind them and add to meat loaf mixtures, to pasta or potato salad, or to yeast and quick breads, puddings, cakes, and cookies. In Asia, seeds are toasted until dark brown and ground for curries. Serve fennel-seasoned dishes with Chardonnay, Petite Syrah, Zinfandel, or Sauvignon Blanc.

Tomato Sauce with Fennel and Thyme

1 tablespoon olive oil

1 cup chopped onion

6 large cloves garlic, chopped

1/2 teaspoon sugar

6 large ripe tomatoes,
coarsely chopped

Bouquet garni of 3 tablespoons
fennel seeds; 8 large sprigs
thyme; 1 bay leaf, crumbled;
 6 peppercorns, lightly crushed;
and 3 lovage or celery leaves
(see page 15)

*Here, a basic tomato sauce is perked up with the addition of a bouquet garni.
Use this sauce on pasta, polenta, or meat loaf.*

✦

*I*n a large, nonreactive skillet or saucepan over medium heat, warm oil.
Add onion and garlic, cover, and cook until onion is soft (about 5
minutes). Sprinkle with sugar and cook, stirring, 2 minutes. Add
tomatoes and mix well.

Lightly smash bouquet garni with a flat mallet to release oils. Place
on top of tomatoes. Bring to gentle boil over medium-high heat. Lower
heat, cover with lid ajar, and simmer, stirring occasionally, 1 hour.

Discard bouquet garni and pass tomatoes through food mill, or
purée in a blender or a food processor fitted with metal blade and then
force through fine-mesh sieve. Return mixture to skillet and bring to a
gentle boil. Cook uncovered, stirring often, until thickened (about
2 hours).

Let cool, cover, and refrigerate up to 3 days or freeze up to
3 months.

MAKES ABOUT 3 CUPS

Fig
Ficus carica

Tender deciduous tree.
Tolerates down to 10° to 15° F.
Young trees can be killed back at
20° to 27° F; old mature trees have been
known to survive 0° F.

Grow from bareroot tree or potted
rooted cutting.

Requires well-drained soil; tolerates poor
rocky and gravelly soils.

Does not usually require additional water
or fertilizer once established.

Bears well with no pruning or with
heavy pruning.

Keep white sap out of eyes and mouth.

Figs share a plant family called *Moraceae* with the mulberry tree, hops, hemp, the tree Buddha was supposedly sitting beneath when he became enlightened, the rubber tree of commerce, and the rubber plant of house-plant fame. One visible similarity between many members of this family is the viscous white sap that oozes from a scarred limb. The sap is latex based and can cause burns to mucous membranes, especially the eyes.

In the summer fig leaves emit a pungent fragrance that is almost hypnotic. The large, heart-shaped, dark green leaves form a bold pattern. The smooth silver-beige bark lends a distinctive tone to the landscape. Older fig trees often develop gnarly, knobby trunks that have a Hobbitt-like character.

Some ancient Greeks considered figs the fruit of philosophers, but we know the fig as that exotic fruit that almost literally drips with honey on a sun-washed summer day. Because of the unique and delectable quality of the fruit, many gardeners outside the tree's natural climatic range go through all kinds of gardening contortions to cultivate it. While the tree prefers to grow only in zones 8 through 10, where temperatures don't drop below 10° to 15° F, the range can be extended with some special gardening tricks.

95

*Complementary
Seasonings and Foods*

Lavender, bay leaf, lemon
verbena; cloves, cardamom, star
anise; honey, fresh ginger, lime,
lemon, vanilla; cream cheese,
Yogurt Cheese (see page 22),
chèvre, Gorgonzola; walnuts,
pecans; apples, melons, pears,
berries; prosciutto, *pancetta*,
bacon, poultry, pork;
sweet wines.

Foremost, fig trees can be espaliered against a south-facing wall, especially a masonry or stucco wall, to huddle in this slightly warmer microclimate against the swirling cold grasp of winter. More ambitious gardeners espalier fig trees within a greenhouse's north wall. Still other gardeners build a shallow glass or fiberglass enclosure to cover their wall-hugging fig tree. Like a skinny greenhouse or tall cold frame, the glazing forms a protective microclimate of trapped warm and moist air. Those who don't have the proper wall or the budget for a greenhouse simply lay their tree over in a shallow trench and cover it with a thin layer of soil and then straw, where it enjoys a seasonal nap beneath a blanket of snow.

All of these cultural tricks are made easier by the fact that fig trees in a good climate yield two crops; they bear fruit on last year's growth as well as the new season's shoots. The first crop, which happens in mid-summer and has a small number of very corpulent and succulent fruits, is born on what were the tips of last year's branch growth. The fall crop usually produces a large number of figs, but they are smaller and, if the early fall has been hot, drier and with a more concentrated flavor. The fall crop is borne on the summer's new growth.

Fig trees offer everything from the full 40-foot-wide shelter of a mature shade tree to a dwarfed espalier forming an attractive silhouette against a whitewashed wall. Because of the fig tree's adaptability to pruning, any shape can be achieved. Some people train their fig trees over a simple trellis to form half of an open arbor. Others train the tree very low to aid in harvesting.

There are four fig classifications: Smyrna, White San Pedro, Adriatic (also called the common fig), and Caprifig (the wild fig). Of these four types, only the Adriatic and White San Pedro will set viable fruit without pollination. Examples of self-fertile figs include 'Black Mission', 'Brown Turkey', 'Kadota', 'Adriatic', and 'Celeste'. The fig wasp is necessary to pollinate the Caprifig and Smyrna fruits, but this wasp cannot live in northern climates.

The fruit itself is composed of many tiny fruits encased in a protective skin. Figs are commonly eaten dried because they do not travel well, but fresh ones are a treat. Harvest when the figs droop on their stems and pull easily from their branches; they should be soft to the touch but not mushy. Eat as soon as possible after harvesting or store in the refrigerator for a few days.

Wash the figs, cut off the stem end, and pat dry with paper toweling. Eat fresh or cooked without peeling, for the skins are thin and tender. Figs go well with sweet or salty foods, and thus can be used with fruits and in desserts as well as in savory dishes. Serve fresh figs for breakfast with crisp bacon and pass the pepper mill, or serve fresh figs and seedless grapes with a variety of dessert cheeses.

Mini Recipes

For an hors d'oeuvre, cut figs lengthwise into quarters. Spread with a mixture of cream cheese and crumbled Gorgonzola cheese softened to a spreading consistency with whipping cream and Cognac to taste.

Wrap whole fresh figs in prosciutto or thinly sliced ham and skewer on toothpicks. Serve as an hors d'oeuvre.

Slit pockets in fresh figs and stuff with a pecan half. Steep in rum for several hours and roll in superfine sugar. Arrange on dessert plates with a dab of Yogurt Cheese (see page 22) mixed with orange juice.

Toss coarsely chopped fresh figs into a green salad with torn arugula, crumbled chèvre or feta cheese, and toasted walnuts.

Heat whole fresh figs in a chafing dish with cooked pork link sausages and serve for brunch with scrambled eggs.

Honey-Roasted Chicken with Fresh Figs

1/3 cup honey

2 tablespoons unsalted butter, at room temperature

1 tablespoon olive oil

1/2 teaspoon salt

1/4 teaspoon freshly ground white pepper

1 chicken (about 3 lb)

1 large handful sprigs parsley, plus 1/3 cup minced parsley

4 rose or apple geranium leaves

1/2 lemon, sliced

3 cloves garlic, lightly crushed

1 teaspoon fresh lemon juice

1/2 cup chicken stock, or as needed

16 figs, halved

To add even more fragrance to this roast chicken, use honey that has been infused with rose petals or rose geranium, thyme, or rosemary leaves (see page 14). Spoon pan juices over baked or steamed yams and snap beans and sprinkle lightly toasted sliced almonds over all.

◆

*I*n a small bowl mix together honey, butter, oil, salt, and pepper; set aside. Preheat oven to 425° F.

Trim fat and loose skin from chicken. Rinse under cool running water, drain, and pat dry inside and out with paper toweling. Stuff cavity with parsley sprigs, geranium leaves, lemon slices, garlic, and 2 teaspoons of the butter mixture. Rub remaining butter mixture over outside of chicken, coating completely, and place breast side up on rack in roasting pan. Add lemon juice and 1/4 cup of the stock to pan.

Roast chicken 20 minutes. Baste chicken with pan juices and turn breast side down. Roast, basting several times, 20 minutes. Add figs to pan and baste them with juices. Roast until juices run clear when thigh of chicken is pierced (about 15 minutes longer). Remove chicken and figs to heated platter. Cover loosely with aluminum foil and let rest 10 minutes before carving.

Skim fat from pan juices and set roasting pan over medium-high heat. Add remaining 1/4 cup stock and deglaze pan by stirring to loosen any browned bits. Add minced parsley, then taste and adjust seasonings with salt and pepper.

Carve chicken and arrange on platter. Pour juices into a bowl and pass at the table.

SERVES 3 OR 4

Fig-Raisin Bars

1 3/4 cups chopped fully ripe figs (about 1 lb or 8 figs)

1/4 cup raisins, chopped or cut with scissors

3 tablespoons sugar

1 tablespoon fresh lemon juice

1/4 teaspoon ground ginger

2 recipes topping for Rhubarb Crisp (see page 178)

1/2 teaspoon baking soda

1/2 cup unprocessed rolled oats

Based on the topping used for fruit crisps, these rich cookies can be frozen in an airtight container for several months. They are even more delicious when eaten straight out of the freezer.

✦

*I*n a nonstick saucepan combine figs, raisins, sugar, lemon juice, and ginger. Bring to a boil over medium-high heat. Reduce heat to low and cook, stirring frequently, until mixture is reduced to approximately 1 1/2 cups (about 15 minutes).

Preheat oven to 400° F. Butter a 6- by 10-inch cake pan. Prepare topping, mixing in the baking soda and rolled oats. Strew half of the topping mixture over bottom of prepared pan. Spread fig mixture in pan and then cover evenly with remaining topping.

Bake until topping is lightly browned and filling is bubbly (about 20 minutes). Cool pan on wire rack 10 minutes. Cut into squares and serve warm or at room temperature.

MAKES ABOUT 18 BARS

Edible Flowers

There are countless varieties of edible flowers. All fall into two major categories, those that are beautiful with no significant taste and those that have both color *and* flavor. The deeper-colored flowers usually have the most flavor. Other edible flowers, such as the nasturtium and clove pink, stand out as spices or flavorings unto themselves. What follows is a selection of edible flowers that truly intrigue both the eye and the palate.

There are a number of important things to keep in mind, however, when cooking or garnishing with flowers. Read the botanical names carefully, and use *only* those flowers with the exact Latin name. Make doubly sure no toxic sprays or systemic pesticides have been used on the plants. If you have pollen allergies, use flowers only for garnishing.

Taste flower and herb blossoms and determine which you prefer, for they can often be used interchangeably. On the day you will be using them, clip flowers early in the morning before the dew has dried. Stand them in a glass of water, cover loosely with a plastic bag, and refrigerate. Before using, mist the blossoms and shake them gently. In some cases it will be necessary to remove the appendage attached to the base of the flower, the stamen, and sepal. Herb blossoms can usually be tossed right into a salad; flower blossoms and petals should be added after the salad has been dressed and tossed. As a general rule, herb flowers, tasting much like their leaves, are used in savory dishes, flower petals in sweet dishes.

Always use nonreactive utensils when cooking with flowers. For a delicate, subtle flavor, infuse petals and/or leaves in milk when warming for custards or in sugar water for poaching fruit (see page 24) or for preparing sorbets and syrups. Infuse honey with petals and/or leaves (see page 13) and serve over pancakes and waffles, ice cream, frozen yogurt, or custard. Prepare infused vinegar (see page 14) for fruit or poultry salads or cold roast lamb. Dip petals in Fritter Batter (see page 23), deep-fry, and sprinkle with confectioners' sugar. Place petals of sweet-tasting blossoms or scented leaves in the bottom of jelly jars before pouring in apple, mint, or Lemon Verbena Jelly (see page 17); flavor cake batters in the same way.

Fold chopped petals into pancake, muffin, and cake batters; whipped cream; softened ice cream; or custards. Use flower-flavored sugar (see page 16) and compound butter (see page 15) for the sugar and butter in your favorite cake or cookie recipes. Sprinkle chopped flower petals over fruit salads, fruit cups, or fruit soups. Freeze small blossoms such as borage flowers in ice-cube trays for summer teas. Candied petals and small blossoms (see page 16) such as pinks and violas make exciting dessert and fruit salad garnishes and are always a conversation piece. Taste, use your imagination, experiment, and enjoy!

Anise Hyssop

Agastache foeniciulum

Not really a hyssop plant, nor related to anise, this is one of the most distinctive, highly flavored, and ornamental of all the edible flowers. The gray-green deciduous foliage of this tender herbaceous perennial grows to three feet tall, with upright branches. The flower stalks rise above the foliage with dramatic hot pink to mauve to pinkish lavender flower spikes up to several inches long.

Both the leaves and flowers are edible. Use the leaves as a garnish or to make a mintlike tea. Add sprigs to poaching liquids (see page 24) or to the cavity of chicken before roasting. Pull the flowers from the sprigs and sprinkle on fruit salads, mix with rhubarb or raspberries in pies, or add to soups or green salads. Combine with other chopped herb blossoms such as pineapple sage and rosemary to garnish roast chicken. Pair with Fumé Blanc.

Tuberous Begonia

Begonia tuberhybrida

Classically used in hanging baskets or containers, this shade-loving plant thrives when grown under the filtered light of a tree. It is usually started from 1 1/2-inch-long tubers purchased in early spring. Shallowly set the tubers in a loamy potting mix and sprout them in a protective spot. Move outdoors to a flower bed or containers when growth is 2 to 3 inches high. In containers use rich, well-drained potting soil and keep moist, but not wet enough to cause the tubers to rot. Plants prefer a humid atmosphere. Use misters to irrigate in arid climates. Feed and water regularly; keep moist but not wet. Tubers are dug up each fall and stored in a dry, cool place until spring.

The gourmet gardener has an enormous array of choices when it comes to tuberous begonias. (Do not confuse tuberous begonias with wax begonias, or bedding begonias, classified as *B. semperflorens* and sold as annual bedding plants.) Both single-and double-petaled varieties come in uniform and blended colors.

The deeper-colored flowers "bleed" when heated in a sauce or custard, imparting a delicate overall color. Pull the begonia petals from the flowers and cut away and discard the lighter-colored, bitter base. Chop the petals, or cut in thin chiffonade, to add a crisp texture and slightly citruslike taste to savory or sweet dishes. Pair with Johannisberg Riesling.

Borage

Borago officinalis

This annual, self-seeding herb grows so well in any climate many gardeners refer to it as an ornamental weed. Planted once, you'll always have this long-blooming plant. To shape a design, simply remove the seedlings you don't want. The bluish green foliage seems to gather and hold dewy droplets better than most plants. From a wide, flat floret of soft-spined foliage a flower stalk grows to two feet. Dozens of flowers open facing the earth, like colorful parasols. The blossoms are pinkish mauve when first opening and gradually flush into a pastel sky blue. (It is this blue color, in part, that makes the plant so attractive to honey bees.) There is a magically pure white version, but the seed is rare and passed from gardener to gardener. This plant grows through the winter in mild climates and will even bloom in mid-winter and very early spring.

Although borage leaves and stems are edible, the pretty starlike flowers, tasting somewhat like cucumber with a tinge of honey, are preferred in the kitchen. Sprinkle them over cold soups, mix them with crumbled blue cheese and sprinkle them over slices of ripe tomato, or toss into green salads just before serving. Pair with Sauvignon Blanc.

Calendula

Calendula officinalis

Calendulas are reliable annuals for a highlight of oranges and yellows in any garden. Plant in full sun in rich soil, add water, and stand back. They will quickly fill in an area with foliage up to two feet high and will soon begin a constant bloom with flowers two to four inches wide. Seeds are sown in seedling trays and transplanted into the garden. Snails and slugs will nibble on the young seedlings; protect accordingly. The plant will self-sow, but the flower size will diminish over the years to a colorful 1/2- to 1-inch button of hot color. As the persistent new blooms overshadow the spent flowers year-round, calendulas rarely need deadheading.

In moderate climates calendulas act as perennials. When plants are mature, snails may gather beneath the foliage during the daylight hours. Some wise gardeners gather up a few plants, along with the napping snails, each day to help control this pesty mollusk. Because the plants are so prolific, the occasional plant sacrificed for snail entrapment will not be noticed.

Known as the "poor man's saffron," ground dried calendula can be substituted for saffron in larger quantities, imparting a vibrant color although no true saffron flavor. Chopped fresh calendula petals lend a tangy and slightly nutty taste to meat dishes, cream soups, chowders, stuffed eggs, scrambled eggs, cream cheese or yogurt dips, and mashed potatoes or turnips. Blend chopped petals into liver pâte, or prepare herb salt (see page 15) or compound butter (see page 15). Pair with Fumé Blanc.

Daylily

Hemerocallis lilioasphodelus

The old-fashioned, fragrant, clear yellow daylily is a tried-and-true garden perennial. Four-inch trumpet-shaped flowers grace tall flower stalks during mid-summer. Unlike the modern hybrid daylilies, this plant can handle a wide range of soils and some neglect. Fertile soil and regular watering will cause the plant to flourish, yet it will bloom handsomely with less fertility and sporadic irrigation. All daylilies will prosper with the addition of a mulch. They tolerate full and partial sun and are often planted in groves beneath shade trees like birches, alders, and maples. Beware of hybrid daylilies, as some people find a few of the thousands of selections to be either bitter or caustic to the back of the throat, often leaving an acrid aftertaste. When sampling other daylily species, try only a small portion, wait to see how your mouth and throat react, and avoid the flower if there is the slightest reaction.

Both the buds and the petals of just-opened daylily flowers are edible. Sauté, braise, or stir-fry the buds, or dip them in Fritter Batter (see page 23) and deep-fry. Chop the petals and add to salads, egg dishes, or soups. Use dried daylily buds and/or petals in Asian dishes, or infuse vinegar (see page 14) with dried buds. Pair with Gewürztraminer.

Scented Geraniums

Pelargonium sp.

There seem to be more obscure strains of scented geraniums than a neighborhood full of cats has lives. The names are poetic, but often require an active imagination to link the named flavor with the actual taste. Some varieties smell so much alike, only the discriminating or easily persuaded gardener can tell the difference. Strangely enough, the rose geranium actually has a lemony smell and taste. Whatever the name, there are dozens of complex, spicy fragrances and flavors from which to choose.

These are frost-sensitive plants that should be brought indoors in all but the warmest winter climates. Some gardeners winter over cuttings under fluorescent lights and pot up the rooted results in the spring. The classic presentation of a scented geranium is in Mexican terra-cotta pottery.

Tasting as you go, select geranium leaves with the aroma that will complement the food to be cooked or garnished. Float leaves in a punch bowl, or use as a bed for chopped garnishes, molded salads, pâtés, or hors d'oeuvres. Cover a cake rack with leaves, turn the just-baked cake out onto them, and let the cake absorb the fragrance while cooling. Crush leaves as a flavoring for soups, poultry, fish, sauces, custards, and fruit puddings. Experiment with geranium flowers, using them as you would other edible flowers.

Marigold

Tagetes tenuifolia

The more reliable edible marigold petals come from varieties with smaller heads and single petals. These types, which are grown from seed, can lend a pleasant lemon or citruslike flavor. Some named varieties to try include 'Lemon Gem', 'Tangerine Gem', 'Citrus Mixed', and 'Lulu'. Watch for snails and slugs when the plants are young. Some marigold petals may have a bitter taste. Sample petals with caution and add chopped petals to scrambled eggs or omelets when eggs are almost set, add to rice cooking water, or sprinkle over soups and chowders just before serving. Pair with Fumé Blanc.

Nasturtium

Tropaeolum majus

Both trailing and bush-type annual nasturtiums offer seasonal color and dramatic foliage in any climate. The unselected forms grow with an attractively shaped blossom in various shades of hot and creamy yellow, clear orange, rusty red, maroon, and crimson. The dark green distinctively shaped, rotundly lobed leaves with lime green veins add a special pattern to the garden and collect little clear droplets of dew around their edges. An especially nice selection is 'Alaska' with its creamy white, pale green, and dark green variegation. In mild areas, all of the annual nasturtiums, with their rampant self-seeding habit, grow as if perennial.

Nasturtium leaves, flowers, and seeds are edible. The larger leaves make marvelous wrappers; lightly blanch the leaves and use in place of grape leaves in Dolmas (see page 118). Cut the leaves in thin chiffonade and use with chives, dill, parsley, and/or sorrel to enhance egg dishes, green salads, and cucumber and tomato salads. Pair with White Zinfandel.

The bright hues of nasturtium flowers add color, texture, and a pronounced peppery bite to a number of dishes. Whole flowers, stuffed with a cream cheese mixture or with crème frâiche and caviar, serve as elegant edible garnishes for any hors d'oeuvre tray. Offer sandwiches of unsalted butter and chopped petals for afternoon tea. Toss chopped petals into green salads, or sprinkle them over cold cream soups or omelets. Make compound butter (see page 15) with chopped petals, savory, thyme, and parsley, or infuse rice wine vinegar (see page 14) with chopped flowers. Nasturtium seedpods, eaten green, add a spicy, crunchy touch to salads. When pickled, they can be used in place of capers.

Pansy

Viola wittrockiana; Sweet Violet (V. odorata)

The proverbial pansy, also known as a viola, is a companion to every grandmother's garden, each Edwardian or Victorian flower bed, and countless plantings in shopping malls throughout America. This cute flower with a puppy-dog face is a tried-and-true favorite. Now, we can add this standby to our list of culinary options. Hybridizers have expanded the color choices beyond anything grandma ever imagined. There is a single- or multicolored pansy to match any design scheme, from gaudy to pastel. The new F_1 and F_2 hybrids are more heat tolerant, but most pansies prefer a rich, cool soil with some shelter from the afternoon's sun. The seed is quite small and usually planted in a cold frame in the very early spring for an early summer bloom, or in mid-summer in a shady spot for fall or winter bloom. The plant will bloom in almost mid-winter in very mild climates. In all cases, watch for slugs, snails, and earwigs when the seedlings are young.

Violets may have smaller petals than pansies, but they pack a punch when it comes to fragrance, thus the species name *odorata*. There is a native and exotic violet for every climate. All are rather diminutive, but dramatic when in bloom. The flowers are borne on short stems just a few inches above the ground. Plant on a raised planting mound, in nooks and crannies in retaining walls, or in pots displayed at eye level to give them the exposure they deserve. Most prefer generous shade in warm climates, but can tolerate full sun in foggy, moderate coastal environments. A rich soil with plenty of humus is preferable and most prosper with regular irrigation.

Pansy and violet leaves and flowers are edible and nutritious. On a weight basis, violet leaves have nearly as much vitamin A as carrots. Flavor syrup or honey with chopped violets or pansies (see page 14) or use to flavor preserves. Garnish cold fruit soups with a dollop of sour cream and violet or pansy flowers. Use violet or pansy leaves as a bed for dessert molds, or cut into chiffonade and add to a steaming pot of potherbs. Pair with Gewürztraminer.

Pink

Dianthus plumarius

This traditional flower, also called dianthus, has graced the perennial flower beds of Victorian and colonial gardens alike; the old-fashioned name is gillyflower. It is most often used as a border plant by a pathway so as to display the bloom as well as the aroma. A close relative is the florist's carnation, but never eat flowers from floral shops as they are usually sprayed. All pinks are hardy and grow best in full sun with a typically rich garden soil. They are usually planted from transplants, but can be grown from seed. Perhaps the most exemplary dianthus is the highly perfumed clove pink (*D. caryophyllus*). This compact perennial plant, to 12 inches, has the typical ruelike blue, thin-leaved dianthus foliage and small carnationlike blossoms. Snip off the calyxes before using.

The pungent true clove fragrance of dianthus can easily be smelled when picked and is strong enough to stand up to many uses in the kitchen. Its natural sweetness complements fruits such as raspberries, strawberries, and rhubarb. Use it in combination with ground cloves and grated nutmeg. Prepare fruit salad dressing with white wine vinegar infused with petals (see page 14). Pair with Gewürztraminer.

Tuberous Nasturtium

Tropaeolum tuberosum

This perennial tuberous nasturtium form contributes brightly colored flowers to any landscape and the exceptional flavor of the tuber to the dining table. The small leaves, two inches or less across, resemble the annual nasturtium but are more deeply lobed and a bluer green. A small yam-shaped tuber, three to four inches long and shallowly planted in fertile soil, will give rise to an attractive vine that grows up to six or eight feet. The tubers continue to proliferate underground, so much so they can become invasive. A curious feature of this ornamental edible is the pendulous, airborne tubers that dangle from the vine like teardrop green earrings.

Tuberous nasturtium flowers have a "flavor remarkably like that of marzipan" and are used in desserts. Dig some of the yellow tubers when you feel the plant is established or you notice the growing spot is being taken over. Scrub them well and taste gingerly, for raw tubers are extremely peppery and spicy hot, making them perfect for pickling. When cooked, however, most of the spiciness is eliminated and the tubers can then be sliced and sautéed, baked or steamed and puréed, or baked whole after sautéing briefly.

Rose

Rosa sp.

*T*here is an entire galaxy of roses: old-fashioned or heirloom, hybrid, and modern. All have petals that are potentially edible, but the range of flavor and scent, or lack thereof, is as varied as their colors. Sample individual petals one at a time to survey what potentially edible roses you may already be growing. Some petals are sweet with a little flavor; others are clove flavored and still others are musky. Beware, though: Many roses, especially the modern hybrid types, are prone to a multitude of pests and diseases and are frequently sprayed with an arsenal of chemicals. Edible rose petals must be harvested *only* from chemical-free plants, including systemic treatments. Some of the old-fashioned roses are able to thrive without a bevy of pesticides and fungicides. Roses need plenty of air circulation to avoid mildews and rusts. Don't overfertilize with nitrogen, as this may lead to pests such as aphids.

Generally, roses taste similar to their smell, so the stronger the smell, the more taste a rose petal will have. Pull off petals, and remove and discard the green or white heel attached to the flower base.

One of the first flowers to become a popular edible, roses can be prepared in any of the ways suggested in the general flower introduction. Steep petals in brandy for three or four weeks and use the brandy in custards, puddings, and dessert sauces, and for flaming dishes. Prepare rose petal jelly, using equal amounts juice and sugar. Rose hips, the berry or fruit left after the flower has withered on the plant, are highly nutritious. They, too, make tasty jams or jellies. Pair rose petals with Chenin Blanc.

Society Garlic

Tulbaghia violacea

*T*his narrow-leaved perennial herb isn't even related to true garlic, yet has similar flavor. The plant is heroic in its drought resistance, surviving extreme heat, to be revived by rain or irrigation. It will tolerate fairly poor soils and thrives in rich soil. The tall, 12- to

18-inch-long, thin leaves resemble large chives. The flowers, which are edible and more delicately flavored than the leaves, are pale lavender-mauve, trumpet shaped, and long-lived on the plant. 'Silver Lace' has silver-white and pink variegated striping on the green leaves. This form grows more slowly than others and is slightly shorter in habit.

Society garlic blossoms make a delightful and tasty garnish for almost any dish. Leave them whole and add at the last minute. The leaves are used in cooking, imparting a delicate hint of garlic to soups, salads, and egg dishes. Compound butter made with finely minced leaves and flowers (see page 15) yields just the right amount of garlic essence.

Tulip

Tulipa sp.

Tulips have made Holland famous in many people's minds. But in Holland the tulip bulb is famous for warding off starvation during World War II. For the modern gardener, it is the vaselike petaled flower that is the object of culinary desire. An endless rainbow of colors can be found in the cornucopia of tulip varieties. The edibility of the bulb does not go unnoticed by gophers and field mice; protect accordingly. In mild or warm winter climates, tulips will not reflower very well the second year. Some gardeners dig up the bulbs and freeze them; others purchase a new set of bulbs each year.

Tulips are classically planted in large groupings or drifts. Or a spot of color is easily achieved with a shallow pot of tulips. According to Ron Zimmerman of the Herbfarm in Seattle, Washington, the 'Red Emperor' tulip has by far the best flavor of all the colors, and he suggests that tulip bulbs be planted at varying depths so as to have an ongoing supply as each group blooms in sequence.

Crisp and tasting "much like sweet garden peas," thinly chiffonade-cut tulip petals can be used for garnishing salads and cooked dishes. Prepare tulip-flavored sugar (see page 16) to use in desserts, or infuse honey (see page 14) for breakfast pancakes. Whole flowers, with stamens removed, make outstanding containers for dips for crudités. To serve as an edible salad container, fill them with seafood, chicken, rice, or pasta salad, arrange on a bed of lettuce, and garnish with watercress sprigs. Pair with Chenin Blanc.

Ensalada de Flores

*E*dible flowers and ornamental kale are a delightful way to enliven a salad, especially in winter when there can be a dearth of salad ingredients. Begin by ringing a salad bowl or plates with leaves of ornamental kale. Mix pieces of the kale with your favorite salad greens ('Lolla Rossa', 'Marvel of Four Seasons', and 'Red Oakleaf' are good choices) and toss with herb and flower petals. Garnish with different-colored rings of petals, a layer of mixed petals, or whole blossoms arranged in a bouquet. Toss with Balsamic Vinaigrette (see page 18) made with the addition of minced garlic, parsley, and basil to taste.

Recipes from Sooke Harbour House

The following recipes, which use some flowers that are not well-known as edible, are chosen from a number donated by the chefs at Sooke Harbour House on Vancouver Island, a restaurant renowned for its gardens and its use of unusual seafood, much of which is raised by the staff. Also considered by many food authorities to be North America's top restaurant for flower cookery, Sooke Harbour House's artistic presentations and innovative approaches to food preparation make it unique in the culinary world.

These recipes call for some hard-to-find ingredients. With advice from the chefs, alternatives have been suggested when possible.

Anise Hyssop Custard with Black Pansy Syrup

Custard:

1 cup milk

1 cup whipping cream

1/4 cup sugar

6 tablespoons chopped anise hyssop flowers

2 eggs plus 3 egg yolks

Black pansy syrup:

1 cup loosely packed black pansy petals

2 cups sugar

1 cup water

Gooseberry purée:

3 cups red English gooseberries

Maple syrup, to taste

For best results, let the anise hyssop flowers steep in the milk-cream mixture overnight. Strawberries or highbush cranberries can be substituted for the gooseberries.

♦

To prepare custard, combine milk and cream in a mixing bowl. Pour half of mixture into a small saucepan and add sugar and anise hyssop flowers. Place over low heat and heat just until small bubbles appear at pan edge, stirring to dissolve sugar. Remove from heat and stir into remaining milk mixture until well mixed. Set aside to cool. Cover and refrigerate overnight.

Preheat oven to 350° F. Have ready six 1/2-cup custard molds. Select a shallow 9- by 13-inch baking dish and add enough hot water to reach halfway up sides of molds once they are placed in dish. Place dish in oven.

In mixing bowl beat together eggs and egg yolks until well blended. Slowly beat in infused milk mixture, then strain through fine-mesh sieve into clean bowl or pitcher. Divide custard evenly among molds.

Garnish:

Anise hyssop flowers and leaves

6 black pansy flowers

Place molds in baking dish in oven and bake until tip of small knife inserted in center comes out clean (25 to 30 minutes). Remove molds to wire rack and let cool completely. Cover and refrigerate at least 1 hour before serving.

To prepare syrup place petals in a food processor fitted with metal blade. Add 1/3 cup of the sugar and pulse 4 times to grind pansies into sugar, then process continuously 30 seconds. Transfer to a small saucepan and add remaining 1 2/3 cups sugar and the water. Bring to a boil over medium heat, stir once, reduce heat to low, and simmer until mixture reaches syrup stage (120° F on candy thermometer). Remove from heat, pour into heatproof container, and let cool completely.

To prepare gooseberry purée, place gooseberries in food processor fitted with metal blade and purée. Force through medium-mesh strainer into a bowl. Sweeten with maple syrup.

To assemble custards run a small knife around edges of molds and invert onto serving plates. Pour some of the black pansy syrup over each custard. Arrange 1 to 1 1/2 tablespoons gooseberry purée around each custard in circular fashion to contain syrup. Decorate each plate with anise hyssop flowers and leaves and a black pansy flower.

SERVES 6

Warm Salad of Shellfish and Tuberous Begonias with Daylily Garnish

8 hazelnuts

2 purple-hinged or giant rock scallops

2 large sea cucumbers (optional)

6 or 8 tuberous begonia stems (each 4 in. long)

6 tablespoons dry white wine

Tuberous begonia petals from 8 variously colored flowers

6 pea tips (each 3 in. long; see page 156)

2 daylily flowers

2 tablespoons unsalted butter

1 tablespoon hazelnut oil, or as needed

If you are unable to find purple-hinged and giant rock scallops, substitute shelled pink swimming scallops or fresh local shelled scallops, with or without roe.

◆

Preheat oven to 325° F. Spread hazelnuts in a single layer on baking sheet and bake until the skins loosen, 12 to 17 minutes. Remove from oven and cool only slightly. Place in a tea towel and rub vigorously between your hands to remove husks. Let cool in a dry place.

Cut meat and roe from each rock scallop shell. Set aside 2 pieces of the orange roe. Trim away all but the white scallop meat; you should have about 2 ounces. Slice the meat very thinly. Set aside. Cut off both ends of each sea cucumber and slice open the body lengthwise so that it lies flat. Run a finger, or knife, if necessary, underneath each of the 5 white muscle strips and pull gently to remove. Set muscle strips aside and discard rest of sea cucumber.

Remove begonia leaves from stems and discard leaves. Peel stems, cut into 1/4-inch-thick slices, and place in a small saucepan. Add wine, bring to a boil over medium-high heat, and cook until stems are soft and wine is reduced (about 5 minutes). Set aside. Pull petals from begonia flowers and cut away and discard lighter-colored base from each petal; set aside. Place pea tips decoratively in center of 2 large white salad plates. Pull petals from daylilies and cut petals lengthwise into strips, about 1/2 inch wide. You should have 12 strips in all. Place strips attractively around and over pea tips.

Place skillet over high heat and add butter. When butter melts and pan bottom is coated, add scallop slices, sea cucumber muscles, and reserved roe. Toss quickly in pan 1 to 2 minutes, being careful not to overcook. Add reserved hazelnuts, stir, and remove from heat.

To serve, arrange scallop slices, sea cucumber, roe, and hazelnuts on prepared plates. Scatter poached begonia stems over salad, garnish with begonia petals, and sprinkle lightly with hazelnut oil.

SERVES 2

Grape

European Grape
(Vitus vinifera)
American Grape
(V. labrusca)

Perennial vine; grows in all but coldest winter areas.

Grow from bareroot or potted rooted cuttings.

Plant in well-drained soil, the richer the better.

Can grow to 100 feet if unchecked, but usually trained to a wire trellis or arbor.

Except for muscadine grapes, self-fertilizing.

Takes three years to come into bearing.

Watch for mildew, anthracnose, black rot, Japanese beetles, and caterpillars; may require netting to control bird damage.

Many a romantic movie has a scene set beneath an arbor or trellis of grapes on a verandah. While commercial vineyards have many versions of trellises with one or more horizontal wires, the traditional place for grapevines in the edible landscape is the arbor. The pale green, classically shaped leaves produce a delightful shade across a patio or deck. In the fall the leaves become infused with crystalline yellows, burnt oranges, and burgundies. Ironically, with wine grapes, the purer the warm yellow colors the better, because the reds and dark oranges often are due to virus-infected plants. The grapevine with the best fall color, *V. vinifera* 'Purpurea', is, alas, usually treated as an ornamental due to the tartness of the fruit. The grapes themselves are rather well-behaved; unlike other fruits, they don't easily fall to the ground to stain patios, walkways, or decks.

Grapes are divided into European and American varieties. American grapes have skins that slip off more easily, are hardier (survive temperatures down to 0° F), have a stronger flavor and aroma, a higher tolerance of humidity, and an ability to ripen in a shorter season (less than 170 frost-free days). They are better known as fresh fruit (table grapes) and juice grapes. Classic examples include 'Concord', 'Golden Muscat', 'Niagara', and 'Interloken Seedless'.

115

European grapes require heat (at least 170 to 180 days of frost-free weather), possess a vigor that demands trellising, and are susceptible to diseases and pests not found in American grapes. Among the best-known European table grapes are 'Black Monukka' , 'Flame Seedless', 'Lady Finger', 'Muscat', 'Perlette', 'Rubier', and 'Thompson Seedless'.

Most classic wine grapes are European varieties, a number of which are also good for eating out of hand, for making juice, and for other kitchen uses. While they do not come in a seedless form, these grapes have a complex and pungent flavor not typically found in table grapes.

Growing grapes solely for their foliage is much easier than for the combined effect of leaf and fruit. Almost all grapevines grown for harvest require sprays, usually strong-smelling sulphur-based compounds, to combat mildew and other fungal diseases. Some of these sprays can also stain stucco and some concrete surfaces. For this reason, grape arbors should be set away from areas that could be damaged.

Harvest grape clusters when the grapes have reached their peak sweetness and color, and when they pull off the cluster easily. Snip clusters with pruning shears or scissors. Once picked, the grapes will not continue to ripen. Refrigerate clusters in a bowl.

Freshly picked grapes are best eaten just as they are. They do, however, combine well with other foods and can be included in any course from appetizer to dessert. Seedless varieties can be used interchangeably in most recipes. Dry them into raisins, or freeze whole for 45 minutes and serve frozen. Halve seedless grapes and add to tuna, chicken, or turkey salad, or toss into mixed green salad dressed with Balsamic Vinaigrette (see page 18). Concord and black Hamburg grapes make especially wonderful juice, jelly, jam, conserve, or flavored vinegar (see page 14).

The grape leaf is also edible and is used primarily as a wrapping for a myriad of fillings. Sampling as you go to be sure the leaves are not bitter, harvest in the spring when the leaves are full size but still lush and tender. Use fresh leaves lightly blanched, or homemade or jarred brined leaves.

To Brine Grape Leaves:

Wash leaves well and cut off all but 1/2 inch of stem. For each bundle, stack 25 to 30 leaves, fold over, and tie with kitchen twine. Bring 2 quarts water and 1/2 cup salt to a rolling boil, stirring to dissolve salt. Dip leaves, a bundle at a time, into the boiling brine for 10 seconds. Remove to hot, sterilized jars, packing bundles tightly. Cover with brine and seal. Store in a cool, dark place at least 1 week and use within 3 weeks. Rinse before cooking.

Mini Recipes

Blend Neufchâtel cheese with Gorgonzola cheese to taste; chill until firm. Roll a small portion of cheese mixture around chilled seedless grapes and refrigerate until well chilled (at least 30 minutes). Roll balls in finely chopped walnuts or pecans and arrange on serving plate. Garnish with sweet cicely or mint sprigs and serve for dessert.

Top seedless grapes with sour cream sweetened with brown sugar. Chill; just before serving sprinkle with freshly grated orange or lemon zest.

Just before serving, toss seedless grapes into a seafood fettuccine.

Garnish chicken liver pâté or cheese torta with chopped or halved seedless grapes or grape clusters.

Make a seedless red grape chutney with onion, tart apples, raisins, and walnuts.

Dolmas

2 cups cooked white or
brown rice

1/2 pound lean ground lamb

1/4 cup finely minced onion

1 teaspoon finely minced garlic

3 tablespoons minced parsley,
plus parsley sprigs, for garnish

1/2 tablespoon minced oregano

3 tablespoons finely chopped
pine nuts

1/2 teaspoon salt

1/4 teaspoon freshly
ground pepper

2/3 cup finely chopped, peeled,
and seeded ripe tomatoes

16 large or 32 small (3 1/2 in.
across) brined grape leaves (see
page 117)

About 3 cups beef stock
or consommé

2 to 3 teaspoons fresh
lemon juice

Yogurt Cheese, to taste (see
page 22)

Serve these lamb-and-rice-stuffed grape leaves warm as a first course to precede roast chicken. You can also form smaller dolmas and serve them at room temperature, with a yogurt dip flavored with garlic and lemon juice, for hors d'oeuvres. Nasturtium or Swiss chard leaves are a good substitute for the grape leaves.

♦

*I*n a mixing bowl combine rice, lamb, onion, garlic, minced parsley, oregano, pine nuts, salt, pepper, and tomatoes. Sauté a small amount, taste, and adjust seasonings.

Rinse grape leaves and spread, shiny side down, on paper toweling. Place about 2 tablespoons filling near stem end of each leaf and roll jelly-roll fashion, folding in sides as you roll. Place rolls seam side down in shallow saucepan or skillet large enough to hold rolls in a single layer.

Combine stock and lemon juice and pour into pan to reach 1/2 inch up sides of skillet. Place a large, heavy plate on top of rolls as a weight, cover pan, and bring to a gentle boil over medium-high heat. Lower heat and simmer until filling is cooked (10 to 20 minutes, depending upon size of rolls).

To serve, remove rolls to heated platter and keep warm. Reduce pan juices by half over high heat, remove from heat, and stir in Yogurt Cheese. Pour over rolls and garnish with parsley sprigs.

SERVES 8

Grape Coffeecake

1 package active dry yeast

1/4 cup lukewarm water (110 °F)

1/2 cup lukewarm milk

1/3 cup plus 2 tablespoons sugar

1 egg

1/4 cup unsalted
butter, softened

1/2 teaspoon aniseed,
roughly crushed

2 1/2 cups flour, plus flour
for kneading

1/2 teaspoon salt

1 1/2 tablespoons vegetable oil

3 1/2 cups ripe seedless 'Red
Flame' or similar grapes

Talented dessert chef Flo Braker is author of two outstanding volumes, The
Simple Art of Perfect Baking *and* Sweet Miniatures: The Art of Making
Bite-Size Desserts. *She developed this delectable coffeecake from a classic
Italian flat bread recipe, schiacciata con l'uva. To preserve taste and
texture, serve the coffeecake, cut into squares, the same day it is baked.*

In a large bowl of an electric mixer, sprinkle yeast over water and set
aside until creamy (about 10 minutes).

Using the mixer on low speed, preferably with paddle attachment,
beat in milk, 1/3 cup sugar, egg, butter, and aniseed. On medium
speed, beat in 2 cups of the flour and the salt until incorporated. Add
remaining 1/2 cup flour and beat to form soft, smooth dough. Turn
dough out onto lightly floured surface and knead until smooth and
satiny (5 to 7 minutes). At first dough will be sticky. Add no more than
1/4 cup additional flour during kneading process. Place dough in large
bowl, cover bowl with plastic wrap, and set aside in warm place until
dough doubles in bulk (1 1/2 to 2 hours).

Spread oil over bottom of a 10- by 15- by 1-inch jelly-roll pan.
Punch down dough. Using your fingertips, pat dough into pan to fit
bottom precisely. At first the dough slides easily over the oiled pan.
Should it resist stretching at some point, just let the dough rest a
minute, then continue to coax dough to the edges. Scatter grapes
over surface.

Cover pan with plastic wrap and let rest until dough is puffy and
almost doubled in bulk (about 1 hour). Remove plastic wrap and
sprinkle 2 tablespoons sugar over top.

Meanwhile, position rack in lower third of oven and preheat oven
to 350° F.

Bake 30 minutes. When done the edges will be golden while the
cake itself will be pale gold. If you like, occasionally baste top of cake
with juice from the grapes during baking. Cool on wire rack.

MAKES 1 COFFEECAKE; SERVES 10 TO 12

Juniper
Juniperus communis

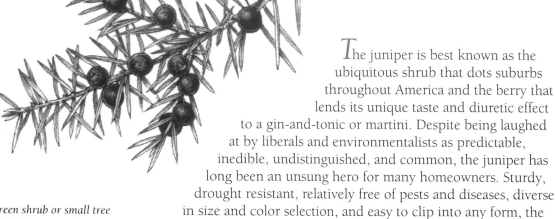

Perennial evergreen shrub or small tree up to 20 feet. Grows in all zones.

Purchase a container-grown, named specimen.

Must have good drainage; doesn't tolerate heavy clay soil.

Prefers full sun.

Do not add amendments to the planting holes, as this restricts the roots and the tree will be more susceptible to wind, snow, and ice loads.

Watch for bagworms, a caterpillar that carries a protective cocoon around while it eats the coniferous foliage; control with Bacillus thuringiensis spray (see Crabapple).

The juniper is best known as the ubiquitous shrub that dots suburbs throughout America and the berry that lends its unique taste and diuretic effect to a gin-and-tonic or martini. Despite being laughed at by liberals and environmentalists as predictable, inedible, undistinguished, and common, the juniper has long been an unsung hero for many homeowners. Sturdy, drought resistant, relatively free of pests and diseases, diverse in size and color selection, and easy to clip into any form, the juniper certainly deserves more respect.

As landscaping plants, junipers come in more options than some ice cream companies have flavors. The tall shrub versions, many of the columnar specimens, and almost all of the low-shrub forms are usually the Asian species, *J. chinensis*. Most of the prostrate forms are a selection of *J. horizontalis*. The native and exotic tree-sized junipers represent various *Juniperus* species.

The true *J. communis* is not known for its landscaping grandeur. Ranging from 12 inches to 20 feet, depending upon the species, it is often described as too large for most gardens. But in the right setting, it adds not only an element of size, albeit with a slightly awkward and rangy habit, but also a pleasant gray-green to the landscape. Junipers can be shaped with persistent shearing to just about any geometrical or whimsical shape, or can be clipped into a hedge or windbreak.

Chances are that any species of juniper with dark blue berries, including some of the more attractive species and cultivars, *could* yield berries that can be used as a substitute for juniper berries, but the specifics aren't well known. If you try the berries from another juniper species, use *extreme* caution; sample only a tiny amount of the berries the first time and wait for one or more days before sampling again.

Harvest *J. communis* berries when they are a rich blue. Be aware that the berries take up to two to three years to ripen fully and the tree is often covered with both immature, greenish yellow berries and mature blue fruits. Lay out the berries in a warm shady area to dry and cure until mostly blackish. Store in airtight containers in a cool, dark place for up to one year.

Juniper berries impart a woodsy flavor to foods in which they are cooked. When crushed, they discharge an aromatic, astringent oil that best complements game or other full-flavored foods such as cabbage. The berries help cut the fat of meats such as pork and are said to purify the air if placed on the coals when barbecuing. Lightly toasting them in a heavy skillet will release their flavor.

Add lightly crushed berries to marinades and stews. Use juniper berry-infused oil (see page 13) for browning venison. Crush berries finely for vinaigrette dressing and sauces, but use with discretion.

Complementary Seasonings and Foods

Bay, parsley, fennel; garlic, onions; cabbage, potatoes; game, goose, ham, lamb, sauerbraten, pork sausage.

Ham Steak with Juniper Berries

1 ham steak (1 1/2 lb and 3/4 in. thick), trimmed of fat

1/4 cup dry vermouth

6 to 8 juniper berries, finely crushed

Ground allspice or cloves, to taste

1/4 cup minced parsley

The flavor of the juniper berries and allspice permeates the ham during steaming, resulting in particularly moist and tasty meat.

✦

Place ham steak in an attractive, shallow heatproof dish. Pour vermouth evenly over steak and let stand 30 minutes.

Strew juniper berries over ham steak and sprinkle lightly with allspice. Set dish on steamer rack over boiling water, cover pot, and steam until ham is heated through (about 25 minutes).

Sprinkle with parsley and serve immediately.

SERVES 4

Juniper Cabbage with Mashed Potatoes

1 tablespoon each butter and canola oil

1/4 cup each minced onion and celery

2 tablespoons minced lovage or celery leaves

2 cups finely shredded cabbage or ornamental kale

6 juniper berries, finely crushed

1/4 cup beef stock

3 cups hot, freshly mashed potatoes (about 1 1/2 lb potatoes)

Salt, freshly ground black pepper, and cayenne pepper, to taste

2 tablespoons each snipped chives and minced parsley

Cabbage seasoned with juniper berries and mixed with freshly mashed potatoes makes the perfect accompaniment to venison chops or steaks.

✦

*I*n a large skillet over medium heat, melt butter with oil. Add onion, celery, and lovage, cover, and cook until soft (about 5 minutes). Add cabbage, juniper berries, and stock, cover, and cook over medium-high heat until cabbage wilts and is just tender (about 10 minutes).

Stir cabbage into mashed potatoes and season with salt and black and cayenne pepper. Spoon into heated serving bowl and sprinkle with chives and parsley.

SERVES 6 TO 8

Kiwi

(Actinidia chinensis, also called A. deliciosa)
Hardy Kiwi (A. arguta); Arctic Kiwi (A. kolomikta)

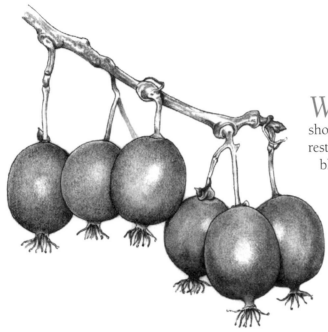

Tender and fairly hardy perennial, deciduous vines.

Plant bareroot vines in fertile, well-drained soil; furnish a sturdy trellis or arbor.

Provide plenty of water and fertilizer on a consistent basis to achieve the best yields.

Rampant growers that require plenty of winter pruning. Prune much like grapevines.

Relatively disease and pest free.

What was once an obscure fruit now regularly shows up in the salad bars of national chain restaurants. The fruit nobody knew "what in blazes" to do with today is featured in fruit-juice blends, a testimony to the size of the commercial crop.

The breakthrough for the gourmet gardener came with the realization that what was called the Chinese gooseberry, which originated in Asia, can be grown in quite a few American climates. This tender perennial vine comes in male and female versions, each on a separate vine. The male vines can tolerate temperatures down to 15° F. The females are tougher, withstanding 10° F.

The vigorous, deciduous kiwi vine requires lots of room to roam. The late-spring flowers are creamy white, delicate looking, and filled with rust-colored stamens. The tendrils of untamed vines can grow 30 feet in all directions and are tipped with a handsome bronze fuzzy texture. The large, round, dark green leaves make a striking pattern against a wall of cool colors. Kiwi vines are not frequently trained against tall walls because of the need for intensive winter pruning and the fall harvest of fruit. Their common location in the home landscape is a sturdy freestanding arbor, because the fruit can total two hundred pounds on a mature plant. Tall arbors, where it's easy to stand and

123

pluck the dangling fruit beneath the foliage, develop a picturesque cascade of rich green foliage that provides an inviting and cool secret hiding place during the heat of summer. Another option is a trellis made of large wooden posts and high-tension wire, which is a bit less aesthetic, but can be much more efficient and productive. Unfortunately, separate male and female vines are necessary to produce fruits on the female vine. If you want to grow lots of kiwis, however, one male plant will handily pollinate up to eight female vines.

Just when cooks throughout the country have come to accept the fuzzy kiwifruit and applaud its tropical-tasting, lime flesh, along comes a close relative of the kiwi that is even more unconventional as a fruit, but more acclimated to our cold winter climates. The *A. arguta*, or hardy kiwi, actually looks more like the common name often given to the fuzzy kiwi, Chinese gooseberry, and the plant is native to areas of northern China. The fruit, which hang in grapelike clusters, are greenish, smooth skinned, and 1 to 1 3/4 inches long. They can be eaten like grapes, popped in the mouth skin and all, and have nearly the same flavor as the better-known kiwifruits.

Besides the incredible convenience of no peeling, the hardy kiwi has a much wider range of adaptability to winter's cold. These plants are also called Siberian kiwis because they can withstand temperatures down to -25° F. Another species, *A. kolomikta*, is originally from Russia and is called the Arctic kiwi by some because it tolerates an amazing, for a kiwi, -40° F.

The hardy kiwis have a dramatically different look in the landscape. The *A. arguta* vine has smooth stems, smaller, more oval leaves, and lighter green foliage. The flowers are white, delicate, and arranged in clusters of three. The male Arctic kiwi is one of the most gorgeous ornamental vines in cultivation. After several or more years, the leaves are mottled in a most spectacular variegation that combines a pastel pink with a creamy white and vivid green. Neither species of the hardy kiwis needs as sturdy a trellis or arbor as the more common fuzzy-fruited vines.

Sweetness comes late in the ripening process, so harvest when kiwifruits are firm but not hard. The fruit should give slightly when pressure is applied with the fingertips. To ripen fully, let stand in a

Complementary Seasonings and Foods

Mint, anise hyssop, basil, cinnamon, crystallized ginger; lime, lemon, and orange juice; yogurt; most fruits; jicamas; liqueurs.

plastic bag, unrefrigerated, up to one or two weeks. To ripen quickly, place in a brown paper bag overnight with a ripe banana or apple. When ripe, refrigerate for up to three or four days until ready to use; do not store near other fruits.

Like the papaya, kiwifruit acts as a meat tenderizer and the pulp, or the peel after pulp has been scooped out, can be rubbed on meats before grilling. As with pineapple, an enzyme in kiwifruit prevents it from combining with gelatin or with milk that is to be gelled or frozen. Kiwi slices dry well and can then be used in mixed dried fruit compotes.

Halve ripe kiwifruits and eat with a spoon, or peel and cut crosswise or lengthwise into slices that will delight you with their color and pattern. Use the slices in fruit salads, compotes, chutneys, custards, and tarts or pies; purée for sorbets. Kiwis will weep if sliced too far in advance; wait until the last moment to decorate custards or pies. If puréeing, do not process or blend more than a few seconds or the seeds will impart a bitter taste. Add lemon, lime, or orange juice; honey; liqueur; or sugar syrup and serve with fresh or poached fruits or over angel food cake.

Mini Recipes

Peel and slice kiwifruits, sprinkle with orange-flavored liqueur, and let stand 1 to 2 hours. Serve over frozen yogurt or ice cream.

Fill a fully baked Walnut Pastry shell (see page 29) with Custard Sauce (see page 25); chill. Just before serving top with sliced, peeled kiwifruits and sprinkle with minced sweet cicely or mint.

Cut slightly underripe, peeled kiwifruits into strips and toss into chicken and sweet pepper stir-fry just before serving.

Compose a fruit salad of sliced, peeled kiwifruits, orange and grapefruit sections, and garden cress; dress with Yogurt Fruit Salad Dressing (see page 20) and crumble feta cheese over top.

Kiwifruit Fritters

3/4 cup flour

1 tablespoon granulated sugar

1/2 tablespoon baking powder

1 teaspoon five-spice powder

2/3 cup water

1 tablespoon vegetable oil, plus oil for deep-frying

1 teaspoon black sesame seed

8 kiwifruits, peeled and each cut into 6 wedges

1 tablespoon cornstarch, or as needed

Confectioners' sugar, for sprinkling

Amiable television chef Martin Yan included this scrumptious dessert recipe in his visually stunning cookbook, ©Everybody's Wokking (Harlow & Ratner, 1991). He originated the idea for these sugar-dusted kiwifruit mouthfuls during his student days in California, adapting them from the deep-fried apples he enjoyed as a child in China. Look for the black sesame seeds in Asian, Indian, and Middle Eastern markets.

◆

To make batter, in a medium bowl stir together flour, granulated sugar, baking powder, and five-spice powder. Gradually stir in water. Add 1 tablespoon vegetable oil and whip with wire whisk until smooth. Cover and refrigerate 2 hours.

Pour vegetable oil into wok, deep-fat fryer, or deep skillet to depth of about 2 inches. Heat oil to 375° F and adjust heat to maintain temperature.

Stir sesame seed into batter. Pat kiwifruit wedges dry with paper toweling. Sprinkle wedges lightly with cornstarch just before you are ready to cook them. Using chopsticks or tongs, dip kiwifruit wedges into batter, letting excess batter drip off, then gently lower fruit into hot oil. Deep-fry several pieces at a time, stirring occasionally, until golden brown and puffy (about 2 minutes). Do not crowd pan. Lift fritters out and drain on paper towels.

Sprinkle with confectioners' sugar. Serve warm.

SERVES 6 TO 8

Chicken Salad with Kiwifruits and Almonds

3 cups cubed Poached Chicken
(see page 72)

1/4 cup thinly
chiffonade-cut basil

Yogurt Fruit Salad Dressing
(see page 20)

2 oranges

6 to 8 cups torn assorted
salad greens

Salt and freshly ground white
pepper, to taste

2 or 3 kiwifruits, peeled and
sliced into 1/4-inch-thick
rounds

1/3 cup sliced almonds,
lightly toasted

For the salad greens, choose one or two soft lettuces and include frisée, arugula or mizuna, garden cress, and salad burnet.

In a mixing bowl toss chicken and basil with 2 or 3 tablespoons of the dressing. Set aside.

Peel oranges. While holding oranges over bowl to catch juice, pull apart into sections; set aside. Strain accumulated juice and set aside.

In a large salad bowl, mix greens with enough of the remaining dressing to coat lightly. Toss in chicken mixture, orange sections, and reserved orange juice to taste. Season with salt and pepper, if needed, and arrange kiwifruit rounds on top. Sprinkle with almonds and serve immediately.

SERVES 4 AS A MAIN COURSE

Lavender

English Lavender (Lavandula angustifolia)
Spanish Lavender (L. dentata)
French Lavender (L. stoechas)

Somewhat tender evergreen perennial.

Plant container-grown cuttings from named varieties.

Comes in a wide range of sizes, foliage colors, and blossom types and colors.

Prospers in full sun in well-drained soil without much fertility.

Virtually pest free. In arid climates, disease free if not overirrigated. In humid climates, prune for a more open habit to allow for air circulation to prevent fungal diseases, stem mildews, and blights.

Prune back once each summer after bloom to maintain a tight form that will hold the flower stalks upright during rains.

While identified with the islands of Greece, the fields of the French Provence, and many an Italian garden, the *Lavandula* genus (a member of the mint family) can be grown in a remarkable range of American climates, and even cultivated on porches and in sunny windows in less suitable areas. English lavender (*L. angustifolia*) is a bit of a misnomer because the plant is native to the Mediterranean. But this species of lavender is the most cold hardy, is revered in all of Europe for its essential oil, and has been extensively cultivated in England.

Most lavenders are not considered cold hardy, but careful attention to your garden's microclimates can greatly extend lavender's range. Check with your local nursery for adaptable varieties.

Lavender plants require good drainage above almost all else; it is even more important than nutrients—even nitrogen. Clay is deadly to lavender, causing crown rot and various root rots, fungal diseases, stem mildews, and blights. When in doubt about the drainage of a particular garden soil, amend raised planting mounds with sand or gravel, not compost, or plant in a container filled with a sandy potting mix.

Never is the perilous jungle of botanical nomenclature more tangled and overgrown than in the case of lovely, innocent lavender. For example, *L. stoechas* is often called Spanish lavender on the West Coast, and *L. dentata* is referred to as French lavender. But the gardening books published on the East Coast swap the Latin names for French and Spanish lavender. Everyone agrees the generic form of English lavender is *L. angustifolia*, however.

This confusion of just two species is simple when compared with the raging debates horticulturists get into over named varieties of lavender. Given the unresolvable debate around lavender nomenclature, it's often best to refer to species of lavender on a "sold as" basis. Get to know the characteristics of the different trade names used by your local nurseries.

Lavenders have many uses in a gourmet's garden. Place larger lavenders, such as Spanish lavender (*L. dentata*), sweet lavender (*L. heterophyla*), and spike lavender (*L. latifolia* or *L. spica*), at the back of an ornamental border, farther from prominent pathways. All of these have a wonderfully rounded, half-spherical form and grow, not including blossom stems, from 2 1/2 to 4 feet high. Spanish lavender has soft, fuzzy, gray-green foliage and leaves that are rounded with large sawtoothed edges. Spike lavender sports a narrow flower on a long, somewhat-branched stem.

One of the sweetest, best-scented, most pungent lavenders is the English lavender (*L. angustifolia*) called 'Provence'. (Others consider this lavender to be a cross between an English lavender and *L. intermedia*.) It has fat flowers, nearly 1 inch in diameter, at the top 1 1/2 or 2 inches of each stem. The flowers are so luxurious that overhead irrigation, even heavy fog, can temporarily knock them over. For sheer drama and rich color of blossom, grow French lavender (*L. stoechas*). It has spectacularly rich, royal purple "flags" that stand straight up from the top of the flower. One particularly showy form is *L. stoechas* 'Otto Quast'.

For subtlety of color that is cool, relaxing, and delicate, use English lavender 'Jean Davis' (*L. angustifolia*). This somewhat petite lavender has small, pale pink blossoms on slender stems and typical gray-green foliage. It fits quite nicely with designs that feature silver-gray and dark green foliage and white or royal purple and blue blossoms.

Plant lavenders in drifts or swales of color for the primary background of a landscape design. The soft tones of blue-gray and green fit nicely with a natural look, providing an intriguing color year-round. Place large clusters of lavender in meandering patterns, to mimic the image of a native plant community. Dark green evergreen plants—rosemary, thyme—provide an interesting foil or counterpoint to the lavender.

Harvest the leaves when they are three to four inches long and the flowers when they start to open. Use fresh or dried lavender with caution, as the fragrance is pervasive and can be overpowering.

Candy lavender blossoms (see page 16) and use as a garnish for fruitades, fruit desserts, and cakes. Infuse honey, vinegar, or oil with lavender, or make flavored sugar (see page 16). Place lavender flowers or leaves in bottoms of jars before pouring in hot lavender or other jelly. Chop flowers and/or leaves with chives and toss into a green salad or vinaigrettes, or add lavender sprigs to beef stew or to the pan when roasting chicken, pork, or lamb.

Honey Ice Cream with Lavender

5 egg yolks

4 cups whipping cream

1/2 cup strong-flavored honey

1/2 tablespoon each chopped lavender blossoms and lavender foliage, or to taste

Dr. Sinclair Philip of Sooke Harbour House, the elegant restaurant and inn on Vancouver Island, maintains that Alice Waters's lavender ice cream is the best. She has graciously agreed to let us publish this recipe from her ©Chez Panisse Menu Cookbook (Random House, 1992). For a stronger lavender flavor, you can add the blossoms and foliage the last 5 minutes of custard cooking time. She suggests using thyme, heather, or tupelo honey.

✦

*I*n top pan of double boiler, lightly beat egg yolks. Blend in 3 cups of the cream and the honey and place over bottom pan of very hot water. Stir constantly with wooden spoon until mixture thickens to the consistency of custard sauce (about 10 minutes). Add lavender blossoms and foliage the last 1 or 2 minutes of cooking time. Strain mixture and stir in remaining 1 cup cream.

Let cool, cover and chill completely, then freeze in an ice cream freezer according to manufacturer's instructions.

Serve in chilled crystal bowls.

MAKES ABOUT 1 QUART; SERVES 8

Lavender Chicken "Pressada"

Vegetable oil

Lavender foliage with some flowers

6 to 8 large boneless chicken breast halves or other boneless cuts

This is a loose adaptation of a recipe for chicken grilled with thyme that horticultural writer Jeff Cox discovered while traveling down the coast of Italy. The word pressada *is an Americanization of the term Italians use for describing chicken pressed between two layers of herbs. You can, of course, grill chicken with lavender sprigs smoking on the coals, but this method gives the chicken a more intense lavender flavor, is more theatrical than any other barbecue technique, and is a conversation piece. You could never afford to buy the amount of foliage this recipe demands. This is a dish for edible landscapers.*

In addition to a grill and standard grilling supplies, you will need a 10-by 20-inch cast-iron pancake griddle, a baking sheet as big or bigger than the griddle, 5 to 10 bricks, and two pairs of long barbecue tongs.

Serve the browned chicken on rice pilaf or atop a bed of colorful salad greens.

✦

Start enough charcoal briquettes in a grill to form a layer 1 or 2 briquettes deep and the same dimension as the griddle. Place a cast-iron griddle atop the grill rack. When the coals heat the griddle to nearly orange hot (when a splattering of oil dances and sizzles on the grill), you're ready to begin.

With a natural-bristle brush (plastic will melt), coat the griddle with some oil. Without hesitation, layer 1 to 2 inches of lavender prunings on the griddle. Be sure lengths of the prunings run in the same direction as the length of the griddle. Cover griddle completely with herbs, leaving no holes.

Quickly lay chicken breasts across surface of lavender, making sure the lengths of chicken are perpendicular to the lengths of lavender. Next, cover chicken with another 1 to 2 inches of lavender foliage. Place baking sheet on top of herbs and put 5 to 10 bricks on the sheet to compress the lavender and chicken into a "sandwich."

The tricky part is to get a feel for how long to wait to turn the sandwich. If the coals have heated the griddle to nearly orange hot, the chicken may only need 5 to 10 minutes per side. A low heat will stretch the time out to 15 to 20 minutes per side.

When chicken is ready to turn, remove bricks and baking sheet. With 2 pairs of tongs, one in each hand, grasp each end of sandwich, slipping tongs as far around sandwich as possible. Very quickly, in one sweeping motion, turn layers over. This is where skill, practice, and barbecue art come into play. You'll either dazzle your friends or reassemble the lavender and chicken layers in humble quiet. Reassemble baking sheet and bricks.

When chicken is done on second side, remove bricks and baking sheet. Pull top layer of lavender off chicken and reserve in a bucket. Lift chicken from its bed of lavender and place on serving platter. Add remaining lavender to bucket and remove griddle from grill. Make sure coals are good and hot, or add a few more hot ones and wait for temperature to increase. Place chicken breasts on grill rack, diagonal to metal ribs. Brown briefly, then move chicken and brown again to create crosshatch pattern. Turn chicken over and grill to form crosshatch pattern on other side in same way, then serve.

SERVES 6 TO 8

Lemon Verbena

Aloysia triphylla

Lemongrass

Cymbopogon citratus

Lemongrass

*O*utside of the citrus belts, authentic lemon flavors from one's own backyard are hard to come by. One perennial herb, lemon balm (*Melissa officinalis*), does have a fairly true lemony taste. But this is one of the seediest, most rampant annual plants to scurry across God's green earth and the cautious gardener will want to skip this pesty plant. The options aren't, climatically speaking, as widely adaptable, but their flavor is more complex and at least equally authentic.

Lemon verbena has a lower profile than lemon balm, but is better behaved. This highly adaptable shrub can be left to grow as a multitrunk plant some 8 to 10 feet high with arching, cascading limbs. Unpruned lemon verbenas need lots of space and belong in the background with other wild plants. The plant can also be trained to a single-trunked specimen with a rounded mass of clipped foliage, called a standard in the landscape trade. A series of almost topiary-shaped lemon verbenas can lend a visual cadence and formal feeling to any landscape.

Regardless of how it is pruned, the leaves of lemon verbena are long, narrow, pointed ovals in an appealing light green. A profusion of pastel pink blossoms grace the long flower stalks and attract butterflies.

134

This woody perennial will survive winters down to 10° F. In mild winter areas, the leaves may cling to the stems throughout winter, but it isn't the showiest seasonal foliage. Where the plant becomes fully deciduous, a well-pruned shrub can reveal a classic branch pattern, like a large bonsai.

Lemon verbena prefers rich, well-drained soil. As the shrub is slow to grow from seed, purchase container-grown plants. Position them in full sun in mild summer climates; they will, however, tolerate afternoon shade in hot regions. Consistent watering is important when the plants are young, but they can become fairly drought tolerant with age. In severely cold climates, grow lemon verbena in a container and move it indoors for winter protection.

Unique for the strength of its scent, lemon verbena can substitute for lemon zest in almost any recipe. Smell your fingers after handling it and you will be reminded of the sweet taste of old-fashioned lemon drops. The flavor of the edible leaves is of highest intensity just before the plant blooms, but the leaves can be harvested at any time.

Lemon verbena is compatible with both sweet and savory dishes and goes well with fruits such as apples, grapes, and bananas; with vegetables such as beets, spinach, corn, broccoli, and asparagus; and with seafood, poultry, and lamb. Use the leafy stem tips to garnish fruit compotes or other fruit desserts. Rub chicken or lamb with the leaves before roasting, or use a handful of leaves to fill the cavity of a fish to be poached or steamed. For a festive touch, float one or two leaves in finger bowls or glasses of ice water in place of a lemon slice. Use leaves to flavor marinades and salad dressings, or place in the jar bottom when putting up apple jelly or in a dish for baked custard. Leaves can also be cooked in stews or sauces. As with bay leaf, however, remove before serving.

Lemongrass is a tropical, highly aromatic plant closely related to the plant from which we get the citronella insect repellent. While its outdoor cultivation is limited to the mildest parts of zones 9 and 10, other gardeners will be rewarded by experimenting with indoor and pot cultivation of this culinarily versatile plant. It has an upright, coarsely bladed, grasslike appearance with gray-green to lime green stalks up to two feet tall.

This is far from a drought-resistant plant and plenty of water and a rich soil are essential. Plants are available in containers in specialty nurseries. Provide as much sun as possible, water frequently, and fertilize when needed. Maintaining high humidity is probably beneficial, as the plant most likely originates in Malaysia.

Harvest the stalks by cutting down through the roots, choosing strong stalks with no blemishes. Discard the top portion of the stalk where the leaves start to branch and store the lower portion in the vegetable crisper of the refrigerator for up to one month.

Bruise the trimmed stalks to release their fragrance and use to impart a slightly sour flavor to soups and fish dishes, chicken stew, or chicken or fish stock. Primarily a seasoning, lemongrass is used in stir-fry dishes, along with sliced fresh ginger and garlic, to impart flavor to the oil; discard before adding the stir-fry ingredients.

Dried lemongrass, in pieces or ground, will last many months. Freezing the stalks softens their fibrous quality somewhat, making it easier to cut them into pieces. Add pieces of fresh, dried, or frozen lemongrass to rice when steaming, or to the steaming water for vegetables, or prepare infused oil or vinegar (see pages 13 to 14).

Steamed Mussels or Clams with Lemongrass and Shallots

4 pounds mussels or clams in the shell, well scrubbed

2 tablespoons peanut or corn oil

3 stalks lemongrass, trimmed and lightly bruised

1/3 cup minced shallot

3 large cloves garlic, minced

3/4 cup coarsely chopped cilantro

3 cups dry white wine

The shape of the pot will determine how long it will take for the shellfish to cook. A tall, deep pot will require longer cooking than a short, wide pot because steam will not circulate as quickly. Serve the shellfish and steaming broth in shallow individual bowls and accompany with French bread.

*P*ull beards from mussels. Discard any cracked or open shellfish.

In a 6- to 8-quart pot with tight-fitting lid, heat oil over medium heat. Add lemongrass, shallot, and garlic and sauté 5 minutes. Add cilantro and shellfish and turn with wooden spoon to coat shellfish with oil and herbs.

Raise heat to high, add wine, cover, and cook until shellfish open (3 to 5 minutes). Discard any shellfish that do not open.

Ladle into heated individual bowls and serve immediately.

SERVES 4

Lemon Verbena Jelly

2 1/2 cups torn lemon verbena leaves

2 slices lemon

2 1/2 cups water, boiling

1 package (2 oz) powdered pectin

2 1/2 cups sugar

1 tablespoon freshly grated lemon zest

Fragrant, delicate, and a lovely pale yellow, this jelly complements roast lamb, pork, chicken, or veal and is equally delicious spread on toast and biscuits. Powdered pectin is generally available in 2-ounce and 1 3/4-ounce packages. Lemon verbena releases no pectin, so the smaller package may not produce as firm a jelly. Whichever size you use, follow package directions carefully.

*P*lace lemon verbena leaves and lemon slices in bowl and pour boiling water over them. Let stand 20 minutes, then strain and discard lemon and leaves. Make jelly, following instructions on pectin package.

Immediately ladle into hot, sterilized jars and seal and store as directed on page 17. Refrigerate unsealed jars no longer than 2 weeks.

MAKES ABOUT 4 HALF-PINTS

Lovage
Levisticum officinale

*L*ovage looks as if it is an overgrown celery plant with a tan. The plant has tall, tight stalks similar to a celery's ribbed stalks, rich earthy green foliage, and glossy leaves that are pointy and cut like a coarse celery leaf. The foliage bursts forth with exuberance to an impressive six or more feet.

Due to its prolific growth, a single lovage plant will produce far more usable forage than any family could possibly need in the kitchen. Nonetheless, the plant deserves a prominent place in any edible landscape by virtue of its graphic foliage. This substantial plant needs brawny-foliaged plants nearby to stand up to its bold form. Examples would include artichoke, cardoon, large-leafed basils, French sorrel, or rhubarb. The royal green of the leaves provides a perfect counterpoint to intense floral colors such as the hot orange of certain calendulas (*Calendula officinalis*), or even the vibrant yellow-green variegated foliage of lemon thyme (*Thymus citriodorus* 'Aureus').

The plant belongs to the parsley family (*Umbelliferae*) and sprouts the classic wide, flat flower heads that distinguish this plant family. The flower head is large, up to 12 inches across, and composed of hundreds of tiny, delicate, greenish yellow blossoms. Because the flowers make plenty of nectar and are small, a myriad of beneficial insects stop by to sup from this plant, fueling up for their attack on pests. Unlike other members of the parsley family, which make fertile seed in abundance,

Hardy perennial Mediterranean herb. Grows in all zones.

Grow from seed or potted seedlings.

Prefers rich soil with consistent moisture and good drainage.

Plant in full sun or partial shade.

May need to be replaced after several or more years.

138

lovage doesn't usually become a weedy pest. To be cautious, remove the seed heads before they ripen.

The leaves, seeds, stems, and roots of lovage are edible. The leaves, which taste much like celery with a hint of lemon, are strong in flavor, so use with discretion. Harvest young leaves and stems at any time after the plant has become established, preferably before the plant flowers. Wrap in a terry towel and refrigerate in a plastic bag for up to three days. Leaves may be dried, or blanched and sheet-frozen. Use fresh, dried, or frozen leaves and chopped stems in bouquets garnis (see page 15), or add to soup stocks and long-cooking ragouts, sauces, and legume soups.

Lovage complements most other herbs and makes a good salt substitute. For a hint of celery, rub your salad bowl with the leaves before adding greens, stuff them into the cavity of chicken before roasting, or use to infuse milk for mashed potatoes. Chop the leaves and add to salads, egg and cheese dishes, root vegetable purées, and other dishes in which celery leaves are commonly used.

Candy lovage stems (see page 16) and use as a dessert garnish, or blanch them and serve as a vegetable side dish dressed with butter. Use dried seeds whole in pickling, or ground as a saltless celery salt in cheese spreads and compound butters (see page 15); potato, chicken, or fish salads; salad dressings; or steamed vegetables. Sprinkle over cooked meat, or add to bread dough.

Ground Venison Patties with Lovage and Sage

4 large cloves garlic, chopped

3 tablespoons chopped parsley

2 tablespoons each chopped sage and lovage

1/2 onion, chopped

1 extra-large egg

1/4 cup low-fat milk

1 large piece whole-wheat or white bread, torn into small pieces

1 teaspoon dry mustard

1 1/2 tablespoons Worcestershire sauce

1/2 teaspoon salt

1/4 teaspoon freshly ground pepper

1 1/2 pounds ground venison

Since lovage is quite pungent, adjust the herb measurements to taste. Serve the patties with Elaeagnus Sauce (see page 86), wild rice, and a steamed green vegetable. If venison is difficult to locate, use ground lean beef in its place.

✦

In a processor fitted with metal blade or a blender, combine garlic, parsley, sage, and lovage and process to mince finely. Add onion and pulse just until onion is minced.

In a large bowl lightly beat together egg and milk. Using a fork stir in garlic mixture, bread, mustard, Worcestershire sauce, salt, and pepper. Let stand until bread absorbs the milk and egg (about 30 minutes).

Using your hands mix meat into bread mixture. Pinch off a small amount of the mixture and sauté; taste and adjust seasonings. Form meat into 8 patties about 3/4 inch thick. Cover and refrigerate for at least 3 hours or up to 24 hours.

Preheat broiler, or prepare fire in a charcoal grill. Broil or grill patties turning once, until cooked to desired doneness (about 5 minutes per side for medium-rare).

Serves 8

Mint

Mentha sp.

Hardy and semitender perennial herb; a variety for every zone.

Grow from rooted cuttings or container plants.

Thrives in fertile, moist soils.

Tolerates full sun in mild summer climates, but prefers shady conditions elsewhere.

Watch out for spreading, invasive nature.

Cut foliage to ground each fall to tidy the garden and remove spent flower heads.

*S*eldom is an edible plant in a shady spot happy as a lark. Mints provide plenty of tasty options for this troublesome place and can grow in full sun in many climates as well. These versatile plants are also adaptable to moist and wet soils, solving another frequent design problem. The one request a mint makes of the gardener is to provide fertile soil.

Mints come in a wide array of foliage tones and hues; every gardener is bound to find at least one that will please. Spearmint (*M.* sp*icata*) has a robust, meaty green, toothed leaf; the golden apple mint (*M. gentilis*) has a smooth, dark green leaf with a clear yellow variegation. The spicy ginger mint (*M. X gentilis* 'Variegata') also has a bright yellow on green pattern—for dramatic highlights in shady areas. Another delightfully variegated plant is pineapple mint (*M. suavaolens* 'Variegata') with its pure white markings over a pale, gray-green hairy leaf. Peppermint (*M. piperita*) has distinctive reddish stems and dark green foliage tinged with musty crimson or purple.

The Achilles heel of a mint plant is its wandering habit. These herbs have more of an urge to roam than a shady aluminum-siding salesman traveling through Kansas. The plant makes vigorous underground stems that travel just below the soil's surface and spread far and wide. But it is fairly simple to design for proper containment as

141

*Complementary
Seasonings and Foods*

*Complementary
Seasonings and Foods*

Oregano, chives, parsley, thyme,
lemon verbena, nasturtiums;
lemon or lime juice; green
beans, fava or shell beans,
carrots, celery, peas, tomatoes;
apples, pineapple, grapefruits,
oranges; fish, lamb, veal;
Cabernet Sauvignon, Pinot Noir,
Gewürztraminer.

a ground cover. (Some mints—spearmint, apple mint, peppermint—are tall enough to resemble a small shrub when mature.) The first option is an area beneath a spreading fruit tree, a place both large enough to accommodate the mature width of the plant and a fair distance from any other herbaceous plants. Arid climates offer a second option to stop or slow the progression of mints: eliminate all irrigation at the perimeter of the planting (although winter rains will foil this plan). Another strategy is to plant mints in sidewalk strips, or anywhere that is surrounded by a wide concrete barrier. Or place mints in pots that sit on top of patios or porches. The frequent recommendation of sinking containerized mints in the ground is misguided. After some time, one of the underground stems is bound to find the drainage hole, no matter how cleverly covered, and escape from captivity.

Harvest young leaves or sprigs any time after the plant is established. Mints wilt quickly, so harvest at the last moment, especially if using the leaves as a garnish. The sprigs will, however, last fairly well up to two days if placed upright in a glass of water, covered loosely with a plastic bag, and refrigerated.

Most mint varieties may be used interchangeably, for all have an aroma, sweet and slightly peppery, that leaves a refreshing aftertaste. Peppermint and apple, pineapple, chocolate, and double mints are usually reserved for flavoring desserts and candies, however. Sweeter and milder than peppermint, spearmint is the favorite for most other culinary purposes. Use the leaves in beverages and in both desserts (custards, ice creams, fruit compotes) and savory dishes. Spicy foods take especially well to mint, and the herb is widely used in Vietnamese, Thai, and East Indian cuisines.

Mini Recipes

Steep chopped mint in melted butter flavored with fresh lemon or lime juice; serve on carrots or lamb chops.

Combine 2 tablespoons melted butter, 1 tablespoon chopped mint, and salt, freshly ground white pepper, and fresh lemon juice to taste. Use to baste fish, lamb, or veal while grilling.

Crush together mint leaves and sea salt in mortar; stuff into cavity of whole dressed trout before frying or grilling.

Candy apple mint leaves (see page 16) and use as a garnish for mint ice cream or frozen yogurt.

Add chopped spearmint leaves to tabbouleh, chicken salad, or coleslaw.

Mint and Roasted Pepper Dip

3 ounces feta cheese

1/4 cup Yogurt Cheese (see page 22)

1/2 teaspoon salt

1/4 teaspoon freshly ground white pepper

1/2 cup finely diced roasted sweet red pepper, or to taste, plus 2 thin strips roasted red pepper, for garnish (see page 160)

1/2 cup thinly chiffonade-cut mint, or to taste

A change from the usual cream cheese-based dips, this colorful green and red hors d'oeuvre is perfect for holiday entertaining. Serve with crudités for dipping, or use as a spread for plain crackers. Chèvre can be substituted for the feta.

◆

*I*n a bowl crumble feta cheese. Add Yogurt Cheese and mash with a fork until smooth. Mix in salt and white pepper and stir in diced peppers and mint. Taste and adjust seasonings with salt and pepper; add additional diced peppers and chiffonade-cut mint, if desired.

Mound cheese in serving bowl and garnish with pepper strips. If not using immediately, cover with plastic wrap and refrigerate up to 2 days. Bring to room temperature before serving.

MAKES ABOUT 1 CUP

Mendocino Quail Salad with Orange-Mint Dressing

4 quail or 2 Cornish game hens, split and backbone flattened

Marinade:

1/4 cup white wine vinegar

2 tablespoons olive oil

1/4 cup Fetzer
Sundial Chardonnay

1/4 cup fresh orange juice

1/4 cup chopped onion

1/4 cup chopped mint

1/2 teaspoon crushed
white peppercorns

Pinch salt

Vinaigrette:

1/4 cup chopped mint

1 tablespoon chopped shallot
or onion

2 tablespoons white
wine vinegar

6 tablespoons fresh orange juice

1 teaspoon honey

1/4 cup plain low-fat yogurt

1 tablespoon walnut oil

Salt and freshly ground pepper,
to taste

Pinch ground cloves

John Ash, culinary director at Fetzer's Valley Oaks Food & Wine Center in Hopland, California, has generously agreed to share his recipe for quail salad. He developed the dish for the Fetzer and Food Report, *a small magazine devoted to wines and food.*

Allow plenty of time for the charcoal fire to reach proper temperature. Or you may slip the quail under a preheated broiler and cook three to four minutes on each side. If serving the salad as a main course, accompany it with baguette slices.

✦

Arrange quail in shallow, nonreactive dish. In a small bowl stir together all marinade ingredients and pour over quail. Cover and refrigerate for at least 2 hours or as long as overnight.

In a small bowl whisk together all vinaigrette ingredients. Cover and refrigerate until serving time.

Prepare a fire in a charcoal grill. When coals are hot, remove quail from marinade and pat dry with paper toweling.

Grill quail skin side down 4 to 5 minutes, turn, and continue cooking until lightly browned and tender (2 to 3 minutes longer). If using Cornish game hens, allow approximately 8 to 10 minutes grilling per side.

Divide greens evenly among individual plates. Garnish with orange sections, mint sprigs, and tomato. Top with quail and drizzle with vinaigrette. Serve at once.

Serves 4 as a first course or serves 2 as a main course

1/2 pound mixed salad greens

1 orange, peeled and sectioned, for garnish

Mint sprigs, for garnish

10 cherry tomatoes, halved, for garnish

Lahmajoon

Pizza Dough (see page 26)

1 pound lean ground lamb

1 cup finely minced onion

1/2 cup minced spearmint

!/4 cup minced parsley

1/2 teaspoon finely minced garlic

1/4 cup finely minced sweet pepper

3 tablespoons tomato paste

3/4 teaspoon salt

1/4 teaspoon each freshly ground pepper, ground cumin, and chile powder

Olive oil, for brushing

Serve this Armenian-style pizza with a fresh fruit salad and cookies for dessert. If you are using only one oven, halfway through the baking time, switch the baking sheets, moving the sheet on the top rack to the bottom rack and vice versa. As you do this, rotate each sheet 180 degrees. This will ensure the pizzas bake evenly.

✦

Prepare pizza dough. While dough is rising, in a bowl combine all remaining ingredients and mix well. Sauté a small amount of the mixture; taste and adjust seasonings.

When dough has doubled in bulk, punch down, knead briefly, and divide into 8 equal balls. Cover with tea towel and let rest 10 minutes. Preheat oven to 400° F.

On a lightly floured board roll out each dough ball into a thin round about 7 inches in diameter. Brush lightly with olive oil. Spread an equal portion of lamb filling on each round. Lightly oil 2 large baking sheets and arrange rounds on them.

Bake until edges are golden and topping is bubbly (about 15 minutes). Serve immediately.

MAKES 8 SMALL PIZZAS

Greek Oregano

(Origanum vulgare subsp. hirtum)
Sweet Marjoram (O. x majorana)

Some oregano species are perennial in moderately cold winter areas; others are perennial only in mild coastal climates. Marjorams are more tender and grow in pots in many cold winter areas.

Grow from rooted cuttings to guarantee authenticity, or from seed.

Plant in somewhat fertile soil with good drainage and water regularly.

Keep flower stalks pruned to maintain the attractive foliage.

Watch for rot and mildew in humid summer climates.

Perhaps it has been some conspiracy promoted by the Greek and Turkish governments, although unlikely given their mutual animosities. Perhaps the spice companies have conspired to withhold information to protect their markets. Perhaps it's just a case of botanical confusion. Ask a number of gardeners "What is true oregano?" and you'll get a different opinion every time. The plants sold as oregano in nurseries run the gamut of species and subspecies, depending upon the source.

The bottom line to oregano is "Does it taste like what I've been buying in the supermarket?" Arthur Tucker, of the Department of Agriculture and Natural Resources, was bemoaning the confusion surrounding "true" oregano in the early 1980s when a colleague, Dr. Raymond Petersen, suggested Tucker simply sprout the seeds in a jar of store-bought oregano, most of which originated from Turkey or Greece, and botanically identify the seedlings. Some 95 percent of the seeds produced a plant identified as *O. vulgare* subsp. *hirtum*. This same plant is sometimes classified and sold as *O. heracleoticum*. (Strangely enough, the other 5 percent of the seeds included another species of oregano, a

*Complementary
Seasonings and Foods*

Bay leaf, basil, thyme; egg and
cheese dishes; garlic, onions,
eggplants, mushrooms,
parsnips, potatoes, squashes,
tomatoes; seafood, poultry and
game birds, lamb, veal, sausage
and meat-loaf mixtures.

pot marjoram, and three species of mints!) While many cultures
around the world use various oregano species and completely different
plants—Mexican "oregano," for example, is actually *Lippia graveolans,*
from a completely different plant family—for an oregano flavor in the
kitchen, most Americans recognize *O. vulgare* subsp. *hirtum* as the
authentic item.

True oregano spreads by underground stems and grows to 2 1/2
feet high. The soft, gray-green foilage is made up of small oval leaves.
The flower stalks, which rise above the foliage, are subtle pink with
purplish overtones. The plant prospers in full sun, but will stand some
partial shade. The roots prefer fairly fertile soil, but must have good
drainage. Adding sand to the planting area will improve drainage, help
prevent frost heaving in cold winter climates, limit fungal problems in
humid summers, and, according to recent research, may enhance the
oil content of the plant, making it more pungent.

Sweet marjoram, also called Italian oregano, also has problems
with botanical nomenclature. Many sources sell *O. vulgare* as marjoram.
Other names for marjoram include *O. marjorana* and *Majorana hortensis.*
The plant looks different from oregano; it has tiny, roundish gray-green
leaves, spikes of white flowers, and foliage only to one to two feet high.
Like oregano, the plant spreads by underground stems in mild winter
climates, but it prefers more moisture and must have full sun.

One particularly attractive plant is *O. vulgare* 'Aureum'. All the
new growth is a pleasantly clear yellow. The small round leaves just
beyond the tip are a warm lime green. Eventually, the older growth
develops a light green color similar to a typical marjoram. The special
color of the foliage makes this an accent plant that should be planted
near a pathway, in a prominent terra-cotta pot, or draped over a
retaining wall. Clipping the bright yellow tips of the 'Aureum' adds a
fantastic color highlight to any salad and a zingy, spicy taste.

Harvest oregano and marjoram sprigs and flowers at any time. If
not using at once, refrigerate in a plastic bag for one or two days. Rinse,
pat dry with paper toweling, snip off the leaves, and chop. Use whole
sprigs in long-cooking dishes, bouquets garnis (see page 15), and
marinades, add to lentils when cooking for a side dish or soup, or steep
with onion and garlic in milk for mashed potatoes. Infuse vinegar or oil

(see pages 13 to 14) with marjoram or oregano sprigs. Use chopped leaves in scrambled eggs, frittatas, quiches, omelets, savory flans, egg or potato salad, stewed tomatoes, or in the stuffing for goose or duck. Prepare oil concentrate or compound butter (see pages 14 to 15) with finely minced marjoram or oregano leaves and blossoms.

Store dried marjoram or oregano in airtight containers in a cool, dark place up to nine months. Store crumbled or ground oregano up to four months. The white, pink, or purple edible flowers of the oregano plant, stronger in fragrance than the leaves, can be chopped with the leaves and used in the same way. They also make an attractive garnish.

Mini Recipes

Add minced marjoram or oregano leaves and flowers to eggplant, bell pepper, and tomato salad.

Marinate feta cheese in olive oil with a generous sprinkling of crumbled dried oregano; break into small pieces and toss into green salad, or mash and use as a spread for sliced baguettes.

Bring out the flavor of tomatoes by marinating slices in olive oil, cider vinegar, minced garlic, and minced oregano.

Braised and Breaded Oxtails

2 pounds oxtails, trimmed of fat

Flour seasoned with salt, freshly ground pepper, and paprika

2 tablespoons canola oil, or as needed

1 large onion, sliced

4 large cloves garlic, minced

1 cup dry red wine

Adapted from a recipe demonstrated by friend Graham Kerr many years ago when he appeared on television as the Galloping Gourmet, these oxtails are without a doubt the best you will ever eat. The preparation may appear long and tedious, but the result is more than worth the effort. Note that it is best to cook the oxtails a day in advance.

If you don't have corn-bread crumbs on hand, use regular bread crumbs. The flavor of oregano is intensified by the use of ground dried oregano. Serve the baked oxtails with their pan juices, baked potatoes, butter-steamed peas, and sliced ripe tomatoes.

Bouquet garni of 6 large sprigs oregano; 3 sprigs parsley; 3 lovage leaves; 1 bay leaf, crumbled; and 6 peppercorns, lightly crushed (see page 15)

2 1/2 cups beef stock, or as needed

1 cup each fine dried bread crumbs and finely crumbled corn bread

2 teaspoons ground dried oregano

1/2 teaspoon salt

1/4 teaspoon freshly ground pepper

1/2 cup Dijon-style mustard, or as needed

Olive oil

✦

*I*n a paper bag shake together oxtails and seasoned flour. Heat 1 tablespoon of the canola oil in a large nonstick skillet over medium to medium-high heat. Shake excess flour off oxtails and, in batches, brown on all sides, adding additional oil as needed; do not allow pieces to touch. As oxtails are browned, transfer to a platter.

When all oxtails have been browned, add a little more canola oil to skillet, if needed. Add onion and sauté over medium heat until lightly browned (about 5 minutes). Add garlic and sauté, stirring, 1 minute. Raise heat slightly, add wine, and deglaze skillet by scraping up any browned bits. Return oxtails to skillet, turn to coat all sides, cover, and boil until wine almost evaporates (about 2 minutes). Add stock and bring to a boil. Lightly bruise bouquet garni and place on top of oxtails. Lower heat, cover, and simmer until oxtails are very tender (1 to 1 1/2 hours). Turn oxtails over several times to insure even cooking and check occasionally to be sure stock has not boiled away. Add more stock as needed; there should be about 1 1/2 cups stock when oxtails are done.

Remove oxtails to a shallow dish, let cool, cover, and refrigerate. Pour pan juices into bowl, cool, cover, and refrigerate.

The following day, spread a piece of waxed paper on a kitchen counter and mound crumbs, oregano, salt, and pepper on paper; toss to mix. Spread each oxtail on all sides with mustard and roll in crumb mixture. Place, not touching, on oiled rack in baking pan. Cover and refrigerate up to 6 hours or overnight.

Preheat oven to 350° F. Drizzle each oxtail with a little olive oil and bake 30 minutes. Raise heat to 375° F and bake until crumbs are golden brown (about 10 minutes). Meanwhile, defat reserved pan juices, transfer to saucepan, and heat to serving temperature. Taste and adjust seasonings.

Arrange oxtails on heated serving platter. Pour the juices into a bowl and pass separately.

SERVES 4

Marjoram-Brie Torta

3 ounces Neufchâtel cheese, at room temperature

2 tablespoons unsalted butter, at room temperature

3 ounces crumbled Gorgonzola cheese (3/4 cup)

3 ounces finely shredded sharp Cheddar cheese (3/4 cup)

1 large clove garlic, pressed or very finely minced

3 tablespoons minced green onion, including tops

2 tablespoons minced parsley

1 tablespoon minced marjoram

One 8-ounce wheel Brie cheese, chilled

Marjoram sprigs and flowers, for garnish

This rich Brie torta will be the star of your next buffet. Give it a place of honor on the table and lavish attention on the garnishes. If your marjoram is not in flower or the sprigs are not full, substitute any colorful edible herb or flower blossoms in your garden. Serve with unsalted crackers.

✦

In a mixing bowl, beat Neufchâtel with fork or wooden spoon until soft. Stir in butter until mixture is smooth. Then stir in Gorgonzola and Cheddar cheeses, garlic, onion, parsley, and minced marjoram. Beat to blend well.

Using a sharp knife, split Brie wheel in half horizontally. Place bottom half, cut side up, on large round serving plate. Spread with cheese mixture, pressing down firmly. Top with second half, cut side down. Cover tightly with plastic wrap and refrigerate at least 3 hours or up to overnight.

To serve, bring to room temperature and garnish with marjoram sprigs and flowers.

MAKES 20 TO 30 HORS D'OEUVRE SERVINGS

Parsley

Curly-leaf Parsley:
(Petroselinum crispum
var. crispum)
Italian or
Flat-Leaf Parsley
(Petroselinum
crispum var.
neapolianum)

Biennial, often grown as an annual.

Grow from seed or purchase transplants.

Plant in rich, fine-textured soil.

Water and fertilize frequently.

Clip off flower stalks to prolong the harvest of leaves.

Watch for swallowtail caterpillars; treat with Bacillus thurengiensis spray (see Crabapple).

*I*n the standard salad bar, parsley is ostracized as a mere garnish. In fact, many of the curly-leaf parsley varieties, *P. crispum* var. *crispum*, have been bred and selected solely for their ornamental foliage with little concern for flavor. Such plants tend to be extremely curled, with deep divisions in each twisted leaf. They make delightful light green, almost chartreuse, tufted border plants for pathways, vegetable beds, and flower border edges. A particularly attractive form, with a luxurious amount of densely curled leaves, is the selection 'Triple XXX', which is also flavorful. Other curly-leaf varieties that are both attractive and colorful include 'Decora', 'Extra Curled Dwarf', and 'Moss Curled'.

For an intense, full-bodied parsley flavor, cooks reach for what is commonly called Italian parsley, *P. crispum* var. *neapolitanum* and sometimes labeled as *P. sativum*. This parsley, also known as French parsley, is a darker, more earthy green, resembling the color of lovage. The flat-leaf varieties are also called fern-leaf parsley because of their broad, flat, deeply cut foliage. The plants are not as compact as the

151

curly forms and are more likely to be relegated to the middle of a dense mixed planting where the floppiness of the foliage is easily disguised.

Both forms require rich soil with plenty of well-aged manure. The plants are heavy feeders and produce more foliage and curlier leaves if well fed and consistently watered. Each species grows well in a container or window box if the initial potting soil is fertile and supplemental fertilizers are used regularly.

All parsley plants are biennial and will produce a three-foot-tall flower stalk. The pale yellow umbel flowers help attract beneficial insects. Clipping off the emerging flower stalk will prolong the harvest. But leaving a few flowers to bloom will add beauty to the garden, enhance its insect ecology, and produce future plants.

Harvest parsley sprigs at any time and, if necessary to store, wash, spin dry in a salad spinner, stand in a glass of water, drape a plastic bag over the top, and refrigerate for several days. The best way to preserve parsley is to prepare a compound butter (see page 15) or oil concentrate (see page 14).

As a versatile herb, parsley has the highest rating because of its compatibility with almost every other herb and food, adding vibrance and color to a vast number of savory dishes. Consider it a vegetable as well as a seasoning.

Curly-leaf parsley is most often used as a garnish, in bouquets garnis, and as a deep-fried side dish. Italian parsley is used in sauces and in dishes such as tabbouleh and hummus. The two varieties are interchangeable. When mincing or chopping parsley, include some of the tender stems, for they contain the most concentrated flavor. Chop in a blender or by hand, however, for most food processors do not do a good job of mincing the stems. Freeze tougher stems for adding to soup stocks.

Roasted Turkey Breast with Parsley Stuffing

3 cups whole-wheat croutons made without butter and oil

1 cup firmly packed parsley leaves

2 or 3 large sage leaves, torn into strips

2 lovage leaves (optional)

Leaves from 6 sprigs thyme

Leaves from 3 sprigs winter savory

2 large cloves garlic

1 onion, chopped (about 3/4 cup)

2 ounces pancetta, diced

1 tablespoon unsalted butter

1/4 cup plus 2 tablespoons dry vermouth

1/2 cup turkey or chicken stock, or as needed

Salt and freshly ground pepper, to taste

1 turkey breast (5 to 6 lb)

2 tablespoons each corn or canola oil and soy sauce

This recipe yields enough stuffing for a five- to six-pound turkey breast or a six-pound turkey leg. Serve the turkey with mashed potatoes and steamed 'Romanesco'.

✦

*I*n a processor fitted with metal blade, whirl croutons to make fine crumbs; remove from processor and set aside. Add all the herbs and the garlic to processor and mince finely. Add onion and pulse several times to mince; be careful not to overprocess or mixture will become mushy.

In a large skillet over medium-high heat, cook pancetta, stirring, until lightly browned (about 3 minutes). Add butter and stir to melt. Add herb mixture and cook, stirring, 2 to 3 minutes. Remove from heat and toss in bread crumbs. Using a fork stir in 1/4 cup vermouth and the turkey stock to moisten to desired consistency. Season to taste with salt and pepper; set aside.

Preheat oven to 350° F. Using fingers carefully loosen skin of turkey up to about 1 inch from edge. Stuff bread mixture between skin and flesh, then fasten skin in place with small wooden skewers or toothpicks. In a small bowl, stir together oil, soy sauce, and 2 tablespoons vermouth. Place turkey breast on rack in roasting pan and brush with oil mixture.

Roast turkey, basting often, until internal temperature reaches 165° F (about 1 3/4 hours). If breast appears to be browning too quickly, cover loosely with aluminum foil.

Remove turkey from oven and transfer to heated platter. Cover with aluminum foil and let rest 20 to 30 minutes before carving.

Serves 6

Ossobuco with Gremolata

4 large veal shanks (about 1 1/2 lb each), each sawed crosswise into 3-inch-wide pieces

1/4 cup fresh lemon juice

2 tablespoons each unsalted butter and olive oil, or as needed

Flour, seasoned with salt and freshly ground white pepper, for dusting

1 1/2 cups dry white wine

4 or 5 ripe tomatoes, peeled and quartered

1/2 cup veal or chicken stock, plus additional stock if needed

4 anchovy fillets, finely minced, or 1 tablespoon anchovy paste

1/2 cup minced parsley

3 large cloves garlic, very finely minced

1/2 tablespoon freshly grated lemon zest

Salt and freshly ground pepper, to taste

The Italian seasoning called gremolata *is a mixture of grated lemon zest and very finely minced parsley and garlic. Often anchovies are added to the* gremolata, *especially when it is used to season veal shanks. Gremolata is also delicious sprinkled over freshly poached or baked fish fillets, poached chicken, or lamb shanks.*

Include small spoons for those who want to scoop the wonderful marrow from the veal bones.

✦

Rinse veal pieces under cool running water, pat dry with paper toweling, and place in nonreactive dish. Pour lemon juice over top and marinate 1 hour at room temperature. Pat veal pieces dry with paper toweling. Mound flour on large piece of waxed paper.

In a large skillet or dutch oven over medium-high heat, melt butter with oil. Working in batches, roll veal pieces in flour to coat lightly, then brown on all sides, being careful not to let pieces touch. Add additional oil and/or butter to skillet, if needed. As the veal pieces are browned, transfer them to a platter.

When all pieces are browned, return them to the skillet, lower heat slightly, and pour in wine. Cook, turning pieces occasionally, until wine evaporates (about 10 minutes). Add tomatoes and stock, cover, and simmer over low heat, adding more stock if pan becomes dry, until meat is very tender and starts to fall off bones (about 1 1/2 hours). Cooking time will depend upon quality of the veal.

When veal is ready, in a small bowl stir together anchovies, parsley, garlic, and lemon zest. Sprinkle anchovy mixture over veal and turn pieces to distribute the flavor. Remove from heat and let stand, covered, 5 minutes before serving.

Serves 6

Pea

Shelling Pea (Pisum sativum var. sativum)
Edible-Podded Pea (Pisum sativum var. macrocarpon)

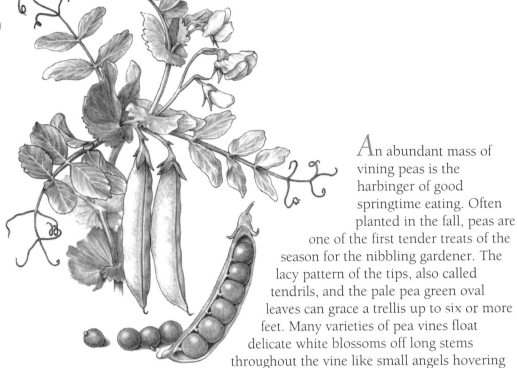

Treat as an annual plant.

Grow from seed or transplants. Inoculate the seeds with a legume inoculant specific to peas; this will insure the plants fix atmospheric nitrogen.

In warm winter areas, plant in the fall; elsewhere plant in very early spring.

Plant in rich, well-prepared soil.

Protect young seedlings from birds with netting and from snails and slugs with a copper foil barrier or by trapping.

An abundant mass of vining peas is the harbinger of good springtime eating. Often planted in the fall, peas are one of the first tender treats of the season for the nibbling gardener. The lacy pattern of the tips, also called tendrils, and the pale pea green oval leaves can grace a trellis up to six or more feet. Many varieties of pea vines float delicate white blossoms off long stems throughout the vine like small angels hovering around the plant.

Plant peas where the afternoon light can illuminate the flowers with dramatic backlighting. The best pea trellises allow the vines to sway in the wind a bit, just for the visual effect, and make fall cleanup easy. Such a trellis has a sturdy single horizontal bar across the top with vertical strings tied to a single horizontal bar near the ground. Following harvest, the strings are cut across the bottom and then the top, and the mass of foliage and string is easily added to a compost heap. Plant a mass of ornamental annual bedding plants—marigolds, salvias, zinnias—at the bottom of the trellis to hide the base of the vines that defoliate and look ugly as the season ages.

Peas are separated into two general classifications: shelling peas

155

*Complementary
Seasonings and Foods*

Mint, tarragon, dill, chervil, basil, parsley; garlic, fresh ginger; walnuts, almonds; water chestnuts, bamboo shoots, onions, artichokes, peppers, potatoes, squashes, seafood, poultry, meats.

where only the peas in the pod are used, and edible-podded peas, where the whole pod is eaten. While edible peas are related to the colorful sweet pea, they should *not* be planted together. Sweet peas, the vine, flowers, *and* pods, are poisonous. Within the shelling pea category, a distinction is made between the regular large-seeded pea and the *petit pois* varieties, which are, when mature, the tiny peas preferred in Europe. Of the edible-podded types there are two subcategories. The first group, variously called snow, Oriental, or Chinese peas, are noted for their thin, delicately flavored pod walls. The other subcategory is the snap pea, which has a thick, sweet, and juicy but not fibrous pod wall. Unlike snow or shelling peas, snap peas can be just as tasty when the peas mature to full size.

Most gardeners consider the snap pea to be a modern "invention." While the varieties we plant (examples include 'Sugar Snap' and 'Super Mel') are from recent breeding experiments, there were, as listed in nineteenth-century European seed catalogs, dozens of varieties of snaplike peas, virtually all now extinct. Basically, modern American science reinvented the culinary wheel with snap peas.

One variety of a semibush plant, 'Dwarf Gray Sugar', is an edible-podded pea that grows to 2 1/2 feet and has fascinating flowers: the upper half of the blossom is a pastel lavender-purple and the lower half is a rich burgundy-purple.

When young and tender, from four to six inches in length, the tips of the pea plant are a delicacy. Snip off, rinse, and quickly steam or stir-fry, seasoning as you would peas. The blossoms of pea plants, too, are edible; sprinkled on soups or green salads, they add variety, color, and a slight zest.

If possible, harvest shelling peas or pea pods just before mealtime, for, once picked, the sugar content of the peas begins to turn into starch. Shell the peas at the last minute. Snow peas usually need only the stem tip removed, but both sides of sugar snap peas need to be strung before cooking. Peas of both categories can be steamed, butter-steamed, braised, stir-fried, or boiled rapidly in a little water. Quick cooking is essential to retain flavor and texture.

To blanch shelled peas and trimmed snow and snap peas, drop into boiling water for 15 seconds, drain, and immediately plunge into iced water. Drain and pat dry with paper toweling. Toss blanched peas into potato salad or into pasta with shrimp and prosciutto, or add to rice stuffing for sweet peppers. Use blanched snow and snap peas for garnishing meat or fish dishes.

Mini Recipes

Butter-steam shelled peas with mint sprigs; discard mint sprigs and sprinkle peas with grated orange zest.

Butter-steam shelled peas with crushed garlic; toss in watercress leaves and garnish with dill feathers or nasturtium blossoms.

Snow Peas Filled with Chèvre

1 pound large snow peas of uniform size (about 70), blanched 30 seconds and drained

1 cup crumbled chèvre (about 1/4 lb)

2 tablespoons whipping cream

2 tablespoons finely minced, well-drained oil-packed sun-dried tomatoes

1 teaspoon each minced parsley, basil, and oregano

Fresh lemon juice, salt, and freshly ground white pepper, to taste

Society garlic blossoms or edible flower blossoms, for garnish

Arranged attractively on a serving plate, these bright green appetizers are a treat to the eye as well as the palate. You will need a second pair of hands in the kitchen to hold the pea open while you pipe. The accolades of your guests will make up for the time and effort it took you to prepare them. Let guests pick up the pea pods with their fingers.

◆

Using tip of a sharp, thin-bladed knife, carefully slit open rounded seam of each snow pea, opening pod to within 1/4 inch of each end; set aside.

In a bowl stir together chèvre, cream, tomatoes, and herbs until well blended. Season with lemon juice, salt, and white pepper.

Spoon cheese mixture into pastry bag fitted with star tip. Pipe filling into each pod. Arrange filled pea pods on a round serving platter in spoke fashion. Garnish with flower blossoms.

MAKES ABOUT *70* HORS D'OEUVRES SERVINGS

Fusilli with Pea Tips and Pancetta

1 tablespoon olive oil

2 ounces pancetta, finely diced

2 large cloves garlic, minced

2 large ripe tomatoes, peeled, seeded, and coarsely chopped

Salt and freshly ground pepper, to taste

1 pound fusilli pasta

4 to 6 ounces pea tips

1/4 cup minced parsley

2 tablespoons snipped chives

Freshly grated Parmesan or Romano cheese

In Italy, names for the same pastas vary from region to region. In some cases, fusilli is a tight corkscrew shape and in others an elongated spiral shape. The latter is preferred for this elegant sauce of tomatoes, pancetta, and wispy pea tips.

If you do not want to sacrifice your future crop of peas and are willing to wait, substitute snow or snap peas for the pea tips and blanch them separately. Serve the pasta with sourdough bread to be dipped in garlic or herb olive oil and a salad of bitter greens.

✦

In a heavy skillet over medium heat, warm oil. Add *pancetta* and garlic and sauté, stirring often, 5 minutes. Stir in tomatoes, bring just to a boil, and season with salt and pepper. Lower heat and keep warm.

Bring a large pot filled with water to a boil. Add salt to taste and pasta. Boil until almost al dente (6 to 7 minutes, or according to package directions). Using a large fork, stir in pea tips. Bring back to a rolling boil and boil for 1 minute, stirring to distribute tips evenly in the pasta. Drain and immediately toss with reserved tomato mixture, parsley, and chives.

Transfer pasta to heated serving dish. Serve immediately and pass a bowl of Parmesan cheese.

SERVES 4 AS A MAIN COURSE OR 8 AS A FIRST COURSE

Sweet Pepper

Capsicum annum

Treat as an annual plant.

Grow from seed or potted seedlings.

Plant in fertile, well-tilled soil.

Needs full sun and plenty of heat to thrive.

Calcium such as oyster shell flour added to the soil helps the plants prosper.

Protect from late frosts with small cloches or other protective covers.

*S*weet peppers offer two seasons of ornamental value to any edible landscape. The majority of the plant's effect is the deep green foliage that stands out in layers almost like the limbs of a Japanese maple tree. The luxuriant color of the leaves provides a wonderful counterpoint to richly colored flowers. Pepper plants often grow to two or three feet. Annual bedding plants with this height, or slightly higher, make great ornamental companions.

Late summer brings the color of the fruit itself, from deep burgundy-purple to hot red to vibrant yellow-orange. All sweet peppers start out as green immature fruits. As the peppers grow older, green still predominates. Once the fruits reach their mature size, the slow progression of color begins. Left to linger on the plant, the fruits provide hints of unique color as each pepper hangs beneath a protective canopy of foliage.

Peppers originated in tropical climates. The most popular sweet pepper in the United States is the bell pepper (*C. annum*, Grossum group). All peppers prefer plenty of sun and heat to prosper and achieve fully colored fruits. Gravel mulches, aluminum foil, white stone walls, water-filled bottles sunk halfway into the ground, and a flagstone

159

*Complementary
Seasonings and Foods*

Oregano, thyme, basil; egg and
cheese dishes; garlic, onions,
eggplants, tomatoes, cabbage,
zucchini, artichokes, corn; fish,
poultry, pork, beef, lamb.

mulch have all been used to improve the light and heat gain in mild summer areas. Where gardeners are desperate, they can grow peppers in cloches, row tunnels, or greenhouses.

In mild winter areas and in greenhouses, astute and ambitious gardeners have been able to revert pepper plants back to their true perennial nature and harvest another crop in the second year. Usually it's difficult to grow the plants past the second season, but the experiment can impress your friends.

The longer they are on the plant, the sweeter peppers become, so harvest as you need them. Remove the ribs and seeds and either slice, dice, or cut into rings or julienne strips. Peppers can be steamed, sautéed, stir-fried, broiled, grilled, or baked.

Raw pepper strips are a refreshing addition to an assortment of crudités and julienne-cut peppers give color and crunch to salsas or to salads such as potato, black bean, or spinach. They can be marinated or made into a relish or jelly, and they add a distinct flavor to stews and casseroles. Pepper rings make attractive garnishes. Whole peppers filled with a variety of stuffings have long been a favorite main course. Chopped blanched peppers can be added to frittatas, quiches, or scrambled eggs.

To bring out their natural sweetness, lightly sauté peppers in olive oil, or roast them (directions follow) to use in tarts, salads, pasta sauces, or spreads.

To Roast Peppers:

Turning frequently, hold peppers over a gas flame (or place on a rack under a broiler) until blackened and blistered on all sides. Transfer peppers to a paper bag, close bag tightly, and let peppers steam 15 to 20 minutes. Working over a bowl to catch the juices, peel and seed peppers. Cut into strips, place in jars and cover with mixture of strained reserved juices, olive oil, minced garlic, chopped oregano, and salt. Cover and refrigerate up to 2 weeks.

Mini Recipes

Sauté bell pepper strips in butter and olive oil until they start to soften. Add Asian pear slices and cook until pears are tender. Sprinkle with shredded Fontina or Muenster cheese.

Thread bell pepper chunks on skewers alternately with turkey or pork link sausages. Brush with olive oil and grill or broil until browned.

Sweet Red and Green Pepper Relish

3 pounds each sweet red and green peppers, seeded, deribbed, and diced

2 1/2 pounds onions, diced

6 large cloves garlic, finely minced

Boiling water, to cover

2 cups cider vinegar

1 1/2 cups sugar

1 teaspoon mustard seed

1/2 tablespoon salt

2 teaspoons celery seed

The yield of this colorful sweet relish may vary, so have several extra sterilized jars and lids ready. Select bell peppers or any other thick-walled sweet peppers for making this relish. It is especially good with pork chops or roast chicken.

✦

Place peppers, onions, and garlic in large, nonreactive pot and pour in enough boiling water to cover completely. Let stand 5 minutes, drain, and again cover with boiling water. Let stand 10 minutes and drain.

Add all remaining ingredients, stir well, and bring to boil over high heat. Lower heat slightly and boil, stirring occasionally, 10 minutes.

Immediately ladle relish into hot, sterilized jars and seal and store as directed on page 17. Refrigerate unsealed jars no longer than 1 week.

MAKES ABOUT *16* HALF-PINTS

Asian Green Pepper Boats

2 dried shiitake mushrooms, soaked in warm water to cover 30 minutes to soften

1 firm white fish fillet (1/4 lb), ground or finely minced

1/4 pound ground lean pork

1/2 cup finely minced green onion, including tops

4 water chestnuts, finely minced

2 to 3 teaspoons soy sauce

4 teaspoons cornstarch

1 to 2 teaspoons dry sherry

1/4 teaspoon Asian sesame oil

1/4 teaspoon each salt and freshly ground white pepper

1 large bell pepper

1 tablespoon peanut or corn oil, or as needed

1/2 cup chicken stock

1 tablespoon water

Cilantro sprigs, for garnish

You will need to use bell peppers for this dish. When cut they form perfect boat shapes and their sturdy walls will hold up under heat. Serve with freshly steamed white rice and a salad of greens and blanched bean sprouts tossed with Hoisin Dressing (see page 19).

◆

Drain mushrooms and remove tough stems (save stems and soaking water for soup stock). Finely mince caps. In a mixing bowl combine mushrooms, fish, pork, onion, water chestnuts, soy sauce, 2 teaspoons of the cornstarch, sherry, sesame oil, salt, and white pepper. Mix well. Pinch off a small amount and sauté; taste and adjust seasonings. Refrigerate several hours to blend flavors.

Cut pepper lengthwise into eighths; remove ribs and seeds and cut each eighth in half crosswise to form a "boat." Use 1 teaspoon of the cornstarch to dust the insides of boats, then fill with 2 to 3 teaspoons of meat mixture. (At this point, filled boats may be covered and refrigerated up to 3 hours.)

Heat peanut oil in large heavy skillet over medium-high heat. When hot add filled pepper sections, meat side down, and fry until lightly browned (about 3 minutes). Carefully turn sections over, add stock, cover, and simmer until meat filling is cooked and peppers are tender but still crisp (about 12 minutes). Remove pepper boats to heated platter and keep warm.

Dissolve remaining 1 teaspoon cornstarch in water and add to juices in skillet. Cook and stir until slightly thickened (about 3 minutes). Pour over peppers and garnish platter with cilantro sprigs.

SERVES 2

Oriental Persimmon

Diospyros kaki

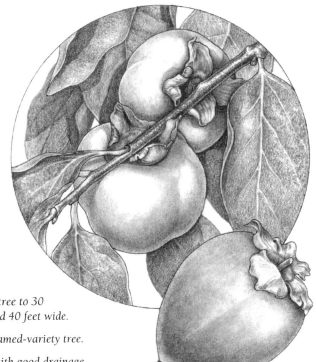

Deciduous perennial tree to 30 feet tall and 40 feet wide.

Plant a bareroot, named-variety tree.

Needs soil with good drainage and fertility.

Do not add any amendments to the planting hole and protect the roots from gophers by lining the hole with wire.

Can tolerate partial shade.

Will become drought resistant with age. Water regularly the first three to five years and then gradually withdraw irrigation.

Prune only for an attractive shape and for branches sturdy enough to hold the weight of the fruit.

An unripe persimmon is the standard by which all tragic and unfortunate culinary experiences are measured. Nobody who has been unlucky enough to taste a persimmon too early in the season forgets the teeth-curling, tongue-defiling ordeal. Unfortunately, such people rarely have the courage to sample the sweetly flavored, fully ripened fruit—regardless of the amount of coaxing.

The tree and the fruit deserve far more use in edible landscapes, however. The Oriental persimmon is not to be confused with the American persimmon. While both trees have an attractive form, well-defined branch pattern, and excellent fall color, the Oriental fruit is three to five times larger than the nickel- to quarter-sized fruit found on American persimmon trees. Oriental trees have large, glossy green leaves that are nearly heart shaped. The intense green of the summer foliage is uncommon on many deciduous fruit trees, and their smooth, gray young branches and attractively textured older bark are appreciated. The fall color makes this tree one of the exceptional examples of an ornamental edible. The leaves turn a translucent color that ranges from golden yellow to pure orange to rusty red. Often one tree will be a single glorious yellow, while another is a palette of vibrant oranges. Occasionally, the full range of color occurs together on the canopy of one tree. The fruits hang on long past leaf fall and look like ornaments on the deciduous limbs. Unharvested fruits will adorn the tree well into the winter, unless the birds take to the sweet treats.

Persimmon trees don't need another tree for pollination. Place a single specimen in a special place where a dark background will provide the canvas for the fall color display. Use an evergreen hedge or the deep green trees of a coniferous forest for the dark backdrop. Give the tree plenty of room so it will be a noticeable accent in the overall design. Most fruits will hang on until the birds finish them off. Because of the bird droppings, plant away from sidewalks, porches, and patios.

One particular advantage to the persimmon tree is its low maintenance. If planted in the right climate, the trees are self-reliant, long-lived, and seldom affected by pest and disease. The recommended range includes areas with moderately cold winters (-5° to -10°F).

There are two categories of Oriental persimmons. The astringent fruit types mentioned above include 'Hachiya' (the pointy-bottomed fruit that is the best-known Oriental persimmon), 'Tamopan', 'Chocolate', and 'Saijo'. The nonastringent fruits don't have to ripen to a mushy, soft texture to be sweet and flavorful; among them are 'Fuyu' (the most common of the nonastringent persimmons), 'Jiro', 'Izu', and 'Ichi Ki Kei Jiro'.

Contrary to popular opinion, astringent persimmons do not have to be subject to frost to ripen fully. In their natural state, astringent persimmons take so long in the season to ripen that frosts often glaze their bright orange skin before harvest. Fruits with two thirds or more of their orange coloration will ripen in a cool shelf, pointy end up, inside the home—away from the predatory birds that seem to love the fruit. Wait to eat the fruit until it has reached a full overall skin color and is nearly puddinglike throughout.

Nonastringent persimmons can be eaten when firm or mushy. The preferred form is a crisp, almost applelike texture. The fruit should be tree ripened when possible. If birds threaten the crop, try to hold the fruit until it has one half to two thirds of its natural orange coloration.

Then bring indoors to a cool shed, garage, or porch. When the skin is fully blushed with color, sample for sweetness and a complex flavor.

Leave the stems on fully ripe Hachiya persimmons and place stem side down on work surface. Cut a cross on the pointed end, peel back the skin, and slice or dice the flesh for use in fruit cups or salads. Cut the persimmon in half, scoop out the flesh with a spoon, and serve as a dessert. Freeze whole persimmons, let stand to soften slightly, and eat this sherbetlike fruit right out of the shell.

To prepare persimmon purée, wash, stem, peel if desired, and seed if necessary. Purée in a food processor fitted with a metal blade or in a blender. Use the purée for jam, jelly, puddings, cookies, cakes, quick breads, sorbets, and ice cream. Hachiya persimmon purée seasoned with fresh lemon juice and grated lemon zest is delicious mixed into softened vanilla ice cream or frozen yogurt.

Nonastringent persimmons, peeled if the skin appears tough, go well with most other fruits and make a refreshing addition to fruit cups and salads. A composed salad of sliced persimmons, kiwifruits, and watercress, or persimmon and avocado slices and grapefruit sections is especially good. Chopped persimmons combined in equal amounts with diced apples can be substituted for the rhubarb in Rhubarb Crisp (see page 178). Halved persimmons, poached with cloves, cinnamon, and ginger mint leaves (see page 24), then laced with brandy, make a refreshing dessert.

Persimmon Chiffon Pie

Walnut Pastry shell (see page 29) or Basic Pastry shell (see page 27), fully baked

2 tablespoons unflavored gelatin

1/2 cup water

1 1/2 cups Hachiya persimmon purée (see page 165)

2 tablespoons fresh lemon juice

1/4 cup plus 1/3 cup superfine sugar

1 tablespoon amaretto liqueur

1 teaspoon freshly grated orange zest

3 egg whites, at room temperature

1/8 teaspoon cream of tartar

Tiny pinch salt

1/2 cup whipping cream, whipped

Small nasturtium, viola, or other edible flower blossoms, for garnish

Shaved bittersweet chocolate, for garnish

This delicate pie deserves to be offered on a special occasion. The crust can be prepared the day before serving and the filling can be made and spooned into the crust the next morning.

✦

Prepare the pie shell and let cool completely.

In a small bowl sprinkle gelatin over water and let stand until softened (about 5 minutes). Place bowl in saucepan of simmering water until gelatin dissolves.

In a large mixing bowl, combine persimmon purée, lemon juice, the 1/4 cup sugar, and the amaretto. Stir gelatin into persimmon mixture, mixing well. Cover and refrigerate until persimmon mixture starts to thicken (about 45 minutes).

In a bowl combine egg whites, cream of tartar, and salt and beat until stiff peaks form (1 to 2 minutes). Then beat in 1/3 cup sugar, 1 tablespoon at a time; beat until smooth and glossy. Stir about one fourth of the beaten whites into persimmon mixture to lighten it, then gently fold in remaining whites, trying not to deflate mixture. Fold in whipped cream.

Spoon persimmon mixture into pie shell, mounding it attractively. Cover and refrigerate 3 hours or up to 8 hours.

Just before serving, decorate top of pie with flowers and chocolate.

Makes one 9-inch pie; serves 8 to 10

Fuyu Persimmon and Yams Baked with Sweet Cicely

1 pound yams, halved crosswise

2 to 3 teaspoons unsalted butter

Salt and freshly ground white pepper

1 large Fuyu persimmon (4 to 5 oz), stemmed and peeled

Sweet cicely feathers

3 tablespoons fresh orange juice

1 to 2 tablespoons dark brown sugar

2 tablespoons brandy

The deep orange of both the Fuyu persimmon and the yams contrasts beautifully with the green of the sweet cicely. This is a slimmed-down version of old-fashioned candied yams. Steaming the yams results in a firmer texture than baking them.

Serve with Ham Steak with Juniper Berries (see page 120), baked ham, or roast turkey and steamed Swiss chard.

◆

Arrange yams on steamer rack over boiling water, cover pot, and steam until just barely tender (about 15 minutes). Remove and set aside until cool enough to handle. Peel yams and cut into 1/2-inch-thick slices.

Preheat oven to 400° F. Using a little of the butter, grease a shallow baking dish large enough to hold yams in a single layer with slices overlapping. Arrange yam slices in dish and sprinkle lightly with salt and pepper.

Cut persimmon into slices 1/4 inch thick. Place persimmon slices so they are slightly off-center of yam slices. Tuck sweet cicely feathers in between yam and persimmon slices and pour orange juice evenly over top. Sprinkle with brown sugar and drizzle brandy over top. Dot with remaining butter.

Bake casserole until yams are bubbly and persimmons are just tender (about 20 minutes). Serve at once.

SERVES *4*

Potherbs

Treat as annual plants.

Grow from potted seedlings or plant divisions.

Plant in soil with good drainage and fertility.

Plant in small blocks so you can tell when to harvest and when to reseed.

Water consistently.

Watch for aphids and leaf caterpillars and control with Bacillus thuringiensis (see Crabapple).

Harvest foliage before seed heads begin to form.

Often times strong-flavored greens that are too foreign, spicy, or pungent for the cook's taste become, by default, potherbs—those leafy greens and stems that are boiled for eating. In many cultures what we call potherbs are esteemed dishes of savory, nutritious greens. What is known in the South as a "mess o' greens" is as important to a meal as a potato is to a steak or corn on the cob to a summer barbecue.

Not only are potherbs quick, easy, and convenient, but the boiling process can make the dish even more healthful. For example, amaranth leaves have a fairly high amount of oxalic acid (1 to 2 percent). Oxalic acid binds up minerals, particularly calcium, in the digestive system and can cause mineral deficiencies. The plant also absorbs nitrates, which are a potential carcinogen. Fortunately, both nitrates and oxalic acid are removed when the leaves are boiled and the water is drained away.

Almost any leafy green vegetable, herb, or wild edible that doesn't totally fall apart during boiling can be used as a potherb. Some examples follow.

Amaranth

Amaranthus sp.

This frost-tender annual grows in all zones with carefree abandon; indeed, it can become a pesty weed if left unchecked. Varieties selected for gardeners have foliage ranging from lush dark green to a rich burgundy-red. Left to bloom, some of the red-leaf forms (*A. hypochondriacus*) develop long, cascading catkinlike, hot red flower heads. All the ornamental varieties, such as 'Love-Lies-Bleeding', have dramatic flowers and foliage. Tasting much like spinach with a slightly sweet accent, the leaves of the cultivated ornamental varieties are edible if picked when very young.

Red Russian Kale

Brassica oleracea, Acephala Group

The fame of ornamental kales as truly tasty edible plants has spread along with the proliferation of edible landscapes. Now, Russian kale, actually an American heirloom variety, lends yet another colorful and flavor-packed addition to the garden. It comes in many colors—creamy white, bluish green, lime green, and hot burgundy-red. The most dramatic form is the 'Red Russian' variety, with large leaves up to two feet high that open out to recall a champagne flute. The leaves are wavy with a highly serrated edge. The foliage can be remarkably blue-green in warm weather. But the leaves' veins turn a dramatic red as temperatures drop and the color can spread to the leaf itself. As with any kale, cold weather, frost, and hard freezes only make the foliage taste sweeter.

Red Orach

Artriplex hortensis

Red orach is a more colorful form of a traditional German potherb. It is related to common spinach and is often called mountain spinach. Orach is usually seeded in the spring and fall, but tolerates far more summer warmth without bolting to seed than does spinach. Red orach's virtue is the vivid crimson color of its spinach-shaped leaves. This unsung plant, which bestows an amazing amount of drama to any garden, should be placed where the late afternoon sun can shine through the foliage like a sun-kissed baroque church window. The uncut foliage can reach up to three feet, and the seed stalks to an astounding nine feet.

Red Perilla

Perilla frutescens atropurpurea

Also known as shiso, this colorful annual deserves more widespread cultivation. What is referred to as either red or purple perilla has an ornately waved, coleuslike foliage with a deep purplish red hue. The compact plant grows to 18 inches and makes a useful accent of leafy embellishment in a vegetable bed or flower border. There are similar varieties with green leaves. Of the two colorations, the red-purple perilla is more pungent and spicier and lends a reddish color to the foods with which it is used. Both have a pleasant, cinnamonlike scent, and they can be used interchangeably in recipes. The red variety, however, makes the most attractive garnish. Raw shiso can be chopped and added to meat loaf mixtures, salads, broths, or stews, or the leaves can be steamed with other potherbs.

With the exception of kale, harvested potherb leaves will not store well for any length of time. Wash, spin dry in a salad spinner, wrap in a terry towel, and refrigerate no longer than one or two days. Kale leaves can be harvested from the base of the plant as they appear, or from the stalk, depending upon maturity, and will store a few days longer. Discard tough stems and midribs before using.

Using nonreactive utensils, steam coarsely chiffonade-cut or whole potherb leaves (except amaranth) on a steamer rack set over boiling water, or boil in lightly salted water until tender. Drain and season with butter, salt, freshly ground pepper, freshly grated nutmeg, and fresh lemon juice. Shred cooked potherbs and toss into risotto just before serving, or add to omelets, quiches, eggs to be scrambled, or mashed or twice-baked potatoes. For additional suggestions, see Swiss chard on page 210.

Kale and Potato Soup

8 cups chicken stock

1 large onion, chopped

1 1/2 pounds thick-skinned potatoes, peeled and sliced

4 cups water

1/4 teaspoon salt

1 pound kale, trimmed and cut into coarse chiffonade

1/2 pound linguiça or chorizo, thinly sliced

1/4 teaspoon freshly ground pepper

1/4 cup minced parsley

Those who love kale are undoubtedly familiar with caldo verde, *the traditional kale and potato soup of Portugal. Serve this version with* broa, *or corn bread, and fruit and cheese for dessert.*

✦

*I*n a large pot combine stock, onion, and potato and bring to a boil over high heat. Reduce the heat to medium-low, cover, and cook until potatoes are soft (about 15 minutes). Working in batches, purée in a food processor fitted with metal blade or in a blender. Return to pot and keep warm.

In a saucepan combine water and salt and bring to a boil over high heat. Add kale and cook until kale is tender (about 5 minutes). Drain and chop finely. Add kale and linguiça to soup and reheat to serving temperature. Season with pepper.

Ladle into heated bowls and sprinkle parsley over top.

SERVES 4 TO 6

Quince
Cydonia oblonga

Hardy perennial tree.

Plant bareroot tree.

Tolerates clay soil, gravel, and low fertility better than most fruit trees.

Water regularly the first 3 to 5 years; will become drought tolerant in later years.

Terminal bearer; makes fruit on ends of limbs on new year's growth.

Needs no pruning to make fruit, but cut out root sprouts to form a single trunk or a 3- to 5-multitrunk specimen.

Diseases and pests not much of a problem, but watch for tent caterpillars.

Quinces are often slandered as being solely a jam or jelly fruit. Their range in the kitchen is much greater than merely gelled condiments though, and their use in the landscape deserves more recognition. Quince trees are well-behaved, somewhat diminutive, reaching 25 feet, relatively pest and disease free, and attractive. The foliage presents a pale, lime green tone with leaves that recall those of an apple tree. Fall brings a delightful earthy yellow to the leaves and plenty of large, lime yellow fruits—like hefty, rotund ornaments—that birds generally avoid. The fruits form at the ends of the limbs and their weight helps to shape the branch into the quince tree's characteristic arching form.

In the spring, the flowers don't open until the tree begins to leaf out, thus escaping most late-season frosts. The pinkish white flowers adorn the tips of the branches as if they're gossamer butterflies. The tree prefers to throw up a thicket of trunks. With considerable pruning, it can be shaped to a single trunk, but the more attractive specimens boast multiple trunks. Selective pruning can leave behind the more gracefully curved and attractive trunks.

Because a mature tree is so prolific and the quince is self-fertilizing, most gardeners and cooks have no need for more than one

172

tree. Place this quince tree where the spring blossoms will be fully visible. A low ground cover—Corsican mint, woolly thyme, woolly yarrow—will allow for a full view of the sculpted trunk.

Pick quinces when still underripe and yellowish green. Arrange, not touching, on the kitchen counter or in a shallow box to ripen. The quinces are ready to eat when they turn an even yellow and emit a strong, pervasive, delightful fragrance.

Quinces should be used immediately upon ripening or the flesh will become mealy. Wash and rub off any fuzzy covering, then peel, halve, and remove the seed. This preparation is tedious and needs a strong hand, but becomes easier with patience and practice.

Quinces cannot be eaten raw. Chop quinces for chutneys, conserves, or marmalades. Slice quinces to combine with apples in a pie or include in a fruit compote of apples and pears. Because quinces have a relatively high acidity, they are a good foil for meats high in fat.

Quince Chutney

1 pound quinces

3 tart apples (approximately 3/4 lb)

2 cups firmly packed dark brown sugar

1 cup each cider vinegar and apple juice

1 cup each raisins and chopped onions

1 tablespoon each finely minced fresh ginger and mustard seed

1/2 to 1 tablespoon finely crushed, seeded dried red chile

1 cinnamon stick (3 in.), broken

For additional texture, add 1 cup chopped walnuts to the chutney the last 10 minutes of cooking. The yield will be slightly larger. Serve the chutney or conserve with roast game or meat.

◆

Peel, core, and dice quinces and apples to measure 2 cups each. In a large, nonreactive pot, combine fruits with all remaining ingredients.

Bring mixture to boil over medium-high heat, stirring to dissolve sugar. Lower heat, cover, and cook at a gentle boil until very thick (about 1 hour). Stir often to prevent sticking.

Immediately ladle into hot, sterilized jars and seal and store as directed on page XX. Refrigerate unsealed jars no longer than 2 weeks.

MAKES ABOUT 5 HALF-PINTS

Stuffed Chicken Breasts with Poached Quinces

Poaching Liquid (see page 24)

2 quinces (about 1 lb)

4 chicken breast halves, boned with skin intact (5 oz each)

1 tablespoon fresh lemon juice

3 fresh shiitake mushrooms (about 1 oz)

2 ounces chèvre, crumbled (1/2 cup)

1 teaspoon finely minced lemon thyme, thyme, oregano, or chives, plus extra, for garnish

1/4 teaspoon salt, plus salt for sprinkling

1/8 teaspoon freshly ground white pepper, plus white pepper for sprinkling

2 tablespoons olive oil

Purchase chicken breasts with skin intact so the cheese mixture can be stuffed under the skin. The quinces can be poached up to two days in advance.

✦

Prepare Poaching Liquid. Bring to a simmer over medium-high heat. Meanwhile, peel, quarter, and core quinces and cut each quarter lengthwise into 4 slices. Add quince slices to liquid, cover saucepan with a lid slightly smaller in circumference than saucepan to keep slices immersed in liquid, and boil gently until quinces are just tender (about 10 minutes). Using tongs, remove quince slices from syrup to shallow dish. Boil liquid 5 minutes and strain over poached quinces. (At this point quinces may be cooled, covered, and refrigerated up to 2 days.)

Rinse chicken breasts under cool running water, pat dry with paper towels, and put on a plate. Drizzle with lemon juice and set aside.

Cut tough stems from mushrooms and finely mince tender stems and caps. Place in a bowl along with cheese, finely minced lemon thyme, 1/4 teaspoon salt, and 1/8 teaspoon pepper. Stir well. Drain chicken breasts and pat dry with paper toweling. Carefully loosen skin from each breast, leaving one end attached, and stuff with cheese mixture. Replace skin snugly over stuffing, securing in place with toothpicks if necessary. Sprinkle skin side of each breast with salt and pepper.

In a large skillet over medium-high heat, warm oil. When very hot add breasts, skin side down, and sauté until golden brown (6 to 7 minutes). Sprinkle skinless sides with salt and pepper and turn breasts. Add poached quinces and half the reduced liquid, cover, and cook over medium-low heat until chicken is tender (10 to 15 minutes). Remove lid, raise heat, and cook until syrup has thickened slightly (about 3 minutes).

Transfer breasts to heated serving platter. Surround with quinces and syrup, and sprinkle minced lemon thyme over all.

Serves 4

Rhubarb

Rheum rhabarbarum

Perennial deciduous herb in most areas.

Grow from large, fleshy rhizomes that are sold bareroot in the early spring.

Requires lots of fertility, prefers an acid soil, and needs good drainage.

Plant in full sun where summers are cool; give afternoon shade in hot climates.

Fertilize with lots of manure each year.

Keep thickly mulched and consistently watered.

Don't harvest a crop for at least one year after planting.

Cut off flower stalk to favor leaf stalk formation the next year.

Stalks are edible; leaves and roots are poisonous.

*E*nglish gardeners know various strains of ornamental rhubarbs for their large, attractive, colorful leaves. Culinary rhubarb can also be used for decorative foliage. The enormous heart-shaped, crinkled leaves are umber-red mixed with dark green, and the veins are laced with the reddish tint found in the stalks. The ample-leaved characteristic of the plant suggests its use in a Victorian-style garden or in any fashion that features the drama of foliage. The flower stalk appears primitive—almost archetypical—as it unfolds. The open flower head has grapelike clusters of inconspicuous flowers. When focusing on harvesting edible leaf stalks, the prudent gardener cuts out the flower stalk before it gets too tall, to conserve the plant's nutrients for the roots and the subsequent stalks.

Rhubarbs are ravenous plants. Plant in the most fertile acidic soil, provide excellent drainage, and water thoroughly and often. Allow the foliage to blossom like a red-green parachute in the midst of a mixed flower border. Silver-gray foliage will highlight the rhubarb's unique green foliage. Examples include silver thyme, low forms of lavender, snow-in-summer, various prostrate artemisias, woolly thyme, and catmint. The rhubarb's foliage dies back to the ground each winter,

175

leaving a hole in your design. Place near evergreen herbaceous plants to hide the hole, or plant annual winter bedding plants where the rhubarb's foliage stood.

Botanically a vegetable, rhubarb is used mainly in the manner of a fruit, the first to appear in the spring. The stalks are edible, but the leaves and roots are poisonous. The length of harvest depends upon the age of the plant: young plants yield for four to five weeks and older plants a bit longer. Harvest crisp, firm stalks about 1/2 to 1 inch thick. Rather than cut the stalks with a knife, which leaves a stub that may decay, grasp the stalks near the base and pull from the plant with an upward and outward motion. Never remove all the stalks and stop harvesting when leaf stalks start to appear slender.

Remove and discard leaves, tips, and root ends from stalks; string them as you would celery if the stalks are very mature. Rhubarb wilts quickly at room temperature, so if not using immediately, refrigerate in a plastic bag no longer than three or four days. Wash well and slice into pieces 1/4 inch to 1/2 inch thick.

Diced rhubarb may be sheet-frozen; tightly packaged, it will keep up to six months. Rhubarb sauce may also be frozen up to six months. Defrost and treat as freshly made sauce.

When cooking rhubarb, always use a nonreactive pan. The ratio of sugar to fruit is high and depends upon how the rhubarb is prepared and with which other fruit it is combined. A good rule of thumb is 1/3 to 1/2 cup sugar to 1 cup sliced rhubarb. Combine rhubarb, sugar and a couple spoonfuls of water in a saucepan over medium heat and cook, stirring to dissolve sugar, until tender, adding more water if rhubarb begins to stick. Cooking time will depend upon size of pieces; 1/2-inch pieces will cook in 6 to 8 minutes. For stewed rhubarb you will want to add water as needed to achieve desired consistency. For rhubarb sauce, use only a small amount of water and cook until the mixture is the consistency of a thick purée.

To use rhubarb in jams, jellies and marmalades, sprinkle rhubarb with half as much sugar as rhubarb. Let stand eight hours or overnight at room temperature, then cook in a saucepan over medium-low heat or in a 300° F oven until tender; it is not necessary to add any water.

Rhubarb combines well with strawberries in a pie or tart or with

Complementary Seasonings and Foods

Cinnamon, cardamom, cloves, nutmeg, coriander; orange and lemon zest and juice; dates, pineapple, blueberries, raspberries, strawberries, oranges, quinces, pears, bananas.

pears for a sorbet. Rhubarb sauce is good on ice cream, meringues, or shortcakes or can be used to make rhubarb ice cream.

Rhubarb Quick Bread

2 cups diced rhubarb

2 eggs, at room temperature

1/2 cup canola oil

1 teaspoon freshly grated lemon zest

1 cup unbleached flour

1/2 cup plus 2 tablespoons sugar

1 teaspoon each double-acting baking powder, baking soda, and ground cinnamon

1/2 teaspoon salt

The quickest of quick breads, this moist loaf is especially good for afternoon tea with unsalted butter or cream cheese lightened with Yogurt Cheese (see page 22). Cool completely and wrap well in plastic wrap. Store at room temperature for up to two days, or freeze up to two weeks. Defrost in the refrigerator.

◆

Preheat oven to 350° F. Lightly butter or oil a 5- by 8-inch loaf pan and dust with flour; set aside.

In a processor fitted with metal blade, combine rhubarb, eggs, and oil; purée until rhubarb is finely chopped (about 30 seconds). Add lemon zest and set aside.

Into a large mixing bowl, sift together all remaining ingredients. Stir in rhubarb purée just until dry ingredients are moistened. Do not overmix. Spoon batter into prepared pan. Bake until bread pulls away from sides of pan and cake tester inserted into center of loaf comes out clean (40 to 45 minutes). Transfer to wire rack and cool in pan 10 minutes. Turn out onto wire rack, turn right side up, and let cool completely.

MAKES 1 LOAF

Rhubarb Crisp

Topping:

1/2 cup each unbleached or whole-wheat flour and unprocessed rolled oats

1/3 cup firmly packed dark brown sugar

1 teaspoon ground cardamom or 1/2 teaspoon ground coriander

1/4 teaspoon freshly grated nutmeg

Dash salt

1/4 cup unsalted butter, cut into bits

Filling:

3 cups diced rhubarb

1/3 cup sugar

1 tablespoon fresh lemon juice

1 tablespoon cornstarch

1 teaspoon freshly grated orange zest

Dash salt

Fruit crisps are extra tantalizing served warm with vanilla ice cream or frozen yogurt. Vary this version by substituting blueberries or chopped Asian pears for half the rhubarb. The crisp may be baked in individual ramekins, in which case shorten the baking time by 5 to 10 minutes.

✦

Preheat oven to 375° F. Lightly butter an 8-inch deep-dish pie plate; set aside.

To prepare topping, in a bowl combine and toss together all topping ingredients except butter. With fingers, work bits of butter into flour mixture until mixture is consistency of coarse crumbs; set aside.

Combine all ingredients for filling and spoon into prepared pie plate. Sprinkle topping over surface to cover thickly. Bake until topping is crisp and fruit is bubbly (about 25 minutes). Cool briefly on wire rack before serving.

SERVES 6

'Romanesco'

Brassica olerscea, Botrytis Group

Treat as an annual.

Grow from seed. Search out 'Romanesco'-named seed.

In cold winter areas, sow in early spring in a cold frame; in mild winter areas, seed mid-summer. Transplant when three to four inches tall.

Requires fertile, well-tilled soil with regular watering and occasional feeding.

Dip the roots of the transplants in a solution of beneficial nematodes to thwart the cabbage root maggot.

Stake if the plants become very large.

Watch for cabbage butterfly caterpillars; pick off caterpillars or control with Bacillus thuringiensis (See Crabapple).

If the *Star Wars* crew were to design a vegetable, 'Romanesco', sometimes called 'Green Point', would be it. 'Romanesco' is, perhaps, the most lovely colored and sculptural vegetable any gardener can grow. The pointy, spiraled head is a fascinating chartreuse—a clear, never muddy tint. The large heads, up to 18 inches wide and a foot tall, are composed of many spiral florets, each a reflection of the cone shape of the overall head. Both the spiral pattern within each floret and the spiral arrangement of the florets themselves have the same curves as a nautilus shell or the pattern of the seeds in a sunflower head.

'Romanesco' also has a special flavor. Even though the plant is not really a broccoli or a cauliflower, and tastes like neither, the seed is usually found under the broccoli section of seed catalogs. People who dislike cauliflower and broccoli, however, find the delicate texture and mild, complex taste of 'Romanesco' pleasing.

This "new" vegetable is actually an heirloom variety with a long tradition in Italy. It has only recently been rediscovered by the culinary

179

vanguard on this side of the Atlantic. Accept no substitutes. One commercial grower in California sells 'Broccoflower', a roundish, cauliflower-shaped head with lumpy florets that is a far cry from the sculptural and culinary glory of a true 'Romanesco'.

The foliage of 'Romanesco' resembles the ordinary blue-green, massive foliage of a broccoli plant. A typical plant grows four to five feet wide and requires plenty of space and copious quantities of water and fertility. Its enormous size means it is often planted in a bed reserved solely for it. Annual bedding plants with hot, vivid colors can be planted between the seedlings for color accents. Examples include cosmoses, zinnias, godetias, clarkias, flowering tobacco (*Nicotiana* sp.), and scarlet flax.

In warm winter climates the largest heads develop on summer-seeded and summer-planted transplants. While the times will vary with each climate, typically the seeds are started as early as mid-July through mid-August and seedlings are set out in the garden from early September through early October. This allows the roots to feed the foliage during the declining light of fall, which prevents premature flowering prior to a head being formed. Then, in mid-winter through early spring, the accumulated mass of foliage drains its nutrition into the forming head for the largest, most enchanting harvest.

The delicate nature of the 'Romanesco' head is much more agreeable as a crudité than many other raw vegetables. This refined vegetable also requires only a fraction of the time a cauliflower demands to be properly steamed. The time, of course, depends upon the size and how long the vegetable has been refrigerated. Straight from the garden, two or three minutes will often be sufficient. Dress steamed 'Romanesco' in any way in which you would broccoli or cauliflower. Browned butter, crumbled Gorgonzola or feta cheese, and buttered bread crumbs mixed with finely minced garlic and parsley are just a few suggestions.

Lightly steamed florets and/or diced tender stems can be added to green salads or to scrambled eggs or omelets. The 'Romanesco' that has not been consumed in one meal can be returned to the steamer and steamed until very soft, then puréed and mixed with an equal amount of mashed potatoes, or used to make cream soup.

'Romanesco' and Gravlax Quiche

Basic Pastry (see page 27)

1 small egg beaten with 2 tablespoons water

1/3 cup freshly grated Parmesan cheese

1 1/2 tablespoons unsalted butter

1/2 cup finely minced shallot

1/4 cup finely minced celery

1 cup flaked Gravlax (see page 84) or minced smoked salmon

1/2 teaspoon freshly grated lemon zest

2 tablespoons each minced parsley and chives

1 cup finely shredded Gruyère cheese

2 cups lightly steamed tiny 'Romanesco' florets

3 eggs

1 1/2 cups half-and-half

1/4 teaspoon each ground dried oregano, salt, and freshly ground white pepper

1/8 teaspoon cayenne pepper

Paprika, for dusting

Halved cherry tomatoes and watercress sprigs, for garnish

A perfect way in which to use leftover gravlax. Lightly steam the 'Romanesco', plunge it into iced water, and drain well. Cut off only the tiny florets. Suggestions for treating the remaining 'Romanesco' head appear in the introduction.

◆

Prepare Basic Pastry as directed, then roll out chilled pastry into a round 1/8 inch thick. Fit into 10-inch quiche pan with removable bottom. Continuing to follow instructions, partially bake, then cool completely on wire rack. Brush pastry shell with egg-water mixture and set aside until coating dries. Sprinkle shell evenly with Parmesan cheese and refrigerate while proceeding with recipe.

In a nonstick skillet over medium heat, melt butter. Add shallot and celery, cover, and cook until onion is soft (about 5 minutes). Let cool completely.

Preheat oven to 375° F. In a bowl gently toss together salmon, lemon zest, parsley, chives, and 1/2 cup of the Gruyère cheese. Using a fork stir salmon mixture into sautéed shallot mixture. Spoon into prepared pastry shell and arrange 'Romanesco' florets evenly on top.

In a mixing bowl beat eggs lightly with cream, oregano, salt, and white and cayenne peppers. Pour egg mixture through fine-mesh sieve into filled pastry shell. Sprinkle surface evenly with remaining 1/2 cup Gruyère cheese. Dust top with paprika.

Bake until cake tester inserted in center comes out clean (25 to 30 minutes). Remove quiche to wire rack and let cool at least 10 minutes, or up to 15 minutes.

To serve, remove quiche from pan by pushing pan bottom up through rim. Transfer quiche to flat serving plate and garnish with cherry tomato halves and watercress sprigs.

Serves 6 to 8

Rosemary

Rosmarinus officinalis

Somewhat hardy perennial herb; grown outdoors where winter temperatures are above 15° F.

Grow from cuttings to maintain trueness to name.

Grows best in a mineral soil without much fertility or organic matter.

Good drainage around the upper root zone is essential to a healthy plant.

Prefers full sun, but tolerates up to two-thirds shade.

Can be pruned to any shape.

Anyone who ambles off the path in almost any Mediterranean country will stumble across rosemary and come back smelling like an Italian salad dressing. Fortunately—and unlike other Mediterranean plants—rosemary can be grown in most of the United States. While the plant is often rated for all zones, prudent gardeners in zones with temperatures below 15° F bring the plant indoors for the winter.

There are dozens of named varieties, including 'Ken Taylor', 'Collingwood Ingram', 'Tuscan Blue', 'Majorca Pink', 'Blue Boy', 'Arp' (perhaps the most cold hardy, down to -10° F), 'Joyce deBaggio', and 'Golden Prostrate'. There is a rosemary to suit virtually any design need. The flowers range from pure white to various shades of pink that border upon lavender, plus there is an entire spectrum of traditional blue, from wispy, pale speckled blue to a sturdy cobalt. The most upright forms, traditionally the best-flavored varieties, tower to six feet, while the most prostrate stay below 18 inches. The branching form includes rigidly upright stalks, branches that gracefully arch out like plaintive upheld arms, rambling limbs that flop up and down as if a serpent, and boughs that smoothly cascade over retaining walls or from containers.

The nomenclature for rosemary varieties is confusing. Plants on the East Coast have names gardeners in the West have never seen in a

182

*Complementary
Seasonings and Foods*

Sage, thyme, marjoram,
lavender; egg dishes; stuffings;
citrus and other fruits; garlic,
onions, cauliflower, lima beans,
dried and shell beans,
mushrooms, potatoes, Swiss
chard, spinach, squashes,
tomatoes; rabbit, seafood,
poultry, lamb, beef, veal, pork;
Cabernet Sauvignon, Zinfandel,
Pinot Noir.

nursery, and vice versa. The solution is to talk to your local nursery, plant a few varieties, and get to know how they perform in your climate and soil.

Rosemary demands superior drainage. The plant is prone to root rot from too much water or heavy clay soils. Always plant rosemary with the crown of the root system, the upper six or more inches, in a planting mound above the level of the surrounding soil. This planting mound can have sand or round gravel added to ensure proper and rapid drainage.

Well adapted to container culture, rosemary can be grown in pots, window boxes, tubs, and terra-cotta and wooden troughs. Use a potting soil with plenty of sand, vermiculite, or perlite to ensure good drainage. Container-grown rosemary can be grown on a sunny, south-facing kitchen window for easy harvest and a pungent, sweet aroma.

This is a plant that can stand on its own merits, yet blends successfully with a number of other herbs. The intense, pungent, sometimes overpowering flavor is considered by some an acquired taste, so use rosemary with caution. Both leaves and flowers are edible; chop or pulverize to release their oil. Young tips are best for cooking and will keep up to four days if refrigerated in a plastic bag.

Rosemary stands up well to long cooking and has the quality to adapt to either sweet or savory dishes; in the latter, its companion, garlic, is almost a must. Use sprigs in marinades, stews, and fricassees, prepare infused vinegar, oil, stock, or honey, or make compound butter (see pages 13 to 16). Stuff sprigs into the cavity of a chicken for roasting or add to water when boiling or steaming potatoes or clams. Tuck needles, along with garlic slivers, into incisions cut into a leg of lamb before roasting. Finely chopped needles enhance the flavor of fruits, cakes, jams, and breads.

Harvest more mature needles for drying. Because of their high oil content, they will retain flavor for at least a year; before using, soak them in hot water 5 or 10 minutes. Dried needles can be ground and stored in an airtight container up to two months. The needles can also be frozen in airtight containers up to a year. If you have large rosemary plants that need trimming, cut branches to place over coals when barbecuing and enjoy the resulting fragrance.

Use the attractive pale blue flower blossoms on their stems as a garnish and the individual tiny flowers to add flavor and color to cream soups or pastas. Infuse oil, vinegar, or honey with blossoms (see page 13 to 16), or place in the bottoms of jars before pouring in hot apple jelly.

Mini Recipes

Sauté finely minced rosemary needles in butter, sprinkle with flour, and stir in a little stock. Season with fresh lemon juice and anchovy paste and serve on steamed fish.

Toss minced rosemary needles and crumbled feta or goat cheese into freshly steamed diced new potatoes.

Strew minced rosemary needles and crumbled Gorgonzola cheese over freshly steamed whole cauliflower.

Sprinkle chopped rosemary needles and/or flowers over pear or persimmon gratinée, or add to fruit sorbets.

Rosemary, Prosciutto, and Asian Pear Pizza

Pizza Dough (see page 26)

Olive oil, for brushing pans and crust

2 or 3 Asian pears, peeled, cored, and very thinly sliced

6 to 7 ounces prosciutto, trimmed of fat

5 ounces mozzarella cheese, shredded

3 to 4 ounces chèvre, crumbled

2 tablespoons snipped rosemary needles

The combination of pear and prosciutto with a hint of rosemary is the inspiration of Gino Lamotta's kitchen at Salute, a favorite Marin County, California, restaurant. Here is an adaptation of that delicious pie.

Purchase lean prosciutto and ask the butcher to slice it about 1/16 inch thick. Serve the pizza as a first course, or as a luncheon or supper dish with Ensalada de Flores (see page 111) and biscotti for dessert.

Prepare pizza dough and set aside to rise. Brush two 12-inch pizza pans with olive oil and set aside. Position oven rack in lower one third of oven and preheat oven to 425° F.

When dough has doubled in bulk, punch down, turn out onto work surface, and knead briefly. Divide in half and form each half into a ball; cover with tea towel and let rest 10 to 15 minutes. Ready remaining ingredients.

Roll and pat dough into two 12-inch circles, and transfer to prepared pans. Pat dough to reach edge of pans and brush lightly with olive oil. Bake until lightly golden (9 to 10 minutes). Remove from oven and prick with fork to deflate any bubbles.

Arrange pear slices in a concentric pattern on dough and cover with prosciutto. Top with mozzarella cheese and then chèvre. Evenly distribute rosemary over top.

Return to oven and bake until golden brown and cheeses have melted (about 15 minutes). Using kitchen shears, cut into wedges and serve immediately.

MAKES TWO 12-INCH PIZZAS

185

Rosemary Bundt Cake

1 cup unsalted butter, at room temperature

2 2/3 cups sifted unbleached flour

1/2 teaspoon each rose water and pure vanilla extract

1 tablespoon finely snipped or chopped rosemary

1 teaspoon freshly grated orange zest

8 egg whites, at room temperature

1/4 teaspoon each salt and cream of tartar

1 2/3 cups rosemary-flavored granulated sugar (see page 16)

Rosemary-flavored confectioners' sugar, for dusting

Candied rosemary flowers (see page 16)

This elegant cake is best made a day before slicing and serving. If you have no rosemary-flavored sugar on hand, increase the measurement of snipped rosemary to 1 1/2 tablespoons. The cake will keep one or two weeks if wrapped in plastic wrap and aluminum foil and refrigerated. It can be frozen up to three months; thaw in the refrigerator.

✦

Preheat oven to 350° F. Butter a 10-inch bundt pan and dust with flour; set aside.

In a large mixing bowl, using a wooden spoon or an electric mixer set on medium speed, beat butter until creamy. Gradually add 1 1/3 cups of the flour, beating until mixture is smooth and fluffy (about 5 minutes). Stir in rose water, vanilla, snipped rosemary, and orange zest. Set aside.

In a bowl combine egg whites, salt, and cream of tartar and beat to soft peak stage. Beating constantly, add the granulated sugar, 1 tablespoon at a time. Continue beating until smooth and glossy (about 3 minutes).

Stir one fourth of the egg whites into butter mixture to lighten it. Then fold in remaining egg whites. At the same time sift remaining 1 1/3 cups flour over batter, a little at a time, and gently fold in to incorporate. Do not overmix.

Pour batter into prepared pan and bake until cake pulls away from pan sides and cake tester inserted in center comes out clean (about 50 minutes). The cake should be a light golden brown.

Remove cake to wire rack and let cool 15 to 20 minutes. Turn out onto rack, turn right side up, and let cool completely. Wrap in plastic wrap and let stand 24 hours before slicing.

Just before serving sieve confectioners' sugar over the cake and garnish with rosemary flowers.

MAKES 1 BUNDT CAKE; SERVES 12 TO 14

Sage

(Salvia officinalis)
Clary Sage (S. sclarea)
Golden Sage (S. officinalis
icterina); Pineapple Sage
(S. gracilistyia, S. rutilans)
Mexican Sage (S. leucantha)

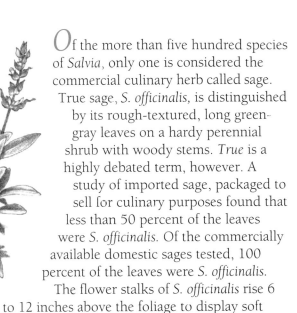

Hardy perennial herb, to -30° F.

Grow from container plants.

Provide good drainage. Fertility is not as important as a sandy, rocky, or gravelly soil.

Prefers full sun and good air circulation.

Compact growth to 18 to 24 inches tall and slightly wider.

Avoid overhead sprinklers; use drip irrigation, but keep the emitters at least 6 to 12 inches away from the base of the plant.

In cold climates, cover with a windbreak to protect from severe winds.

Of the more than five hundred species of *Salvia,* only one is considered the commercial culinary herb called sage. True sage, *S. officinalis,* is distinguished by its rough-textured, long green-gray leaves on a hardy perennial shrub with woody stems. *True* is a highly debated term, however. A study of imported sage, packaged to sell for culinary purposes found that less than 50 percent of the leaves were *S. officinalis.* Of the commercially available domestic sages tested, 100 percent of the leaves were *S. officinalis.* The flower stalks of *S. officinalis* rise 6 to 12 inches above the foliage to display soft violet-blue flowers. The flowers offer a delightful pastel haze floating above the foliage. Because of the moody flower color and the soft sagebrushlike foliage, sages are perhaps best grouped in masses or with other herbs of similar tone: woolly or silver thyme, lavenders, low species of *Artemisia,* catnip, dittany of Crete, or horehound. If you want to use a green-foliaged companion, choose a rich, deeply colored one such as mother-of-thyme, rosemary, salad burnet, or anise hyssop. The ornamental sages with more dramatic blooms are usually much more tender than *S. officinalis,* bushier, often

187

taller, more herbaceous, and less woody.

There are several attractive cultivars of common sage: a deep, smoky purple-leaved form called *S. officinalis* 'Purpurascens' or 'Purpurea', a variegated form with pale lime green, chartreuse, and typical dark sage markings called *S. officinalis* 'Aurea' or 'Golden Sage', and another variegated form with a mixture of the normal sage green, creamy white, and purple called *S. officinalis* 'Tricolor'. All of these offer distinctively colored foliage for accent in an herb or flower border. But upon close examination with a comparison tasting, most gardeners find the foliage of these colorful forms is either more resinous tasting, slightly more acrid, or less authentic than regular common sage. Yet, in certain recipes, especially herbal breads or wild game meats, a wide range of sage leaves, both European and native, can be added for a more varied and complex flavor.

Common sage can adapt to −10° F if covered with a protective bower of evergreen limbs or straw. (Many other species of *Salvia* will expire just below the freezing mark and are either treated as annuals or relegated to temperate winter climates.) It demands well-drained soil, preferably a rocky, gravelly soil rather than a loamy one. Too much compost will hold onto moisture that can cause the sage's roots to rot. According to some authorities, gravelly soil may also actually enhance the volatile oil content, and therefore the flavor, of the foliage. In humid climates, sandy soil at the base of the plant and judicious pruning to a more spacious habit will enhance air circulation and soil drainage and help the plant prosper.

The strong aroma and somewhat bitter, astringent taste of sage are easily released and can overwhelm the foods in which the herb is used. The leaves can be harvested at will, but are most flavorful just before the flowers open. Gather the leaves from the young shoots near the top of the plant and use fresh, or dry or freeze for later use.

Whole or chopped sage leaves can be used fresh in marinades and salads, or can be cooked in foods such as crêpes, omelets, and sausages. The large leaf of clary sage (*S. sclarea*) is a natural for dipping in batter and deep-frying, or as a wrapping for chicken breasts, small game birds, or Cornish hens to be roasted. Pineapple sage (*S. gracilistyia, S. rutilans*)

Complementary Seasonings and Foods

Savory, thyme, parsley; egg and cheese dishes; artichokes, green beans, onions, tomatoes, squashes, corn, cabbage, lentils; oranges; poultry, pork, game and game birds, sausage mixtures; Chardonnay, Fumé Blanc, Pinot Noir.

adds interest and tang to fruit desserts, jams, and jellies.

The bright red flowers of pineapple sage and the woolly lavender-purple blossoms of Mexican sage, which feel like pussy willows, add dynamic color to salads and desserts. Harvest them when they are in full bloom. Infuse vinegar, oil, or honey with sage flowers and/or leaves, or prepare compound butter (see pages 13 to 15). Add chopped sage leaves to the skillet when cooking fish or calves' liver, or add chopped leaves and flowers to grits just before serving. Stuff chopped sage leaves and minced garlic under the skin of chicken before roasting.

When dried or frozen, sage leaves retain their aroma better than most herbs. Whole dried sage leaves can be stored up to six months; use leaves whole, or crumble or grind. Add crumbled dried leaves to bread crumb coatings or to batter breads. Rub pork roast with ground sage before roasting. Frozen leaves will remain fragrant up to nine months and can be used in marinades, steamed dishes, and stews and other long-cooking dishes.

Mini Recipes

Marinate goat cheese in olive oil and chopped sage leaves; serve on toast rounds with a thin sliver of drained oil-packed sun-dried tomatoes.

Add chopped sage leaves sautéed with snipped chives and minced Canadian bacon to a filling for an omelet; garnish with a tiny sage sprig or blossom.

Steep fresh pineapple slices in port wine and chopped sage; broil until heated through and lightly browned.

Sauté chiffonade-cut clary or large leaves of other sages in butter or olive oil until crisp; use as a garnish for dishes in which sage is used as a seasoning.

Dip clary or other sage leaves in Fritter Batter (see page 23) and deep-fry; serve as an accompaniment to roast pork.

Rolled Flank Steak Stuffed with Herbs and Veal

Stuffing:

1 egg

1 large clove garlic,
finely minced

2 tablespoons each finely
minced sage and parsley

2 teaspoons finely minced
lemon basil

1 teaspoon finely snipped
rosemary needles

1/2 teaspoon salt

1/4 teaspoon freshly ground
white pepper

1/2 pound ground veal

2 cups plain croutons

1 flank steak (about 1 1/2 lb)

2 tablespoons dry vermouth
mixed with 1 tablespoon
olive oil

1 cup beef stock

2 teaspoons cornstarch
dissolved in 2 tablespoons water

Sage sprigs, for garnish

Combining sage, parsley, basil, and rosemary results in an unusual com-bination of flavors. Serve these spirals with Polenta with Sweet Pepper and Savory (see page 202) and Mixed Green Salad with Blossoms (see page 199).

◆

To prepare stuffing, in a mixing bowl beat egg lightly. Mix in garlic and all herbs and seasonings. Using your hands gently knead in veal, mixing thoroughly. Sauté a small amount, taste, and adjust seasonings. Using a fork toss in croutons; set aside.

Preheat oven to 350° F. Trim fat from flank steak and pound with meat mallet to even thickness of 3/8 inch. Spread stuffing evenly on steak, leaving 1-inch border on all sides. Starting at one long edge, carefully roll up steak like a jelly roll. Tie in 6 or 8 places with kitchen twine. (At this point, roll may be covered with plastic wrap and refrigerated up to 3 hours. Preheat oven and let roll come to room temperature before proceeding.)

Place beef roll in roasting pan. Roast, basting several times with vermouth-oil mixture until tender when pierced with a fork (about 45 minutes). Do not overcook or the meat will dry out and toughen. Transfer roll to heated plate, cover loosely with aluminum foil, and let rest 10 minutes.

Meanwhile, place roasting pan with juices over medium-high heat. Add stock, deglaze pan by loosening any browned bits, and bring to a boil. Remove from heat, blend in cornstarch mixture, and return to heat. Boil gently, stirring almost constantly, until sauce thickens; keep warm.

Remove twine from beef roll and, using a sharp knife, cut roll crosswise into 8 to 12 slices. Arrange slices in concentric pattern on round heated platter. Pour warm sauce over and fill center with sage sprigs. Serve at once.

SERVES 4

Salad Greens

Frost-tender and frost-hardy annuals; grow in any climate, according to the season.

Grow from seeds in the garden or from transplants.

Prepare well-drained soil with plenty of fertility and a fine seed bed.

Water regularly and occasionally side dress with fertilizer, or foliar feed with fish emulsion or seaweed powder solutions.

Protect from birds, snails, slugs, earwigs, and other pests.

Reseed on a regular basis for an extended, successional harvest.

Plants usually get too bitter to eat after the flower head forms.

Salad greens can be divided into two basic groups, the lettuces and the chicories. The lettuces, in turn, fall into three major categories: erect, relatively tight heads, such as romaine; cabbageheads, which are round and made up of crispheads and butterheads; and the looseleaf varieties, such as oakleaf and mâche. All of them can be decorative, making them ideal for tucking in among flowers and herbs in the garden. The most attractive lettuces, however, are the various butterhead types, including Batavian crispy lettuces, Bibb or Boston, and limestone.

The ornamental chicories are robust plants with a pleasantly bitter tang. They include the coarse-textured chicory, also known as curly endive; frisée, a variety of curly endive with finely cut, spindly leaves; loose-headed escarole, which looks like an oversized butter lettuce; and the richly veined, semiheading radicchio, which ranges in color from light red to a deep maroon.

Four additional decorative salad greens that fit into neither of these basic groups are mizuna, a popular Japanese green with deeply notched leaves on a long, slender, white stem; arugula (sometimes called rocket or roquette), a peppery green with tiny edible flowers; leafy giant red mustard, another Japanese green that imparts a subtle

191

mustard flavor to a salad bowl; and ornamental kale, also known as salad savoy and formerly planted only as a striking ornamental, which has become a popular addition to the salad bowl.

Although it is touted that greens should never be washed until just before using, it is more convenient and sometimes better if the greens are washed a number of hours, or a day ahead, spun dry in a salad spinner, wrapped in a terry towel, and stored in a loosely closed plastic bag in the crisper of the refrigerator. Dressings will not cling to damp leaves and thus be diluted. This method ensures dry leaves and longer storage. Soft lettuces and greens such as oakleaf lettuce and garden cress will remain crisp for up to two days; sturdier greens such as radicchio will store well for up to one week.

When composing a salad, use your imagination and what you have on hand. Keep in mind complementary flavors, colors, texture, shape, and eye appeal.

Mesclun salad mix is a refreshing approach to salad making born in the south of France. In its present evolution as an American culinary product, mesclun is a delightful blend of tender young salad greens, the succulent shoots of immature edible wild plants, the small tips of various herbs, and a sprinkling of edible flowers.

According to Alice Waters, the renowned owner of Chez Panisse, who first sampled mesclun salads in the Nice area some 20 years ago, the origin of mesclun was thrifty market gardeners who harvested their seedling thinnings, gathered them into a tablecloth, and sold the premixed blend of young lettuces and greens at the local market. While there are probably a thousand definitions of mesclun, Waters is quite adamant that "of all the many blends of greens, the dominant theme was, and is, the inclusion of arugula and chervil. Without these two ingredients I wouldn't call it mesclun."

Arugula

Eruca vesicaria

What a mere 15 years ago was an obscure, strange-tasting leafy vegetable consumed in America only by gardeners with an interest in Italian and French greens is now a "required" ingredient in mesclun.

This salad green defies a definitive description. Usually it is referred to as having a peppery, nutty, spicy flavor that adds a brilliant, tangy highlight to any salad.

Arugula grows like a weed; it is fast to sprout, quick to bloom in warm weather, and prolific in the number of seeds it will make if left alone. This is a temperate-weather plant that thrives throughout the winter in mild winter climates or early spring and late fall elsewhere. Successive plantings are required to keep a steady supply. If left to bloom, the flowers are just as flavorful—if not spicier—as the foliage. Allow a few flower heads, which resemble a vivid yellow radish blossom, to mature seed. With the next mild season you will find a stand of sprightly arugula. Allow some seedlings to grow amidst other vegetables for a wilder, more informal look in vegetable beds.

Frisée

Chicory endivia

Frisée is a showy, green-leaved chicory that is a close relative to curly endive. The plant produces a frothy mound of foliage that is so exquisitely articulated the passerby can't help but stop and notice. Plant in long sweeping swards or drifts for a truly stunning effect. Or plant a single specimen against a rich brown mulch for a highlight.

Cultivation of frisée is very similar to radicchio, which follows, except timing for coloration is not a consideration.

Ornamental Kale

Brassica oleracea, Acephala Group

For the gourmet gardener, ornamental kale is far from being *just* decorative. This dramatic plant, with swirls of vibrant pinks, creamy whites, hot rose, bluish green, and boastful ruby reds, is just as sweet when brushed with a fall frost or winter freeze as any other kale.

Due to their heroic color presentation, ornamental kales deserve a special spot in the landscape. Place a small grouping near the front door, by the mailbox, or along the main walkway to the house. Mound up the soil to bring this visual drama closer to the viewer. If planted too late in the spring, kales quickly go to flower, which ruins the painterly look of the colorful whirl. In many climates, these kales thrive with fall transplanting and keep their attractive form for many months. Where it's too cold to grow kale through the winter, the earliest spring plantings provide the longest period of prebloom display.

The frilly leaves of ornamental kale are sturdy and store well. They impart a refreshing crunchiness to any salad, or can stand alone as the primary green in turkey, chicken, or shrimp salads. Harvest single leaves from the outside of the kale, or take up the entire plant. Use the tender inner leaves raw mixed with other greens. Wilt the larger leaves with a hot dressing to soften them slightly. If overcooked, the leaves will lose their color.

Soft Lettuces

Lactuca sativa

*T*hese are open-leaved lettuces—sometimes called looseleaf lettuces—that do not form tight heads nor the even looser head of a classic butter lettuce. There are hundreds of wonderful lettuces from which to choose. What follows is a mere nibble of the amazing selection of modern and heirloom varieties available to the lettuce lover.

'Lolla Rossa': A delightfully colorful lettuce from Italy. The heart of the head is a clear, cool green. But the leaves gradually change tone until the outer curly portions are an intense crimson hue. The heads are rather dense, but ruffled in a swirl of frilly, crinkly foliage.

'Marvel of Four Seasons': This French selection is noted for its unique color. Again, the ruby outer portion graduates to a rich green throat. Its name belies the ability of this lettuce to withstand the heat of summer.

'Red Oakleaf': All oakleaf lettuces add a unique foliage to the garden. The name accurately describes the multilobed leaf, resembling a white oak tree's foliage. This variety has the striking advantage of a range of reddish colors, from pastel burgundy to rich cranberry to bright crimson, depending upon the season. Oakleaf lettuces are more heat tolerant than many other lettuces, help extend the season for succulent salads well into summer, and grow fine in mild seasons.

Mizuna

Brassica rapa var. nipposinica

*T*his little-known green deserves much more visibility in both seed catalogs and gardens. The glossy dark green leaves form a magnificent rosette of finely cut foliage. The 18-inch-wide rosette is composed of gracefully arching leaves that sprout forth like an airy, green, bubbling fountain. Place individual plants far enough apart so they don't touch, with a healthy amount of dark mulch below, so as to present each specimen like a sculpture in a gallery.

Mizuna is a fairly hardy plant, tolerating down to 3° F in protected places. Unlike some salad greens, it is adaptable to a wet area and shade. This is a bolt-resistant plant. Therefore, early spring sowings will not form seed heads in late spring as readily as most Asian greens. Late summer or early fall seedings in mild winter areas will provide an ornamental and edible addition for many months until late spring brings forth the flower stalk. Watch for slug and snail damage when seeding directly into garden soil.

Radicchio

Cichorium intybus

*T*hese tangy, bitter salad greens actually come in many colors other than pale lime green: variegated creamy white and pastel crimson, motley earthy red and bronze-green, deep burgundy and pure white, and deep metallic green brushed with hints of rose. Famous in Italy for their unique flavor, some named varieties of radicchio we can grow have a history going back at least five generations. There are leafy forms, like rangy leaf lettuces, and heading types, which resemble tightly formed butter lettuces. Because certain radicchios are unique among other vegetables for their tight heads of dramatically variegated wine red and white foliage, they deserve a prominent place in the landscape.

Until recently, one could only buy radicchios that displayed their best burgundy colors and gathered a hint of sweetness along with their distinctive pungent flavor with the breath of fall's first frosts. Now imported seed is available that can be spring-planted and develops the tight little heads and classic red tones associated with radicchio during the heat of summer. Read your seed catalogs carefully to make sure you're getting the right seed for the season.

Some gardeners enhance the tightness of the heads and the brightness of the red foliage by growing the plant through the summer and then cutting off the top one inch above the soil line to force a new head—much the way Belgian endive, the close cousin of radicchio, is grown. In cold winter areas, seeding in the middle of June begets a fall harvest, and a late August seeding in a cold frame produces a crop next spring.

For a bittersweet flavor, texture, and color, add torn or chiffonade-cut radicchio leaves to the salad bowl. Use small individual leaves as a garnish; use large ones as cups to hold salads or spreads. Slice heads into halves or quarters lengthwise, brush with a little olive oil, and braise, grill, or bake to serve as a vegetable side dish. Wrap large leaves around chicken breasts or fish fillets to be baked.

Salad Burnet

Poterium sanguisorba

This hardy perennial is native to the rocky limestone soils of Europe. It can take amazing neglect and abuse, thriving in the gravelly shoulder of a summer-arid California country road. The deeply toothed leaves are arranged in a prostrate whirl to 12 inches, with an undramatic flower stalk to over two feet. Salad burnet is best suited to the wilder areas of the landscape and the rougher soils, and is drought resistant. Because it so freely self-sows, once established it can become a bit of a weed. Grow it in a container to control its spread.

The cucumberlike flavor of the pretty, blue-green, round leaves is predicated on the use of fresh leaves only. Harvest at any time and use as soon as possible. Leaves, flowers, and seeds are edible, and the leafy stems make an unusual garnish. Use leaves and flowers in green or vegetable salads or to flavor vinaigrettes. Simmer chopped leaves and snipped rosemary in butter to serve on fish fillets, or sprinkle on steamed vegetables. Use seeds to make vinegar or compound butter (see pages 14 to 15), to season cheese spreads, or in marinades.

Potato Salad with Arugula and Basil

1 pound thin-skinned potatoes

3 sprigs thyme, lemon thyme, summer savory, or oregano

1/4 cup each plain nonfat yogurt and mayonnaise

1/2 cup diced white or red sweet onion

1/2 cup julienne-cut green sweet pepper, plus green sweet pepper rings for garnish

1 cup thinly chiffonade-cut arugula

4 large basil leaves, cut into thin chiffonade

2 tablespoons snipped chives or garlic chives

2 ounces Monterey jack cheese, cut into thin strips

Salt and freshly ground white pepper, to taste

'Lolla Rossa', 'Marvel of Four Seasons', or 'Red Oakleaf' lettuce leaves

Halved cherry tomatoes, for garnish

Three varieties of thin-skinned potatoes, Ruby Crescent, Yellow Finn, and Rose Fir, are ideal for making potato salad. Serve this colorful salad for lunch or supper with whole-grain rolls and Honey Ice Cream with Lavender (see page 13) for dessert.

✦

Place potatoes on steamer rack set over boiling water. Strew thyme sprigs over, cover pot, and steam until potatoes are just tender (about 15 minutes); do not overcook. Remove from steamer and let stand until cool enough to handle. Discard thyme sprigs. Peel and slice or dice potatoes; set aside.

In a large bowl whisk together yogurt and mayonnaise until blended. Add potatoes and toss with two forks to coat thoroughly with dressing. Toss in onion, julienne-cut pepper, arugula, basil, chives, cheese, salt, and white pepper. Taste and adjust seasonings.

Make a bed of lettuce on individual salad plates. Mound salad on bed and garnish with sweet pepper rings and cherry tomatoes.

SERVES 4 TO 6

Coleslaw with Cress and Salad Burnet

6 cups finely shredded cabbage
(about 3/4 lb)

1 carrot, peeled and shredded
(about 2/3 cup)

1 small sweet pepper, seeded,
deribbed and cut into very thin
julienne (about 2/3 cup)

1/2 small sweet onion, very
thinly sliced

1 to 1 1/2 cups loosely packed
salad burnet leaves

1/3 cup garden cress or
watercress leaves

Yogurt Salad Dressing (see
page 19)

Salt and freshly ground
white pepper

Here is a basic recipe for coleslaw that encourages the chef to use his or her own imagination. Try mixing in chiffonade-cut young ornamental kale, radicchio, or arugula; finely julienne-cut cucumbers, kohlrabi, or jicama; or slivered almonds. Serve as an accompaniment to sandwiches or soup, or add julienne-cut cooked seafood, poultry, or meat and serve as a main dish on a bed of lettuce.

✦

In a large salad bowl, toss together cabbage, carrot, sweet pepper, onion, salad burnet, and cress. Toss in about 1/3 cup of the dressing; add more dressing to taste.

Season with salt and white pepper and serve immediately.

SERVES 4 TO 6

198

Pasta with Shrimp and Radicchio

1 tablespoon olive oil

2 cloves garlic, minced

3 cups loosely packed torn radicchio

1/2 pound gemellini pasta

1 pound large shrimp, peeled and deveined

Herbed Tomato Vinaigrette (see page 18)

2 ounces feta cheese, crumbled (1/2 cup)

1/2 cup snipped chives

Serve this light pasta dish with crusty bread for dipping in garlic olive oil.

✦

*B*ring a large pot filled with water to a boil.

In a large skillet over medium-high heat, warm oil. Add garlic and radicchio and sauté, tossing to coat with oil, 3 minutes. At the same time, add the pasta to the boiling water and cook until al dente.

Meanwhile, raise heat under radicchio and add shrimp. Stirring with fork, quickly cook shrimp until they turn pink and opaque (2 to 3 minutes). Timing will depend upon size of skillet; do not overcook. Add vinaigrette and heat, stirring, 2 minutes.

As soon as pasta is ready, drain well and immediately add to skillet with sauce. Add cheese and toss well. Remove from heat.

Transfer to large heated serving dish and sprinkle with chives. Serve immediately.

SERVES 4

Mixed Green Salad with Blossoms

1 1/2 cups torn red oakleaf or other looseleaf lettuce

1 cup each torn radicchio, frisée, and arugula

2 tablespoons snipped chives

3 tablespoons Balsamic Vinaigrette (see page 18)

1 cup raspberries (optional)

3 to 4 tablespoons edible herb and/or flower blossoms

Croutons

Soft lettuces and hardy bitter greens are enhanced by the addition of herb or flower blossoms. Nasturtium, Mexican or pineapple sage, arugula, anise hyssop, or society garlic blossoms are particularly tasty. Use them whole or lightly pulled apart.

✦

*I*n a large salad bowl toss together lettuce, radicchio, frisée, arugula, chives, and vinaigrette until greens are evenly coated. Gently toss in raspberries (if used) and sprinkle blossoms over top.

Serve immediately. Pass a bowl of croutons at the table.

SERVES 4 AS A SALAD COURSE

Savory

Summer Savory (Satureja hortensis)
Winter Savory (S. montana)

Annual and perennial herbs.

Grow from seed.

Prosper in rich, loamy, well-drained soil.

Prefer full sun.

Water regularly.

Summer savory is the herb that many consider the perfect partner to all manner of legume dishes. Traditional German cookery can't do without this hardy, aromatic annual herb. As summer savory does not keep its flavor in dried form, the garden is the best source of this desirable herb. The 12- to 18-inch plant has gray-green foliage, lavender-tinted long stems, and pale lavender blossoms that are noted for their long bloom.

Culinary purists find winter savory to have a slightly coarser flavor than the annual form. Hardy to 10° F, the plant has attractive foliage with narrow bright green leaves; white or pale purple blossoms are produced on short flower stalks. In traditional European herb gardens, this appealing plant is often clipped to sculpt a tight, low formal hedging.

The savories can be used interchangeably; use almost twice as much summer as winter savory. Savory is a mellow and congenial herb that acts as an "herbal enhancer." Its somewhat peppery, lemony tang brings out the flavor of other herbs and of the foods with which it is cooked. When rubbed between the fingers, savory seems strong and pungent, but becomes subtle when combined with other ingredients. Snip sprigs any time after the plant is established. The tiny flowers, sweeter in flavor, can be used along with the leaves.

Add savory sprigs to the water in which potatoes, pasta, legumes, or vegetables are cooked. Infuse white wine vinegar with savory sprigs (see page 14). Prepare oil concentrate or compound butter with chopped leaves and flowers (see pages 14, 15), or add to cream cheese dips, eggs to be scrambled, egg yolks for deviled eggs, stuffings for fowl, or fricassees. Chop summer savory leaves for chowders, sausage mixtures, or stuffing for veal. Toss summer savory leaves and/or blossoms into green salad or potato salad, cooked rice or pasta, or oyster stew.

When dried, winter savory retains its aroma better than summer savory. Crumbled dried savory will remain pungent for four or five months; ground savory will keep three months. Use crumbled dried or ground savory in bread crumb coatings, meat loaf mixtures, for rubbing on poultry or meats before roasting, and in consommés, chowders, and bean soups.

Polenta with Sweet Pepper and Savory

1 tablespoon olive oil

1/3 cup very finely minced onion

1/3 cup very finely minced red sweet pepper

1 large clove garlic, very finely minced

2 tablespoons finely minced winter savory, or 3 tablespoons finely minced summer savory

3 1/2 cups stock or 1 cup milk and 2 1/2 cups water

1 cup coarse-grind cornmeal (polenta)

1/2 cup freshly grated Parmesan cheese (optional)

Salt and freshly ground pepper, to taste

Coarsely ground cornmeal, preferably nondegerminated, is a must for this satisfying dish. Polenta complements almost any main course, but is especially good with lamb and veal.

✦

In a heavy saucepan over medium heat, warm oil. Add onion and sweet pepper, cover, and cook until onion starts to soften (about 3 minutes). Add garlic and savory and cook 2 minutes. Add stock, bring to a boil, and gradually stir in polenta. Bring back to a boil, lower heat, and cook, stirring, until mixture begins to thicken (about 10 minutes).

Continue cooking on low heat, stirring often and keeping mixture at very slow boil, until polenta pulls away from the sides of the pan and is thick and creamy (about 30 minutes). Add cheese (if used), remove from heat, and stir until cheese melts. Season with salt and pepper and serve at once.

SERVES 4

Poached Orange Roughy with Winter Savory and Mustard

4 orange roughy fillets (each 5 to 6 oz and 3/4 in. thick)

2 tablespoons Dijon-style mustard

2 tablespoons fresh lemon juice

1/3 cup minced shallot

1/2 cup dry vermouth

4 sprigs winter savory

Minced parsley and lemon wedges, for garnish

Search out fresh rather than previously frozen orange roughy; the fresh flesh firms up and develops a texture similar to crab meat.

✦

Rinse fillets and pat dry with paper toweling. In a small bowl stir together mustard and lemon juice and spread one fourth of mixture over top of each fillet. Set aside for 10 minutes but no longer than 15 minutes.

In a large skillet over medium high-heat, combine shallot, vermouth, and savory and bring to a boil. Lower heat slightly and boil until shallot is tender and vermouth is reduced by half (about 6 minutes). Place fillets in skillet, mustard-coated side up, and top each with a savory sprig. Bring back to a boil, lower heat, cover, and cook at gentle boil until fillets are firm and flesh is opaque (7 to 8 minutes); do not overcook.

Using slotted spatula transfer fillets to heated serving plates. Discard savory sprigs and pour pan juices over fillets. Sprinkle generously with parsley and place a lemon wedge alongside.

SERVES 4

Sorrel

French Sorrel (Rumex acetosa);
Buckler's Sorrel (R. scutatus)

A hardy perennial herb. Grows in all zones.

Grow from rooted rhizomes or potted plants.

Likes fertile, moist soil.

Drought resistant, but dies back to the ground without water.

Control its spread by weeding religiously.

Fairly pest and disease free; watch for beetles and treat with rotenone or pyrethrum sprays.

The extended upright leaves of French sorrel are easily illuminated by the morning or afternoon sun. The pale green foliage turns into a vibrant shimmering lime yellow with dramatic backlighting. A small grove of this striking foliage adds a bright spot in any landscape. In mild winter areas, the foliage holds its form and color through the season. In colder climates, you may want to cut the foliage to the ground with the onset of winter. The flower stalks are an impressive reddish color and tower a foot or more above the foliage.

All sorrels are rambunctious plants that spread by underground roots. Plant in a container sunk into the ground with a wire mesh covered drainage hole. Even then, these persistent roots may find a way out. The safer bet is to grow sorrel in containers on a deck or patio where the roots have no chance of escaping.

Sorrel, a vegetable as well as an herb and known in the wild as sour grass or dock, has a lemony tang that makes it a favored culinary herb. When the plant is established, cut the leaves at will. Remove stems and center ribs of large leaves. Stuff whole sorrel leaves into the cavity of chicken to be roasted, or cut into thin chiffonade to use in green or navy bean salad, in bread or corn bread stuffing for whole fish, or in soups and sauces. Small tender leaves and the leaves of Buckler's sorrel, both of which can be eaten raw in salads, need no trimming.

Sorrel leaves are very tender and wilt quickly, so they should be cooked rapidly. Always use nonreactive utensils. Steam on a rack over boiling water, butter-steam, or cook with other foods. Whole sorrel leaves or cooked chiffonade-cut sorrel can be frozen up to three months; use in soups or sauces.

Complementary Seasonings and Foods

Chervil, dill, garden cress, savory, thyme; eggs; lemon juice; celery, garlic, leeks, lettuce, mushrooms, onions, shallots, potatoes, sunchokes, spinach, tomatoes; seafood (especially salmon and scallops), chicken, beef, veal.

Chiffonade of Sorrel

2 tablespoons unsalted butter

3 cups coarsely chiffonade-cut sorrel leaves

2 to 3 tablespoons whipping cream or evaporated low-fat milk

Pinch sugar

Salt and freshly ground black or white pepper, to taste

Serve as a garnish for salmon steaks, fillet of sole, veal piccata, or cream soups, or as a filling for omelets. Double or triple the recipe and serve as a side dish with roast goose or pork, or as a vegetable side dish topped with seasoned croutons.

◆

In a skillet over medium heat, melt butter. Add sorrel, cover, and cook until sorrel darkens and softens (about 3 minutes). Stir in cream, sugar and salt and pepper.

Heat through and serve at once.

MAKES ABOUT 1 CUP

Sorrel, Celeriac, and Tuna Salad

1 large celeriac (celery root), peeled and cut into 1/2-inch dice

1 teaspoon plus 1 tablespoon fresh lemon juice

Salted water, to cover

1/4 cup mayonnaise

1/4 cup Yogurt Cheese (see page 22)

3 cups firmly packed thinly chiffonade-cut tender sorrel

1/2 cup finely minced celery

1 can (7 oz) water-pack tuna fish, drained and flaked

2 hard-cooked egg whites, chopped

Salt and freshly ground white pepper, to taste

Herb Vinaigrette to moisten, if needed (see page 17)

Looseleaf lettuce

Minced parsley and chives, ripe tomato wedges, and sliced cooked artichoke bottoms, for garnish

A satisfying low-fat, low-calorie luncheon salad. Accompany with melba toast rounds and serve fresh fruit for dessert.

◆

*I*n a saucepan combine celeriac, the 1 teaspoon lemon juice, and salted water to cover and bring to a boil. Boil until barely tender (about 3 minutes). Drain, return to saucepan, place on burner, and heat until all moisture evaporates (1 to 2 minutes); set aside to cool to room temperature.

In a salad bowl stir together mayonnaise, Yogurt Cheese, and 1 tablespoon lemon juice. Toss in reserved celeriac, sorrel, celery, tuna fish, egg whites, and salt and pepper. If desired, moisten with vinaigrette.

Make a bed of lettuce on individual plates. Mound salad on top and sprinkle with parsley and chives. Garnish with tomato wedges and artichoke bottoms.

Serves 4 to 6

Sweet Cicely

Myrrhis odorata

At last, a bold, showy herbal plant that actually *prefers* shade. The especially attractive foliage grows into a two-to four-foot upwelling of lacy leaves on arching stems. The fountain of soft green foliage thrusts up tall stalks with white umbel flowers in early summer. The remarkable resemblance to a cross between a fern and a feverfew makes this plant a welcome edible for shade spots. Beneath taller trees with their lower limbs removed, plant sweet cicely in large informal clusters to display its airy foliage. Like most shade-loving plants, sweet cicely prefers a fairly rich soil that is high in humus, drains well, and is moist.

Sweet cicely's pronounced anise flavor comes as a pleasant surprise, reminding one of tangy licorice candy with a hint of celery. The sweetest of all the many herbs, sweet cicely has been said to make sweet foods sweeter by cutting down on the acidity in tart fruits. It also makes it possible for the cook to cut down on the amount of sugar.

The feathery leaves and tender stems, flowers, seeds, and roots of sweet cicely are edible, with the most concentrated and spiciest flavor

Perennial herbaceous plant hardy to all zones.

Grow from seed or container plants.

Prefers rich, loamy soil.

Place in partial or full shade.

Water regularly.

Leaves, stems, flowers, and seeds are edible.

207

in the seeds and roots. Harvest sprigs when the plant is established and continue throughout the growing season. Stand them upright in a glass of water, cover with a plastic bag, and refrigerate for up to three days.

Chop sweet cicely leaves and flowers and use them in green salads, fruit soups, dessert sauces, custards, ice creams, and fruit salads. One tablespoon chopped leaves is enough for approximately one cup of fruit. Sweet cicely helps reduce the acidity in fruits for jams and jellies. Use the sprigs as a garnish for iced or fruit desserts, or to infuse syrup when poaching fruits.

The slightly oily seeds should be harvested shortly before they turn brown. Use the seeds green or snip off the seed heads and hang to dry as directed for coriander (see page 74). Unripe seeds, with their sweet, slightly nutty flavor, can be used whole in apple pie or chopped and added to green or fruit salads, fruit cups, ice creams, sorbets, or cakes. Steam sliced carrots and rutabagas or parsnips, toss in melted butter, and sprinkle with chopped seeds. Use dried seeds in place of caraway seeds in baked goods.

If you have an abundance of plants, dig up the roots, wash well, peel, and candy whole (see page 16). Or grate raw roots into quick breads or salads or slice raw roots and butter-steam with sliced carrots or add to stir-fry dishes.

Sweet cicely combines well with mint, tarragon, and most other herbs, and goes especially well with root vegetables such as turnips, potatoes, and yams.

Sorbet of Sweet Cicely and Rose Geranium

1 1/2 cups plus
2 tablespoons sugar

3 1/2 cups water

24 sprigs sweet cicely (about
6 in. each)

24 rose geranium leaves

1/2 cup fresh lemon juice, or
to taste

Rose geranium blossoms,
for garnish

This delicate and refreshing dessert recipe (© The Herbfarm, Ltd., 1988) comes from Ron Zimmerman of the Herbfarm just outside Seattle, Washington. He describes the role of the sweet cicely this way: "[It] lends the sorbet just a hint of anise and reduces the amount of sugar needed."

◆

In a saucepan combine about three fourths of the sugar with all the water. Bring to a boil over high heat, stirring to dissolve sugar. Remove from heat and let cool to room temperature.

In a food processor fitted with the metal blade, combine the remaining sugar, sweet cicely and geranium leaves and process to a fine blend (3 to 4 minutes). Stop as needed to scrape down sides of processor bowl. Add to cooled sugar syrup, stir well, and let stand 1 to 3 hours.

Strain through fine-mesh sieve or several layers of cheesecloth. Stir in lemon juice. Place in an ice cream freezer and freeze according to manufacturer's directions. Or pour mixture into metal bowl and place in freezer; scrape down sides every hour or so until frozen (allow at least 3 to 4 hours).

To serve, spoon into chilled glasses. Garnish each glass with a rose geranium blossom.

MAKES ABOUT 1 QUART; SERVES 6

Swiss Chard

(Beta vulgaris, Cicla Group)

Somewhat frost-hardy annual vegetable.

Grow from seed.

Plant in rich, fertile soil.

Select a sunny spot.

Water regularly.

Watch for snails, slugs, and earwigs while seedlings are young.

Trim lower leaves to reveal the vibrant colors of the midribs when backlit by the afternoon sun.

The grand dame of edible landscaping. When the genera of ornamental edible gardening first looked around for specimens to consider, the Swiss chard was one of the first candidates. The classic example is the 'Ruby', with its clear crimson stalk. The curled, wide, tall leaves, up to two feet, are a mixture of burgundy-green foliage with bright red veins. But the translucent ruby stalks are what sets this vegetable apart. With the sun behind the plant, Swiss chard's midribs light up like the best stained-glass window in a lofty European cathedral. Place where backlighting will reveal its greatest virtue. The plant does well in a container, making it easy to move with the season's changing light. Other varieties offer white or carrot orange midribs; this last variety is quite rare. Some seed companies offer packets of mixed varieties. Sprout the seeds and, as the color is revealed, single out most, if not all, of the common green forms and favor the colorful versions.

Harvest Swiss chard after the plant reaches maturity and continue until the plant has gone to seed. Before the stalks become too thick, cut them one or two inches from the crown so new leaves can be produced. Although very tender young leaves can be torn or cut into chiffonade for green salads, Swiss chard is usually served cooked. Prepare in any way in which spinach is prepared, noting that chard does not cook down as much as spinach.

Steam chard on a rack over boiling water before chopping finely to use in ravioli filling, timbales, quiches, frittatas, custards, stuffings, soufflés, and ground meat or poultry mixtures. To serve Swiss chard as a vegetable side dish, cook chopped stems in garlic olive oil, or in olive oil with several bruised garlic cloves, in a covered pan two or three minutes. Add coarsely chiffonade-cut leaves and cook, tossing occasionally, until tender (just a few minutes). If the chard is freshly washed, it will need no additional water for cooking other than the washing water clinging to the leaves. For additional flavor, add a sprig or two of rosemary while chard is cooking, or sprinkle steamed chard with freshly grated Parmesan or Romano cheese.

If using large leaves to line a terrine or as a wrapper for chicken breasts or fish fillets, trim as above and blanch lightly. Substitute blanched leaves for grape leaves in Dolmas (see page 118).

Complementary
Seasonings and Foods

Rosemary, thyme; butter, olive oil, cream; lemon juice; egg dishes, hard-cooked eggs; Parmesan cheese; pine nuts; garlic, shallots, onions, other leafy greens, sweet peppers, fresh or dried mushrooms; lamb, pork.

Mini Recipes

Add thinly chiffonade-cut Swiss chard leaves to vegetable, minestrone, lentil, or white bean soup the last few minutes of cooking.

Finely chop well-drained cooked Swiss chard and add to White or Mornay Sauce (see page 22), transfer to shallow baking dish, cover with shredded Italian Fontina or Monterey jack cheese, and sprinkle with paprika. Bake in 350° F oven until heated through and cheese melts (15 minutes).

Add finely chopped young chard leaves to low-fat cottage cheese mixed with Yogurt Cheese (see page 22); season with minced garlic, fresh lemon juice, minced rosemary, salt, and pepper. Serve as a dip for crudités.

Ham, Scallop, and Swiss Chard Ramekins

1 pound scallops, halved or quartered if large

2 tablespoons fresh lemon juice

2 to 2 1/2 tablespoons olive oil

1/3 cup minced yellow onion

1 1/2 cups diced cooked ham (about 1/2 lb.)

1/2 pound fresh mushrooms, sliced

3 tablespoons chopped green onion, including tops

2 large cloves garlic, finely minced

1 1/2 cups thinly chiffonade-cut tender Swiss chard leaves

Flour seasoned with freshly ground white pepper, for dusting

1/2 cup dry white wine

1/2 cup evaporated low-fat milk or half-and-half

1/4 cup freshly grated Parmesan cheese

2 tablespoons fine dried bread crumbs

1 1/2 tablespoons unsalted butter, melted

For lunch divide the scallops and other ingredients among six ramekins. The ramekins may be filled several hours ahead, cooled, covered, and refrigerated. Bring to room temperature before baking. Serve with corn bread and a fruit salad.

✦

Place scallops in shallow bowl. Sprinkle with lemon juice, toss, and let stand 10 minutes. Transfer to colander and set aside to drain.

In a large skillet or saucepan over medium heat, warm 1 tablespoon of the oil. Add yellow onion and sauté until soft (about 5 minutes). Add ham, mushrooms, green onion, and garlic. Cook, stirring often, 3 minutes. Add chard and continue cooking until chard wilts (about 2 minutes). Remove chard mixture with slotted spoon to a bowl and set chard and pan aside.

Preheat oven to 400° F. Lightly butter 6 ramekins or large scallop shells; set aside.

Pat scallops dry with paper toweling and dust with seasoned flour. Return pan to medium-heat and add remaining 1 to 1 1/2 tablespoons oil. When hot, add scallops and sauté quickly, turning often, 3 minutes. Add wine, stir well, and cook until slightly thickened (about 45 seconds). Pour in milk, return chard mixture to skillet, stir to combine, and transfer to prepared ramekins. In a small dish stir together cheese and bread crumbs. Sprinkle evenly over ramekins. Drizzle with melted butter.

Bake until bubbly and lightly browned (about 10 minutes). Serve at once.

Serves 6

Thyme

Thymus vulgaris

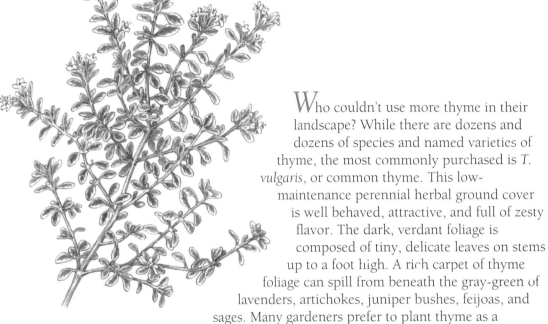

Hardy perennial evergreen herb.

Grow from potted plants or root divisions.

Provide well-drained soil; fertility is not as important.

Water frequently only when trying to root stems for new plants. Otherwise likes dry soil; do not overwater.

Shear back hard once after blooming to keep a compact form.

Relatively pest and disease free.

Who couldn't use more thyme in their landscape? While there are dozens and dozens of species and named varieties of thyme, the most commonly purchased is *T. vulgaris*, or common thyme. This low-maintenance perennial herbal ground cover is well behaved, attractive, and full of zesty flavor. The dark, verdant foliage is composed of tiny, delicate leaves on stems up to a foot high. A rich carpet of thyme foliage can spill from beneath the gray-green of lavenders, artichokes, juniper bushes, feijoas, and sages. Many gardeners prefer to plant thyme as a rambling drift of forest green ground cover. Each summer, thyme bears a sea of flowers, of mauve, miniature lollipops floating a few inches above the foliage. (Bees seem to prefer thyme over most other flowers in the garden, a boon to the beekeeper and a bane to those allergic to bee stings.) With a bit of seasonal clipping, thyme can be kept quite low, dense, and without flower. In fact, fastidious gardeners can shape thyme into a small boxwoodlike hedge to border a flower or vegetable bed.

Thyme spreads by rooting its stems as they touch moist mulch or soil. To further its spread, maintain a weed-free mulch and water overhead by sprinkler on a regular basis. To speed up the process, sift some fine compost into the foliage and wash it in with a hand-held hose

213

sprinkler. The stems will readily root into the thin compost layer. Once the plant has spread to the desired width, back off on irrigation and the plant will become fairly drought resistant.

Common thyme can be used interchangeably with lemon, golden lemon, or lime thyme, even in desserts. Silver thyme is milder, and caraway thyme is distinctly reminiscent of caraway, which makes it perfect for potatoes, pork, sauerkraut, or any dish in which the flavor of caraway is desired. Both the leaves and flowers of the thyme plant are edible. Harvest the sprigs at any time, especially just before the plant blooms. Add the sprigs whole to stocks, sauces, and stews, or use them to infuse vinegar, honey, or syrup (see page 14), or to make jelly. Strip the leaves from the sprigs (not always easy to do) and chop or crush to release their oil. Use them in cheese, egg, seafood, poultry, or meat dishes, and in stuffings, gravies, stocks, soups, and sauces. Add caraway, lemon, or lime thyme to coleslaw or shredded carrot salad. Prepare compound butter, oil concentrate, or herb salt with minced thyme (see pages 14 to 15). Add to muffin or bread batter, or to fruit cups or salads. Use the flowers in salads or as a garnish.

Dried thyme retains flavor for four or five months. Use crumbled or ground thyme as a seasoning for any of the above suggestions.

Complementary Seasonings and Foods

Parsley, savory, marjoram, rosemary, sage; garlic, onions, carrots, eggplants, chayotes, sweet peppers, peas, potatoes, mushrooms, rhubarb (lemon thyme); seafood (especially clams), poultry, meat; Cabernet Sauvignon, Zinfandel, Fumé Blanc, Pinot Noir, Sauvignon Blanc.

Mini Recipes

Tie thyme, parsley, marjoram, rosemary, and savory sprigs in a bundle and stuff into cavity of whole fish for poaching.

Combine mayonnaise and Yogurt Cheese (see page 22); add chopped thyme and serve as a dip for crudités or as a sauce for fish.

Combine olive oil, fresh lemon juice, Dijon-style mustard, and minced thyme leaves. Use for marinating chicken and for basting while grilling.

New England Clam Chowder

3 tablespoons unsalted butter

1 cup minced leek and/or green onion, white part only

2 large cloves garlic, minced, plus finely minced garlic, for serving

1/4 pound salt pork, cut into small dice

3 cups chicken stock

Bouquet garni of 4 large sprigs thyme or lemon thyme; 1 bay leaf; 3 allspice berries, lightly crushed; and 4 peppercorns, lightly crushed (see page 15)

2 or 3 thick-skinned potatoes, peeled and cut into 1/4-inch dice (about 2 1/2 cups)

3 dozen clams in the shell, shucked and minced, and their liquor

1 cup bottled clam juice

2 cups half-and-half

Salt and freshly ground black or white pepper, to taste

Paprika, for garnish

Finely chopped thyme or lemon thyme, for garnish

Serve this aromatic chowder on a wintry night with crusty French bread.

✦

In a large saucepan over medium heat, melt butter. Add leek, minced garlic, and salt pork and sauté until leek is soft (about 5 minutes). Add stock and bouquet garni and bring to a boil. Lower heat, cover, and simmer 10 minutes. Add potatoes and bring back to a boil. Then lower heat, cover, and boil gently until potatoes are starting to soften (about 10 minutes); they should remain firm.

Discard bouquet garni. Add clams and their liquor and clam juice. Bring to a boil and boil for 2 minutes. Stir in half-and-half and reheat without boiling. Taste and adjust seasonings with salt and pepper.

Transfer chowder to a heated soup tureen or ladle into heated individual soup bowls. Sprinkle with paprika and thyme and pass a bowl of minced garlic at table.

SERVES 4 TO 6

Herbed New Potatoes with Gruyère

4 white new potatoes (4 to
5 oz each)

1 1/2 tablespoons garlic olive oil

Salt and freshly ground
white pepper

Leaves from 8 or more thyme or
flavored thyme sprigs, chopped

1/4 pound Gruyère or Monterey
jack cheese, shredded

Thyme sprigs with flowers,
for garnish

*As an accompaniment to seafood, meat, or poultry dishes, these attractive
and delicious potatoes can be made with any savory herb. Select white new
potatoes 3 1/2 to 4 inches long and about 2 1/2 inches in diameter. Carry
plate directly from the steamer to the table; spoon accumulated steaming
juices over the potatoes when serving.*

✦

Scrub potatoes and pat dry with paper toweling. Work with 1 potato
at a time. Place on cutting board and position the handle of a wooden
spoon just in front of potato. Using a sharp knife, cut potato into 1/4-
inch-thick slices, being careful to cut just short of all the way through;
let handle of spoon prevent cutting too deeply. Arrange potatoes cut
side up in a colorful ceramic 9-inch pie plate.

Carefully pull slices apart without detaching and drizzle oil
between and over slices. Tuck about 1/4 teaspoon thyme leaves
between each slice and place plate on steamer rack set over boiling
water. Cover pot and steam until potatoes are just tender (20 to
30 minutes).

Sprinkle cheese evenly over potatoes and steam until cheese melts
(about 5 minutes). Garnish plate with thyme sprigs.

SERVES 4

Poisonous Plants

Learn to identify these common garden plants and make sure they are treated solely as nonedible ornamentals. All species of plants with sp. following the botanical name are poisonous.

Common Name	Botanical Name	Common Name	Botanical Name
Amaryllis	*Hippeastrum* sp.	Henbane	*Hyoscyamus niger*
Azalea	*Rhododendron* sp.	Hydrangea	*Hydrangea* sp.
Belladonna Lily (Naked Lady)	*Amaryllis belladonna*	Iris	*Iris* sp.
Bird of Paradise	*Strelitzia reginae*	Lantana	*Lantana* sp.
Buckeye	*Aesculus* sp.	Larkspur	*Delphinium* sp.
Buttercup	*Ranunculus* sp.	Lily-of-the-Valley	*Convallaria majalis*
Caladium	*Caladium* sp.	Lupine	*Lupinus* sp.
Cardinal Flower	*Lobelia cardinalis*	Mandrake	*Mandragora officinarum*
Carolina Yellow Jessamine	*Gelsemium sempervirens*	Monkshood	*Aconitum* sp.
Castor Bean	*Ricinus communis*	Narcissus	*Narcissus* sp.
Clematis	*Clematis* sp.	Oleander	*Nerium oleander*
Crocus, Autumn	*Colchicum autumnale*	Poinsettia	*Euphorbia pulcherrima*
Daffodil	*Narcissus pseudonarcissus*	Sweet Pea	*Lathryus* sp.
Daphne	*Daphne* sp.	Rhododendron	*Rhododendron* sp.
Datura	*Datura* sp.	Star-of-Bethlehem	*Ornithogalum* sp.
Deadly Nightshade	*Atropa belladonna*	Tansy	*Tanacetum vulgare*
Euphorbia	*Euphorbia* sp.	Thorn Apple	*Datura stramonium*
Foxglove	*Digitalis purpurea*	Wisteria	*Wisteria* sp.
Glory Lily	*Gloriosa* sp.		

Resources for the Gourmet Gardener

Abundant Life Seed Foundation
Box 772
Port Townsend, WA 98368
206-385-5660

Features organically grown, open-pollinated, and untreated seeds. Includes a good selection of vegetables, small grains, herbs, and flowers suited to the Pacific Northwest climate and elsewhere. A nonprofit institute for plant diversity and the preservation of heirloom plants. Catalog is $2.

Bountiful Gardens
Ecology Action
18001 Shafer Ranch Road
Willits, CA 95490
707-459-6410

A full listing of organically grown heirloom vegetable, green manure and cover crop, small grain, herb, and flower seeds. Also biointensive gardening supplies and organic pest controls. Income from the catalog supports the nonprofit work of John Jeavons and friends as they research and train others in sustainable, biointensive mini farms. The catalog is free, but send a donation; they do good work.

The Cook's Garden
Box 535
Londonderry, VT 05148
802-824-3400

Extensive listing of gourmet vegetables, with a special emphasis on lettuce varieties. Features untreated, open-pollinated, and organic seeds. Catalog costs $1.

Edible Landscaping
Michael McConkey
Box 77
Afton, VA 22920
804-361-9134

An amazing collection of rare and unusual fruits, edible vines, nut trees, and berries. Excellent selection of hardy kiwis. Has obscure edibles such as Pakistan mulberries, jujubes, edible dogwood, and unusual figs. Free catalog.

The Herbfarm
32804 Issaquah-Fall City Road
Fall City, WA 98024
206-784-2222

One of the few places, if not the only place, where you can visit demonstration plantings filled with herbal, ornamental, and edible plants; purchase hundreds of varieties of potted herb plants; and dine on a sumptuous multicourse meal of seasonal vegetables and herbs grown at the Herbfarm. Those who can't visit can ask for their listing of over 450 varieties of ornamental and edible herbs and plants, which are available by mail order. Most of the herbs mentioned in this book are offered. Catalog is $3.50.

Highlander Nursery
Box 177
Pettigrew, AR 72752
501-677-2300

Lists both hardy and low-chill varieties of blueberry plants. Free catalog.

Johnny's Selected Seeds
Foss Hill Road
Albion, ME 04910
207-437-9294

Good source for seeds acclimated to the northern climates. Nationally known for a wide range of short-season vegetables, many carrot varieties, and seeds for greenhouse crops. Free catalog.

Native Seeds/ SEARCH
2509 North Campell Avenue, #325
Tucson, AZ 85719

An extensive offering of seeds of
traditional crops planted in the
Southwest and in northwest Mexico.
Only good source for seeds of many
obscure ethnic ingredients. A
nonprofit organization dedicated to
conserving the genetic and ethnic
diversity of the region. Send $1
for catalog.

The Natural Gardening Company
217 San Anselmo Avenue
San Anselmo, CA 94960
415-456-5060

The only mail-order source of live,
certified-organic ornamental flowers,
edible flowers, gourmet vegetables,
and culinary ornamental herbs. A
wide selection of annual and
perennial plants. Also organic pest
controls, organically grown and
commercial vegetable seed, wild-
flower seed, drip irrigation supplies,
and high-quality garden tools.
Free catalog.

Nourse Farms, Inc.
41 River Road
South Deerfield, MA 01373
413-665-2658

Excellent choice of named-variety
strawberry, raspberry, blackberry,
and blueberry plants. Also, rhubarb,
horseradish, and asparagus. Free
catalog.

Pacific Tree Farms
4301 Lynwood Drive
Chula Vista, CA 92010
619-422-2400

The single best mail-order source for
tropical and semitropical fruiting
plants, shrubs, and trees. Carries
named varieties of feijoa and the
hard-to-find goumi. Also miniature
avocado trees, over forty citrus
varieties, bananas, and cherimoyas.
Free catalog.

Pinetree Garden Seeds
Box 300
New Gloucester, ME 04260
207-926-3400

Over six hundred varieties of
vegetable and ornamental seeds, at
reasonable prices. The seeds come in
small packets—perfect for those
gardeners who never safely store and
religiously reuse leftover seeds.
Extensive selections grouped by
country, culture, or region—Italian,
French, Continental, Asian, and so
on. Has specialty items such as seed
for the purple Italian artichoke.
Mostly untreated seed. Free catalog.

Plants of the Southwest
Agua Fria Route 6, Box 11-A
Santa Fe, NM 87501
505-471-2212

Source of edible plants indigenous to
the American Southwest, as well as
many species of ornamentals and
native grasses. Also focuses on plants
for mountains, high plains, and higher
elevations. Catalog is $3.50.

Raintree Nursery
391 Butts Road
Morton, WA 98356
206-496-6400

An impressive selection of heirloom
and modern fruit trees, nut trees,
berry plants, edible vine crops, and
edible shrubs. Has mulberry trees.
Focuses on plants suited to the
Pacific Northwest, but many species
will thrive elsewhere. Very
informative free catalog.

Redwood City Seed Company
Box 361
Redwood City, CA 94064

One of the standard sources for
unusual and rare edible and
ornamental seeds. Specializes in seed
for Mexican, European, and Oriental
edibles. A must. Catalog is $1.

Richters Herb Catalogue
Goodwood, Ontario
Canada L0C lA0
416-640-6677

The ultimate herb catalog. A
cornucopia of seed for all kinds of
annual and perennial herb plants.
An excellent selection of basil
varieties. Catalog is $2 in US dollars
and in Canadian dollars.

Roses of Yesterday and Today
802 Brown's Valley Road
Watsonville, CA 95076
408-724-3537

The definitive source of heirloom roses, some of which are disease resistant and don't require massive spraying to bloom abundantly. Great source for roses to be used for edible petals and rose hips. Send $3 for catalog.

Seeds Blüm
Idaho City Stage
Boise, ID 83706
FAX 208-338-5658

An outstanding listing of herb, heirloom vegetable, edible flower, and old-fashioned flower seeds. Exceptional listing of unusual potato varieties. Fun, "homemade," personal catalog ($3) with solid gardening tips, organized by plant families with good index.

Seeds of Change
PO Box 15700
Santa Fe, NM 87506-5700
505-438-8080

A large selection of organically grown vegetable, herb, edible flower, small grain, ornamental, and fiber plants. Interested in preserving Southwest native food plants by keeping them in commerce. Catalog is $3, credited toward first purchase.

Shepherd's Garden Seeds
Shipping Office
30 Irene Street
Torrington, CT 06790
203-482-3638

An excellent listing of specialty vegetables, herbs, edible flowers, and ornamental flowers. Mouth-watering descriptions of numerous European, heirloom, and modern vegetables and salad greens. Catalog is $1.

Sonoma Antique Apple Nursery
4395 Westside Road
Healdsburg, CA 95448
707-433-6420

These avid orchardists offer much more than just dozens of heirloom apple trees. Good listing of Asian pear, persimmon, chestnut, fig, and other deciduous fruit trees. Many of the apple varieties are certified organically grown trees. Send $1 for an informative catalog.

Sunrise Enterprises
Box 330058
West Hartford, CT 06133-0058

The best listing of seeds for Asian edibles. A particularly extensive selection, including perilla, Asian parsleys, and edible-podded peas. Includes live plants, mostly ornamentals. One of the few sources of live lemongrass plants. Free catalog.

Taylor's Herb Gardens, Inc.
1535 Lone Oak Road
Vista, CA 92084
619-727-3485

Perhaps the single best source for live herb plants. Very good selection of unusual varieties and old standards. Carries many types of rosemary, sage, thyme, lavender, and scented geraniums, as well as lemongrass, society garlic, and lovage. Send $3 for catalog.

Vermont Bean Seed Co.
Garden Lane
Fair Haven, VT 05743

The definitive catalog for many types of snap, pole, bush, lima, and dried beans. Also, a good selection of other vegetables, herb seeds, and Asian greens and root crops. Free catalog.

INDEX

Biographical Notes

CORALIE CASTLE is a food consultant and the author of nine other cookbooks, with more than three decades of experience in developing new recipes and innovative adaptions of classic dishes. Among her best-sellers are *Soup*, *The Hors d'Oeuvre Book*, *Real Bread*, and *The Complete Book of Steam Cookery*. She has operated a successful catering and baking business and owns Coralie Castle Cookware, manufacturers of the Ultimate Expandable Steamer, a product she designed. An active member of the International Association of Culinary Professionals and the American Institute of Wine and Food, Ms. Castle has made numerous appearances on television and radio to discuss food and gardening. When not traveling abroad to collect ideas and recipes for her books, she lives in Marin County, California, where she and her husband tend a one-acre garden filled with fruits, vegetables, herbs, and edible flowers.

ROBERT KOURIK is the author and publisher of the widely acclaimed *Designing and Maintaining Your Edible Landscape—Naturally*, *Gray Water Use in the Landscape*, and *Drip Irrigation for All Landscapes and Every Climate*. He also is coauthor of *Composting* and *The Naturally Elegant Home*. A self-taught horticulturalist who began as a maintenance gardener in the early 1970s, since 1976 Mr. Kourik has been defining and promoting the concept of "edible landscaping" through his work as a landscape designer, environmentalist, publisher, and writer. He resides in Occidental, California.